Hope for America's Last Generation

Galyn Wiemers

Last Hope Books and Publications
A division of Generation Word Bible Teaching Ministry

Last Hope Books and Publications
A Division of Generation Word Bible Teaching Ministry
P.O. Box 399
Waukee, Iowa 50263

Visit www.lasthopebooks.com or www.generationword.com.

Unless otherwise indicated, all scripture passages are from the New International Version

Cover design by Clint Hansen
Photography by Paul Blaser

ISBN-13: 978-0-9794382-0-2
ISBN-10: 0-9794382-0-9

To Toni.

Thank you for the years, the love, the respect, the memories, the trust, the encouragement, the joy of being in love with you, but, most of all, thank you for calling me your best friend.

May God help us to finish strong.

ACKNOWLEDGEMENTS

Much appreciation goes to Clint Hansen who designed the cover and illustrations. You can see some of Clint's outstanding work at www.clinthansen.com.

Thank you to Paul Blaser and Blaser Photography in West Des Moines, Iowa for the photographs used on the back cover. Visit Blaser Photography at www.blaserphotography.iowacom.net.

I especially appreciate Jennifer Ruisch for encouraging me to write this book and doing all the editing. You can buy Jennifer's book *Faith and the City: A Girl's Search for Post-College Meaning* at most bookstores or on Amazon.com.

Finally, I want to recognize the Monday night Bible study crowd that started meeting in our home in the spring of 2002. These believers represent the faithful people in our country during this fourth generation. As always, thanks for coming to Bible study!

TABLE OF CONTENTS

The Coming Delusions

I OPENED UP the newspaper on Easter morning to find the headline "Best-Sellers Challenge the New Testament." At the end of this lengthy article about *The Da Vinci Code* and the *Gospel of Judas*, the writer finished by saying, "...making a case that the New Testament isn't the last word. Maybe not even the first word."

It sounded a lot like the original line used by Satan in the Garden of Eden. "Did God really say...?" With articles like this, we can see that from Genesis 3 until present day, the story hasn't changed. The theme of skepticism remains.

I preached a message that Easter Sunday about the consistency of God's promises. He promised a savior first to Adam and Eve and then to Abraham, Jacob, David and the prophets Jeremiah, Isaiah, Daniel, and Ezekiel. I reminded everyone that these promises were recorded and documented over a 4,000 year period. The gospels also record the life and death of Jesus in great detail with historical accuracy. They tell of Christ's execution and resurrection—events all foretold with amazing precision in the Old Testament. I explained to the Easter crowd that we are all part of this continuum, a process that began long ago. It's a story that continues to unfold today.

Then I paused to announce the "shocking" news report from the paper that morning. I pulled out the article and said that, according to this story, the New Testament may all be a hoax. I announced that this might very well be the last Easter we ever celebrate since 6,000 years of history, prophecy, documentation, and experience has just been undermined by a best-selling novel. Though I was obviously joking, the part that wasn't funny was that, for some Christians, the undermining I spoke of was actually true.

I went to buy *The Da Vinci Code* right after it first came out, but when I went to Barnes & Noble, I couldn't find it. (This was early on, before the front tables in bookstores prominently displayed stacks upon stacks of the red book.) I eventually gave up my search and asked an employee for help. The young boy immediately knew what the problem was. "Oh," he said. "You're in the wrong section. *The Da Vinci Code* is in fiction."

I was confused. Wasn't this the book that had Christians in a state of panic? As I began reading the book, I immediately recognized that the facts concerning apologetics, church history, and the origin of the scriptures had been terribly misrepresented. Because I had previously studied those things, I wasn't the least bit bothered by the book. In fact, I thought it was a great novel, and read it straight through.

The Da Vinci Code didn't bother me because I knew that the false information it presented could easily be countered. There are hundreds of pieces of historical evidence that could quickly disprove this small fictional work from the 21st century. There were manuscripts authenticated long before the year that the ancient church supposedly began tampering with scripture (325 AD). These texts include John Ryland's manuscript, dated 100-125 AD; the Bodmer Papyrus, dated 125 AD, which includes nearly all of the Gospel of John; some of the Oxyrhynchus papyri, dated 100-150 AD; the Chester Beatty Papyri, dated 200 AD, which contains much of the New Testament; the Codex Vaticanus, dated 325, containing most of both the Old and New Testaments. Remember, these are actual copies of scripture, some within a generation of the original writers, and they all agree with what we find in our Bibles today.

In addition to these ancient manuscripts of the New Testament itself, we have many writings from early pastors, teachers, and others who quoted portions of the New Testament in their books, notes, and sermon outlines. More than 36,000 of these Biblical quotations are dated prior to 325 AD. Scholars say that all but eleven of the verses in the New Testament are found in these writings dated 100-300 AD.

Knowing all this, I realized I had far more important things to do than try to convince people Dan Brown's story wasn't real. The fact that so many Christians were confused by the book was proof that my time might be better spent teaching on church history, apologetics, and the veracity of ancient Biblical texts.

The Da Vinci Code, The Lost Gospel of Judas, and other works that attack scripture simply do not stand up against historical, archaeological, philosophical, scientific, and linguistic evidence. It is absolutely clear that the authenticity of the New Testament has been preserved accurately for two-thousand years. *The DaVinci Code* attacking this evidence could be likened to a canoe attacking a fleet of battleships.

If your faith has collapsed because of some novel or movie then understand that the naval fleet of your soul has been conquered by a canoe.

We read in II Thessalonians 2:9-12 that in the last days God will send a powerful delusion to the people who have rejected him. If *The Da Vinci Code* has confused you, then the bad news is that you will become even more confused in coming days. If your faith has collapsed because of a book or a movie or whatever else you might stumble across in our culture today, then you should know that the naval fleet of your soul has just been conquered by a canoe.

What's Going On?

Chapter 1: Confusion

I AM A teacher, and I coach the boys' track team at our school. Track practice takes place every weekday after school throughout the season. It's always been that way, and probably always will be. One week I learned that a school dance was scheduled for Friday afternoon right after class ended. Because the dance was going to go well into the night, I told the boys we'd have track practice after school like usual, and they could head over to the dance when they were finished. I told them I was well aware of the dance, but practice was still on. I thought I'd made everything clear as the boys headed to their locker room after Thursday's track practice.

On Friday, about five minutes before the last bell rang, I noticed a DJ setting up his sound equipment for the dance in the school gym. Since our track team practices right outside the gym, I knew the boys were going to be frustrated when they heard the music and saw fellow classmates dancing. I wondered if some boys might still be tempted to skip practice, so, for good measure, I decided to make one final announcement over the intercom as a reminder. The announcement was, "There *will* be track practice as usual immediately after school today for the *entire* boys track team."

Right as the announcement ended, eight boys from the track team walked into my classroom dizzy with confusion. One boy conjured up his best look of bewilderment and asked, "Coach, do we have practice tonight? We were wondering because nobody really knows." When I again confirmed that we did, another boy quickly asked, "What happens if we don't come?" My reply was simple: "You'll be punished."

Confusion was not limited to this group of boys. Many members of the track team lingered in the hallway debating about whether or not there was track practice. One boy approached a team manager to inquire about it. The manager supposedly told him, "I think there's practice…but it might be optional." That was all that the boy needed. Now armed with words straight from the mouth of the team manager, he could claim ignorance to later justify the reason he followed his desires and went to the dance. As I left my classroom to head to the track, another boy stopped me to ask about practice. I looked right at him and said, "Yes, we have practice." He went to the dance.

The track boys who chose to go to the dance could actually see their teammates running warm up laps on the track outside as they walked into the gym. Yet these boys remained "confused" as to whether or not there was track practice.

Confirmations about track practice that had taken place:

1) I had announced there would be practice on Friday and even warned the boys that there might be some confusion because of the dance, but that shouldn't change anything.

2) An announcement was made over the loud speaker moments before the boys had to decide whether or not to go to track practice.

3) Some of the boys had approached me even after hearing the announcement, and I told them face-to-face, "Yes we have track practice."

4) The fifty-eight boys who showed up for track practice were running right outside the gym, and the boys who were at the dance could actually see their teammates running—thus confirming that practice was indeed taking place.

When all seventy track boys showed up on Monday, I asked why twelve of them had missed Friday's practice. The excuses varied but all came back to the same claim: they were in a state of ignorance due to so much confusion. Some insisted that I hadn't made it clear. One blamed the manager for saying practice was optional. Others swore they forgot. And all the boys who went to the dance confirmed each other's confusion by contending that there was just no way of knowing whether or not we had practice. Their strategy involved insisting on confusion. They figured if enough people said they were confused, I would have to accept it as a legitimate excuse. But I didn't. The confused boys lost the privilege of running in our first track meet.

Claiming to be confused
after rejecting the truth
is no different
than claiming to be
in the dark after
you shut off the light.

As I stood there on Monday surrounded by the track team it became clear to me that, in life, people *choose* to be confused. I couldn't have done anything more to get them to track practice short of picking them up and carrying them from the school to the track. (Even then some of the boys probably would have slipped away to the dance while I wasn't looking.) After all my effort to communicate obvious truth, still almost 20% of the boys I spoke with chose to remain confused.

Today the people of the United States of America have become just like those junior high boys. It's a growing cultural pandemic to be confused about what's right, true, and moral. It's hip to claim ignorance and say, "I don't think we can ever really know for sure about things we can't see." In fact, claiming ignorance is the quickest way to avoid any kind of personal responsibility to know and understand the spiritual side of life.

But just because there so are many conflicting beliefs in this world doesn't mean we can claim to be "confused" about what's right without facing serious consequences. And just because certain Bible teachings may baffle us doesn't give us a free pass to skip over them. Just because some Christian doctrines are hotly debated doesn't mean we aren't accountable for examining the evidence ourselves.

We can't hide behind our claims of confusion any longer. We must stop making excuses and admit that things can be known for certain. It's time for us to quit being lazy and get busy gaining the understanding we lack. Like the track boys, the excuse of, "I just wasn't sure which way was right," is not going to cut it in the end.

Chapter 2: God Communicates with Us

THE TRUTH OF *God can be known*. His very nature involves the desire to reveal himself to us, and he loves to communicate with us.

"The heavens declare the glory of God; the skies proclaim the work of his hands. Day after day they pour forth speech; night after night they display knowledge. There is no speech or language where their voice is not heard. Their voice goes out into all the earth, their words to the ends of the world." Psalm 19:1-4

"You saw no form of any kind the day the Lord spoke to you at Horeb out of the fire." Deuteronomy 4:15

"Do you not know? Have you not heard? Has it not been told you from the beginning? Have you not understood since the earth was founded?" Isaiah 40:21

"Did I not proclaim this and foretell it long ago?" Isaiah 44:8

"When he, the Spirit of truth, comes, he will guide you into all truth. He will not speak on his own; he will speak only what he hears." John 16:13

"He has not left himself without testimony." Acts 14:17

"What may be known about God is plain to them, because God has made it plain to them." Romans 1:19

"I have become its servant by the commission God gave me to present to you the word of God in its fullness – the mystery that has been kept hidden from ages and generations, but is now disclosed to the saints." Colossians 1:25

"This is the message we have heard from him and declare to you: God is light; in him there is no darkness at all." I John 1:5

God has communicated with man throughout human history beginning with Adam in the garden and continuing with the patriarchs and the prophets. Finally, God manifested himself to humanity as a man named Jesus. Hebrews 1:1-2 says:

"In the past God spoke to our forefathers through the prophets at many times and in various ways but in these last days he has spoken to us by his Son."

God has continually revealed his nature to us in countless ways. We learn about his character through history, philosophy, and science. Through written text, we learn his plan for the future of mankind. He lets every generation know what he is doing during their time on earth so they can understand what's going on around them.

If you personally don't understand what God is like or what he's doing in the world, you have no one to blame but yourself. You may feel like you can't know God, but it's not because God has failed to communicate with you—it's because you've failed to study hard enough to understand him. This may sound harsh, but it's true. God has gone out of his way to reveal his plans to us, including salvation and a standard of morality that goes above and beyond, calling us to righteousness. As Christians, we should no longer accept the attitude of ignorance or confusion when it comes to the spiritual realm. We should stop nodding in agreement with people who say things like, "Some parts of the Bible are just too confusing for us to comprehend..." or "I'm sure everything will work out fine in the end..." or "I guess we'll just have to wait until we get to heaven to understand it."

As human beings, we are generally rather distrustful of strangers. So when Proverbs 3:5 tells us to trust in God with all our hearts, we can understand why this would be a silly command if God was a total stranger to us. If our creator is merely an entity we can't know much about, why on earth would we be asked to trust him completely? Isn't it therefore logical that God would reveal parts of himself and his plan to us *first*, and expect us to have faith in him *second*?

"God's very nature involves the desire to reveal himself."

Asking for a Sign

In Matthew 16:1-5, the religious leaders in Christ's day were trying to make a decision about who Jesus was. So far they had rejected the available information they already had about Jesus, including:

1. The witness of John the Baptist
2. Jesus' own words
3. Scriptural testimony
4. Jesus' miraculous works

The Pharisees and Sadducees (religious leaders) came to Jesus and tested him by asking him to show them a sign from heaven. Jesus replied:

> "When evening comes, you say, 'It will be fair weather, for the sky is red,' and in the morning, 'Today it will be stormy, for the sky is red and

overcast.' You know how to interpret the appearance of the sky, but you cannot interpret the signs of the times. A wicked and adulterous generation looks for a miraculous sign, but none will be given it except the sign of Jonah.' Jesus then left them and went away." Matthew 16:1-4

Although the Pharisees and Sadducees presented themselves as open-minded seekers who wanted to know the truth, the fact was that they would only hear the truth on their terms. Jesus' response to them indicates that he didn't view them as real seekers desiring revelation from God, but, rather, men who had rejected the truth time and time again. We too can deduce that those who reject God's available revelation while still presenting themselves as "open-minded truth seekers" will be rebuked just like the Pharisees and Sadducees.

Jesus says, "A wicked and adulterous generation looks for a miraculous sign." Why does he say this? Because only a morally corrupt generation would reject all the revelation God had already provided. Jesus made it clear that no miraculous sign would be given. In other words, God will not ever split the sky, step out of the heavens, and appear in all his glory just long enough for a *New York Times* photographer to snap his picture and a CNN cameraman to catch it on film. Although that would be very impressive proof of the reality of God's existence, our creator knows that even an incredible supernatural appearance would do mankind little good. Why? Because as soon as God vanished back into heaven, everyone who'd rejected all his previous revelations would begin to explain away the latest miracle. If men have already found a way to disprove God's revelation in nature, logic, scripture, and history, they won't hesitate to again use their science and philosophy to explain away even the most obvious revelation of God's existence.

Consider the Exodus generation. They were a generation of people enslaved in Egypt when Moses first spoke to Pharoah concerning their freedom. He then called upon signs from God and struck Egypt with ten terrible plagues. The Exodus generation experienced all of the ghastly plagues and later walked through the Red Sea after it was parted by the very hand of God. They were led through the wilderness by a pillar of cloud and fire, and they experienced an incredible manifestation of God on Mt. Sinai. And yet, even after witnessing all these miraculous works of God, the Exodus generation still didn't believe he would lead them into the Promised Land. Because of their disbelief, they spent the rest of their lives wandering in the wilderness. Hebrews 3:16-18 says:

> "Who were they who heard and rebelled? Were they not all those Moses led out of Egypt? And with whom was he angry for forty years? Was it not those who sinned, whose bodies fell in the desert?"

All the excuses of the Exodus generation amounted to nothing more than mankind's continually rebellious attitude toward the obvious truth of God, (truth revealed with crystal clarity, in their case). God was angry that they were so quick to discount his past revelation, and he remained angry for forty years.

I have to imagine Jesus rolling his eyes when the Pharisees and Sadducees asked him for "a sign." After all, he had already performed numerous signs including public healings and miracles. He had brought the dead back to life; he had walked on water; he had cast out demons. There were eye-witnesses at all of these events, and yet many people still wanted "a sign" that Jesus was who he said he was.

Jesus makes it clear that his generation had evidence to make an informed decision about him. In Matthew 16:3, Jesus said, "You know how to interpret the appearance of the sky, but you can not interpret the signs of the times." His generation had paid such careful attention to the signs of the natural world that they had even learned how to predict the weather, but they still couldn't utilize the signs revealed by God to understand what he was doing in their generation.

The problem Jesus had with his generation is the same problem we have today. We are a group of people more aware of our natural world full of trivial concerns than the spiritual realm which is everlasting. We pay no heed to II Corinthians 4:18, "For the things which are seen are temporal, but the things which are not seen are eternal." This is a great travesty because we will all eventually step into that "eternal" world someday, and we will all be held accountable.

Chapter 3: Knowing the Signs

JOHN THE BAPTIST knew the signs, and, therefore, knew that Christ was the Messiah. The wisemen knew the signs, as did Simeon, an old man who met Jesus' parents at the temple when Jesus was an infant. Anna, the prophetess, also recognized Jesus when he was just a baby. These people had been careful to study previous revelation from God. They didn't need additional signs. They already knew what God was up to.

Distractions from the Signs

The parable of the sower says:

> "The one who received the seed that fell on rocky places is the man who hears the word and at once receives it with joy. But since he has no root, he lasts only a short time. When trouble or persecution comes because of the word, he quickly falls away. The one who received the seed that fell among the thorns is the man who hears the word, but the worries of this life and the deceitfulness of wealth choke it, making it unfruitful." Matthew 13:20-22

This is a warning about the things that will keep us from being productive in our spiritual lives. These things include:

1. Trouble
2. Persecution
3. Worries
4. The deceitfulness of wealth
5. Times of testing
6. Riches
7. Pleasures

The seed in the parable represents the word of God revealed to us. The above distractions hinder the growth of that seed after its been planted. The distractions can even render our knowledge of God completely ineffective. They can stop us from maturing in our Christian life. These seven dangers make us vulnerable to the influence of our culture and can cause us to slowly adjust ourselves to the standards of the declining world around us.

If we can overcome these dangers, the word of God will take root in our lives and we will mature and become like Christ, producing more and more righteous deeds. We will begin to positively influence those around us, changing our immediate environment and eventually changing our culture.

They Knew the Times

Many people were not surprised when David became the king of Judah. They knew beforehand that David would be crowned king because God had sent word through the prophets. Abigail knew. Jonathan knew. King Saul knew. Amazingly, even the Philistines knew. They indicated this knowledge when David walked into Achish's palace in Gath several years before he actually became king. I Samuel 21:11says:

> "But the servants of Achish said to him, 'Isn't this David, the king of the land? Isn't he the one they sing about in their dances: 'Saul has slain his thousands and David his tens of thousands'?"

This information had been made available to everyone but most people were too distracted to try to understand it. The problem with their lack of knowledge didn't arise until much later. After the tribe of Judah made David their king, the northern tribes of Israel had to decide if they wanted to unite with Judah under King David and form one nation *or* resist King David, fight against Judah, and try to become their own nation.

I Chronicles 12:32 says, "The men of Issachar knew the times and knew what to do." The men of Isachar were men from one of the northern tribes of Israel. They knew what God had been preparing, and they understood the times they were living in. These men are described in I Chronicles 12:23 as "the men armed for battle who came to David at Hebron to turn Saul's kingdom over to him as the Lord had said." These men were in the midst of a serious, political battle for their land. They were on the verge of a civil war. Yet God had already made a plan to save them from a national catastrophe. What separated these men from other men was their knowledge of the times. They knew which decision to make. They understood the correct course of action. Like the men of Isachar, we must understand the times so we know which decisions are best.

Lights, Maps, and Road Markers

If you are driving on a strange road in the darkness with no road map and no street signs ahead, you are going to have a difficult time knowing which way to go in order to get to your destination. But, if the sun begins to rise, you'll at least know which way is east and which way is west. And if you stop to buy a map, you'll be able to really stay on course. Best of all, if you finally drive past a sign on the road, you'll immediately know exactly where you are. From there, you can use the map to trace a path from where you are to where you want to be.

It's the same way with God's plan for mankind. We find ourselves on life's strange road in the darkness, not understanding why we're here or in which direction we should travel. But then, the sun comes up, and we begin to experience the light of the spiritual realm—something that lets us know God may actually be real. This is much better than being alone in the dark, but the presence of light alone won't help us find our way to a destination. We must then stop to buy a road map. As cheesy as it always sounds, the road map to life is the word of God. Once we begin to understand the Bible, we will have a much better picture of what's going on around us and where we need to go to get to our final destination.

But in order to know where we are on the road of life right now, we need some kind of sign. We must be able to identify some of the events or activities happening in our world during our time on earth, so that we, like other faithful believers before us, can know exactly where we're at in history. Only when we grasp God's entire plan for mankind can we find out what he wants us to accomplish in our generation.

God knows that men must be given a certain amount of information in order to find their way in the world—to make the right choices and do right things. That's why God gives us the sun, the road map, and, the part that isn't talked about as often, the many signs along the road we travel.

God knows that men must be given a certain amount of information to find their way.

Chapter 4: Staying Alert

THE APOSTLE PAUL started a church in the Greek town Thessalonica in Macedonia. Because of persecution, he had to flee town and ended up in Corinth, a city in the Greek province of Achaia. While he was there, the believers in Thessalonica sent him a letter with some questions about Christianity. One of those questions asked about a timeline for the Lord's return. Paul answers their question in I Thessalonians 5:1:

> "Now, brothers, about times and dates, we do not need to write to you, for you know very well that the day of the Lord will come like a thief in the night." I Thessalonians 5:1, 2

The Greek words for "times" and "dates" are:

1) chronos – translates as "times" and refers to a space of time or interval—a period of time. Ephesians 3:9 calls the present church age an "oikonomia" which is a Greek word for the administration or stewardship of a household or estate. -

2) kairos – translates as "dates" or "seasons" and refers to the length of a time or the character of a time. The character of a time would include its specific features (e.g. temple worship in the age of Israel, the ministry of the Holy Spirit during the church age, etc.).

Basically, Paul is saying, "Concerning the periods of time and the character of that time," or "concerning the various dispensations..." He says he does not need to write about these things because the people should already know them. They should be familiar with past dispensations after reading the Old Testament, and they should understand the current dispensation from Jesus' teaching and Paul's own teaching. Paul says in the NIV that they understood these things "very well." "Very well" comes from the Greek word "akribos" which means "exactly or perfectly." Other translations say they "know full well" or "know perfectly or thoroughly." Paul says they know "that the day of the Lord will come like a thief in the night." "The day of the Lord" is a reference to the seven year period of time leading up to Christ's physical manifestation in the sky when he descends the Mount of Olives and enters Jerusalem. The seven year Tribulation period comes directly after the church age and is known as "the day of the Lord" in II Thessalonians 2:1-4.

To say Christ will come as a "thief in the night" is the perfect analogy because so many people will be spiritually asleep, and the Messiah's return will catch them completely by surprise. In Matthew 24:37-39, Jesus describes what those last days will be like:

"As it was in the days of Noah, so it will be at the coming of the Son of Man. For in the days before the flood, people were eating and drinking, marrying and giving in marriage up to the day Noah entered the ark; and they knew nothing about what would happen until the flood came and took them all away. That is how it will be at the coming of the Son of Man." Matthew 24:37-39

Peace and Safety

Paul spoke about the worldview of the last generation before Christ returns. He says:

"While people are saying, 'peace and safety,' destruction will come on them suddenly, as labor pains on a pregnant woman, and they will not escape." I Thessalonians 5:3

The generation that sees the beginning of the Tribulation will be talking about "peace and safety." World events will have finally reached a temporary state of calm, and there will be total cooperation among nations. The false hope of world peace will lull nations into a political trap that will end in a world war. The cultural turmoil, economic upheaval, and cataclysmic events of the tribulation will serve as warning signs that Jesus is about to return.

These warning signs can be likened to the signs of a pregnant woman. A woman doesn't just wake up one day and give birth to a baby. She first has nine months of pregnancy, and, when the birth is imminent, she experiences many hours of labor pains. So it will be with Christ's second coming. It should not take us by surprise because there will be plenty evidence far in advance that it is going to happen. Although Jesus said we will not know the day or the hour of his return (Mark 13:32; Matt. 24:36), Paul stresses that we *should* know the times and the seasons. A woman may not know what day or hour she'll give birth, but she definitely knows she's pregnant, and the moment she goes into labor, she knows the time is very near. Those who do not believe in the promise of Christ's return will not interpret the events of the tribulation correctly and will be stunned when it actually happens. Had they paid attention to the seasons, they would not have been caught unaware. It's as though they've watched the season change to winter, but have refused to notice the bare tree branches, the shorter days, the dropping temperatures. So when the first snow comes, they ask, "Is it winter already?" Because they missed all the signs, they've failed to make winter preparations. They have no warm clothes, no ice scraper, no snow tires, no shovel.

Jesus said:

> "Understand this: if the owner of the house had known at what time of night the thief was coming, he would have kept watch and would not have let his house be broken into. <u>So you also must be ready</u>, because the Son of Man will come at an hour when you do not expect him." Matthew 24:42-44

Paul addresses those who believe Jesus is coming back someday. He says:

> "But you, brothers, are not in darkness so that this day should surprise you like a thief. You are all sons of the light and sons of the day. We do not belong to the night or to the darkness. So then, let us not be like others, who are asleep, but <u>let us be alert</u> and self-controlled."

Anyone who knows the Bible should not be surprised by Christ's return. Paul calls believers "sons of the light and sons of the day." He says believers should not be asleep, but alert. "Alert" has been translated from the Greek word "gregoreuo" which means "to keep awake, to be watching, to be vigilant." It is in the present tense here which means "continuous action." "Self-controlled" has been translated from the Greek word "nepho" which means "to not be drunk with wine, to be sober, to watch." It's talking about avoiding the influence of the world while waiting for Christ's return. Together, these two words ("gregoreuo" and "nepho") urge believers to pay attention to the teachings they already "know very well" concerning the times while applying those teachings to their daily lives.

Keeping Your Clothes

Revelation 16:15 says:

> "Behold, I come like a thief! Blessed is he who stays awake and keeps his clothes with him, so that he may not go naked and be shamefully exposed."

If this verse has ever baffled you, perhaps some background will be helpful. In the Roman world, enemy combatants were stripped of their clothes to expose their weakness and shame. Even the dead were often stripped of their clothing as a final sign of having been conquered. In other words, a fully clothed soldier will live to fight another day—a naked one, probably not. Any soldier who is not prepared for battle will surely be defeated, captured, stripped, and shamefully exposed.

In addition, the nightly temple guards in Jerusalem where required to stand, salute, and greet the Captain of the Temple as he made his rounds throughout the night. If any guard fell asleep, the Captain would know immediately because that guard would fail to stand up as usual and say, "Officer of the Temple Mount, peace be to you." If the guard had fallen asleep and thereby missed his cue, the Captain would take his torch and set the guard's clothes set on fire. If the guard survived the fire, he would be shamefully exposed in the morning walking around in his burnt clothes.[1]

We are the temple guards of the church age. We will be exposed by the enemy if we don't stay alert. Satan would love to strip us of the garments that prove our righteous position and character. Our mission is to "guard the good deposit that is entrusted to us" (II Timothy 1:14).

If we fall asleep, we will be exposed at the judgment seat of Christ:

Chapter 5: Judgments and Rewards

II Corinthians 5:10 says:

> "For we must all appear before the judgment seat of Christ, that each one may receive what is due him for the things done while in the body whether good or bad."

"Appear" is the Greek word "phanerothanai," and it means "to make clear, to manifest." The meaning of this word *is not* "to show up," or "to be there." The verse means that everyone's life and character will be crystal clear. Hidden motives will all be made obvious. I Corinthians 4:5 says:

> "Therefore judge nothing before the appointed time; wait till the Lord comes. He will bring to light what is hidden in darkness and will expose the motives of men's hearts. At that time each will receive his praise from God."

Proverbs 21:2 says:

> "All a man's ways (*actions*) seem right to him, but the Lord weighs the heart (*motives*)."

Two people may do the same good deed for very different reasons. Consider those who were preaching Christ just because they were envious of Paul and felt competitive with him.

> "It is true that some preach Christ out of envy and rivalry, but others out of good will. The latter do so in love, knowing that I am put here for the defense of the gospel. The former preach Christ out of selfish ambition, not sincerely, supposing that they can stir up trouble for me while I am in chains. But what does it matter? The important thing is that in every way, whether from false motives or true, Christ is preached." Philippians 1:15, 16

Notice that both were doing the same work: preaching Christ. The difference was only in their motives:

1) out of envy and rivalry, selfish ambition
2) out of good will, in love, in knowledge, sincerely

Jesus warned about wasting our lives in service to others while actually just honoring ourselves.

> "Be careful not to do your acts of righteousness before men, to be seen by them. If you do, you will have no reward from your Father in heaven. I tell you the truth, they have received their reward in full." Matthew 6:1, 5

"Judgment seat" comes from the word "bema." In Jesus' day, the "bema" was a platform where officials sat to deliberate on decisions. It was where official judgments were made and rewards were handed out. In John 19:13, Jesus himself appeared before the "bema" of Pilate.

"Due" comes from the word "komizo" and it means "to get for oneself, to receive, to receive as recompense." It refers to receiving something that belongs to you. God has set up a reward system for all believers. When a believer has done the work asked of him, a reward is "due" him according to God's standards.

"Bad" here means "worthless, of no account, good-for-nothing." It doesn't necessarily mean these actions were sinful or evil; they were just worthless. The wood, hay, and straw of I Corinthians 3:12, 13 is burned up at the bema of Christ. The "bad" things here are those things that may have had some earthly value but are of no value in light of eternity.

Thankfully, we who trusted Christ to save us will not have to account for all the sinful things we did on earth because we are forgiven. Jesus has already made the payment for our sins. The following verses help confirm that the judgment seat of Christ is not a judgment of our sin.

> John 3:18: "Whoever believes is not condemned."

> John 5:24: "I tell you the truth, whoever hears my word and believes him who sent me has eternal life and will not be condemned; he has crossed over from death to life."

> John 6:37: "All that the Father gives me will come to me, and whoever comes to me I will never drive away."

> Romans 5:1: "Therefore, since we have been justified through faith, we have peace with God through our Lord Jesus Christ."

> I Peter 2:24 "He himself bore our sins in his body on the tree."

> Romans 8:1: "Therefore, there is now no condemnation for those who are in Christ Jesus."

> I Corinthians 11:32: "When we are judged by the Lord, we are being disciplined so that we will not be condemned with the world."

The judgment seat of Christ deals entirely with our service for the Lord and has nothing to do with sin. Jesus already paid for our sin on the cross, so believers will not be judged for their sin, but rather, evaluated on their production.

Quality of Works Revealed by Fire

We know that the quality of our works on earth will be revealed in heaven. I Corinthians 3:10-15 says:

> "By the grace God has given me, I laid a foundation as an expert builder, and someone else is building on it. But each one should be careful how he builds. For no one can lay any foundation other than the one already laid, which is Jesus Christ. If any man builds on this foundation using gold, silver, costly stones, wood, hay, or straw, his work will be shown for what it is, because the day will bring it to light. It will be revealed with fire, and the fire will test the quality of each man's work. If what he has built survives, he will receive his reward. If it is burned up, he will suffer loss; he himself will be saved, but only as one escaping through the flames."

The "building" spoken of here is the life of a believer. The foundation is Jesus Christ. You cannot build a true Christian life with out first laying the foundation—faith in Jesus. There are two groups of building material that can be used to build a Christian life:

1) Gold, silver, and costly stones – these are all very valuable and were used to build temples in the ancient world. These materials will endure in fire/be purified by fire.

2) Wood, hay, and straw – these were also considered legitimate building materials in the ancient world, and we still use wood today when we build homes. But these materials, however common, are not lasting and would be consumed if a fire broke out.

Notice that neither group of building materials is bad. But one set of materials is used to build places that honor deities, whereas the other set of materials is used to build homes for common men. If you want to build your Christian life as a house for men to applaud, feel free to use wood, hay, and straw. But if you want to build your life as you would a dwelling place for God, you must use gold, silver, and costly stones.

At the bema seat of Christ, your life (your "building"), including the foundation of Jesus Christ, will pass through the fire of evaluation. This evaluation is not a judgment to determine whether or not you get eternal life. That was already secured when you determined your foundation. This judgment is for believers only. There is a separate judgment for those who did not build on the right foundation. It's called the Great White Throne judgment, and it comes at the end of the millennium as described in Revelation 20:11-15.

Paul tells us that at the bema seat of Christ, the building materials we've chosen to use "will be revealed with fire, and the fire will test the quality of each man's work." This fire will do one of two things to our work:

1) Consume the "bad" or "worthless" (wood, hay, or straw)
2) Purify the "good" (gold, silver, and costly stones)

With the consumption of the "wood, hay, and straw," some believers will "suffer loss" of their entire life's work. They are fortunate that their foundation, which is Jesus, has endured the fire. But they will enter into eternity with little or no reward for what they built during their lives.

God rewards believers for their faithful service. The believer who has been saved for many years and lived a faithful life will have more opportunities for rewards than one who got saved at the last minute or one who never truly walked in obedience to God.

It is possible to spend your life thinking you are serving the Lord but earn no reward in the end (I Corinthians 3:15; 9:27). Rewards are only given for actions that involve:

1) Pure or sincere motivation—(doing the right thing for the wrong reason won't earn a reward)
2) Serving God in truth—(having a sincere motive but doing the wrong thing won't earn a reward)

The Protestant Problem

The Protestant Reformation of the 1500s was a rebellion against the Roman Catholic church. The Protestants emphasized salvation by faith in Christ alone—and rightly so. But now, this doctrine has been taken to the extreme in many Protestant churches, neglecting the need for good works. Yet good works (and subsequent rewards) are foundational to the Christian faith, as seen in these verses:

Services That Result in Rewards:

1. Persevering under trial (James 1:12)
2. Diligently seeking after God (Hebrews 11:6)
3. Martyrdom (Revelations 2:10)
4. Faithfully doing God's will (II Timothy 4:8)
5. Looking forward to Christ's return (II Timothy 4:8)
6. Faithfully serving as a pastor (I Peter 5:4)
7. Leading people to a saving faith in Christ (I Thessalonians 2:19-20)
8. Faithful stewardship (I Corinthians 4:1-5)

9. Acts of kindness (Galatians 6:10)
10. Hospitality (Matthew 10:40-42)

Each man is born with a sin nature. All the good works he performs (works that stem from that sin nature) are "as filthy rags" to God. When a man trusts in Jesus, however, he receives:

1) A new nature
2) A plan from God
3) The Holy Spirit
4) Specific good works to do

When a man walks in the Spirit, he will learn the plan God has for him and the "good works God prepared in advance for him to do" (Ephesians 2:10). The man who walks in obedience will receive rewards from God for good deeds done in the power of the Holy Spirit. If even our "good works" have been prepared for us, we can rest assured our rewards have also been prepared.

To avoid the problems the Protestant and Catholic churches have dealt with regarding salvation/works, keep these points and verses in mind.

Salvation is a gift.
Rewards are earned.
Salvation cannot be lost.
Rewards can be lost.

1. Salvation is described in the Bible as a free gift.

> "If you knew the gift of God and who it is that asks you for a drink, you would have asked him and he would have given you living water." John 4:10

> "The gift of God is eternal life in Christ Jesus..." Romans 6:23

2. Rewards are earned through works.

> "And if anyone gives even a cup of cold water to one of these little ones because he is my disciple, I tell you the truth, he will certainly not lose his reward." Matthew 10:42

> "Do you not know that in a race all the runners run, but only one gets the prize. Run in such a way as to get the prize. Everyone who competes in the games goes into strict training. They do it to get a crown that will not last; but we do it to get a crown that will last forever." I Corinthians 9:24, 25

(Also read: II Timothy 4:7, 8; Revelation 2:10; Revelation 22:12; Luke 19:17)

3. Salvation is something we can possess right now during our lifetime.

"Your faith has saved you, go in peace." Luke 7:50

"Whoever believes in the Son of God has eternal life." John 3:36

(Also read: John 5:24; John 6:47)

4. Rewards cannot be possessed until a future time, after the Lord returns.

"For the Son of Man is going to come in his Father's glory with his angels, and then he will reward each person according to what he has done." Matthew 16:27

(Also read: II Timothy 4:8; Revelation 22:12)

5. Salvation cannot be lost. Rewards can be lost.

"No, I beat my body and make it my slave so that after I have preached to others, I myself will not be disqualified for the prize." I Corinthians 9:27

"Disqualified" here is the word "adokimos." The root word "dokimos" or "dokimozo" means "to test to approve as one tests metal in a fire." The prefix "a" in the Greek means "the opposite of" or "anti." To be "adokimos" is to be "the opposite of one approved or accepted after the testing." It means "to be rejected after the testing." Apparently, people can lose rewards they were supposed to have received.

"I am coming soon. Hold on to what you have, so that no one will take you crown." Revelation 3:11

"Watch out that you do not lose what you have worked for, but that you may be rewarded fully." II John 8

God offers the lost salvation through faith in Christ, and he offers believers rewards for faithful service. You can see the confusion in doctrine that occurs when the above areas get mixed up. When salvation and rewards are confused, false teaching develops from lack of understanding. Some false teaching might include:

1. Salvation is earned.
2. Rewards in heaven are distributed equally.
3. We get rewards on earth.
4. We can lose the salvation we worked so hard for.
5. God offers salvation only to the person who does good works.
6. Good works don't matter at all.

Crowns in Scripture

Our rewards will include special crowns.

"Do you not know that in a race all the runners run, but only one gets the prize? Run in such a way as to get the prize. Everyone who competes in the games goes into strict training. They do it to get a crown that will not last; but we do it to get a crown that will last forever." I Corinthians 9:24, 25

The word "crown" here is the Greek word "stephanos" which means "the victor's crown." The victor's crown was the ultimate symbol of victory given out to the winners of Greek games. The word "stephanos" can also be used in a way that means "ornament for a festivity or celebration." It's used this way in: Proverbs 1:9; Proverbs 4:9; Song of Solomon 3:11; Isaiah 28:1. People wore this type of "stephanos" to indicate that they were publicly honoring someone who had distinguished service—someone who'd been proven worthy of praise. People wore these kinds of crowns during the Parousia (the return of a king in the Greek and Roman world). Likewise, we will wear these crowns when Jesus returns.

The "diadema" was the kingly crown. (Remember the lyrics "bring forth the royal diadem?") A diadema is worn only by nobility—someone occupying a royal position. Believers will not earn this type of crown; it is for the king alone.

There are several specific crowns mentioned in scripture. Each one is connected to a different aspect of the Christian life.

1. **Incorruptible Crown** (I Corinthians 9:25). This crown indicates mastery over the sin nature.

   "Therefore, I do not run like a man running aimlessly; I do not fight like a man beating the air. No, I beat my body and make it my slave so that after I have preached to others, I myself will not be disqualified for the prize." I Corinthians 9:25

   The Corinthians are urged to live the Christian life in such a way as to receive a prize in the end. The emphasis here is self-control.

   Note the other things we should learn from the analogy of life as a race:
   1) Only those who run the race according to the rules can earn a reward. If a track runner runs the wrong way around the track or leaves the track and runs around the buses in the parking lot, he will not win the race regardless of how fast he is.
   2) A crown eventually becomes old after the victory is over. But what the crown symbolizes (the prestige and fame of the winner) will never fade.
   3) Paul does not run aimlessly—meaning he does not live his Christian life without purpose or direction. Nor should we live without direction. Think about what would happen if someone entered a race without knowing how far they'd be running. There is a great difference between running 100 meters, 400 meters, and 1600 meters. If you don't know how far the race is, it's hard to pace yourself, making it extremely tough to win.
   4) The undisciplined believer who misses the purpose of life is like a zealous boxer who fails to land his blows.

2. **Crown of Righteousness** (II Timothy 4:7-8). This crown is for those who live righteously in the world as they look forward to Christ's return. It's for those who are not captivated by this world, but instead hunger and thirst for righteousness.

> "I have fought the good fight, I have finished the race, I have kept the faith. Now there is in store for me the crown of righteousness, which the Lord, the righteous Judge, will award to me on that day—and not only to me, but also to all who have longed for his appearing." II Timothy 4:7-8

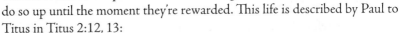

This is a crown earned for living an upstanding life. "Have longed for" is in the perfect tense here which suggests people who've greatly anticipated Christ's return in the past and are continuing to do so up until the moment they're rewarded. This life is described by Paul to Titus in Titus 2:12, 13:

> "[The grace] teaches us to say 'no' to ungodliness and worldly passions and to live self-controlled, upright, and godly lives in this present age while we wait for the blessed hope—the glorious appearing of our great God and Savior, Jesus Christ."

"Fought" is the word "agonizomai" and, though sometimes it can refer to a military fight, here it is clearly a reference to training and competing in athletics. It is the same word translated "competes in the games" in I Corinthians 9:25.

- "make every effort" in Luke 13:24
- "struggling" in Colossians 1:29
- "wrestling" in Colossians 4:12
- "strive" in I Timothy 4:10
- "fight" in I Timothy 6:12

3. **Crown of Life** (James 1:12; Revelation 2:10). This crown goes only to those who've endured great trials. The believe who moves forward in faith in the midst of great adversity will receive this special crown.

> "Blessed is the man who perseveres under trial, because when he has stood the test, he will receive the crown of life that God has promised to those who love him." James 1:12

> "Do not be afraid of what you are about to suffer. I tell you the devil will put some of you in prison to test you, and you will suffer persecution for

ten days. Be faithful, even to the point of death, and I will give you the crown of life." Revelation 2:10

Testing and trials are part of every life. Sadly, when faced with great hardship, many Christians turn back on God rather than continuing on the path he has called them to. Jesus said we would have trouble: "I have told you these things, so that in me you may have peace. In this world you will have trouble. But take heart! I have overcome the world" (John 16:33). He also said, "If the world hates you, keep in mind that it hated me first" (John 15:18).

Paul writes to Timothy:

> You, however, know all about my teaching, my way of life, my purpose, faith, patience, love, endurance, persecutions, sufferings—what kinds of things happened to me in Antioch, Iconium, and Lystra, the persecutions I endured. Yet the Lord rescued me from all of them. In fact, everyone who wants to live a godly life in Christ Jesus will be persecuted." II Timothy 3:10, 11, 12

The doorway to the next level of fulfilling God's plan is to endure everything life throws at you and make the sacrifices that are required for you to keep living a godly life. The reward comes for "persevering" and remaining faithful. The reward is *not* given to those who are quickly delivered from trials and tests.

4. **Crown of Joy** (Philippians 4:1; 1 Thess.2:19). This crown is for those who lead others to Christ or who demonstrate great fruitfulness in their lives, thus influencing others toward righteousness. We won't just be rewarded for how we choose to live our own lives, but we'll also receive rewards for the influence we had on others and how they chose to live their lives.

> "Therefore, my brother, you whom I love and long for, my joy and crown, that is how you should stand firm in the Lord, dear friends!" Philippians 4:1

> "For what is our hope, our joy, or the crown in which we will glory in the presence of our Lord Jesus when he comes? Is it not you? Indeed, you are our glory and joy." I Thessalonians 2:19

In Daniel 12:3, Gabriel tells Daniel:

> "Those who are wise will shine like the brightness of the heavens and those who lead many to righteousness, like the stars forever and ever."

5. **Crown of Glory** (I Peter 5:4). The greatest achievement is to fulfill your calling and finish the work God has asked of you.

> "To the elders among you, I appeal as a fellow elder...One who will share in the glory to be revealed: be shepherds of God's flock that is under your care...and when the Chief Shepherd appears, you will receive the crown of glory that will never fade away." I Peter 5:4

This scripture is specifically about pastors who complete their work diligently, but the Crown of Glory is not just for pastors because every believer has a gift, calling, and purpose. The crown is for anyone who chooses to fulfill their God-given assignment.

Here Jesus is seen as the Chief Shepherd, paying the workers he contracted to tend his sheep while he was gone.

A Brief Review of Crowns

1) Incorruptible Crown for mastery over the sin nature
2) Crown of Righteousness for living a holy life in a sinful world
3) Crown of Life for enduring trials while staying true to the faith
4) Crown of Joy for leading others to Christ and spurring them onto righteousness
5) Crown of Glory for fulfilling a calling and finishing the work assigned

In the final chapter of the Bible, Jesus again tells us to stay alert because he is coming back. He also reminds us that we will be rewarded for the things we've done during our time here on earth:

> "Behold, I am coming soon! My reward is with me, and I will give to everyone according to what he has done." Revelation 22:12

Chapter 6: Dispensations

THERE IS A valuable principle in life that involves knowing where you've been and knowing where you're going. It is the only way to effectively determine what you need to do right now.

What's your life all about? Do you know why you're here? Trying to answer some of these questions can be likened to staring at one piece of a puzzle and trying to grasp the whole picture. The single piece you hold in your hand might seem meaningless, and it is, in fact, very confusing by itself because it doesn't present the whole image—or even a sensible part of it. Yet you know it must fit in there somewhere. It came in the puzzle box, after all.

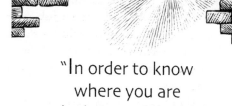

So where does the puzzle piece of your life belong? In order to find out where you fit, you must first know which puzzle pieces have already been fitted into place. In other words, you need to know what's already been done in order to know what to do next.

"In order to know where you are and what you should do you need to know where you come from and where you are going."

The Time Before Man

There are four "beginnings" mentioned in the Bible that help to set up the chronology of events in the ancient world:

1) The beginning of God, (not the literal beginning of God, but the starting point for our story)
2) The beginning of angels
3) The beginning of the physical universe
4) The beginning of man

John 1:1 says:

> "In the beginning was the Word, and the Word was with God, and the Word was God. He was with God in the beginning."

This verse is not about the beginning of God himself; it's about the beginning of the account of God's plan revealed to men. It's a reference to the most ancient point in recorded history.

Before the universe was created, and before mankind came into being, the angels were created. We know this because in Job 38:4-7, God asks Job:

> "Where were you when I laid the earth's foundation? On what were its footings set, or who laid its cornerstone while the mornings stars sang together and all the angels shouted for joy?"

The angels actually witnessed the creation of the physical universe. In Isaiah 14:12, the phrase "morning star" is the translation of the Hebrew word "helel" which, in the Greek, is "eosphorus" or "dawn-bearer" and in the Septuagint (Latin version from 200 BC) is "lucis" or "light." In 1611, the English King James translators utilized the Latin phrase "lucis ferre" ("ferre" means "to bring"). This phrase was translated into English as "Lucifer." Thus, "Lucifer" or "Morning Star" is an actual personality from the angelic class of the cherubim.

It is interesting to note that all the angels (including Lucifer and his fallen comrades) not only believe in God (James 2:19), but they know for a fact that he is the creator.

The physical universe was created in Genesis 1:1 at God's command:

> "For he spoke, and it came to be; he commanded, and it stood firm."
> Psalm 33:9

The Angelic Rebellion

Genesis 1:2 says:

> "Now the earth was formless and empty, darkness was over the surface of the deep."

Most people understand these verses to mean that before God created everything, the earth was empty and dark. But throughout scripture the Hebrew words that translate into formless, empty, and dark (used here) are words used to describe the effects of God's judgment. Being empty, without form, and in darkness isn't merely the result of being without God, but is a direct consequence of having been condemned by God. In other words, it sounds as though planet earth was condemned by God long before the six days of creation occurred.

All scholars, teachers, and pastors who accept the Bible as the inspired word of God generally agree on a few basic things regarding Satan. They agree that he was originally created by God as sinless, but he chose to lead an angelic rebellion and was eventually cast out of heaven. Although these are widely accepted doctrines in most orthodox theologies, it seems few people bother to ask the question "when?" When did the rebellion and fall of Satan occur?

Did it happen:

1) sometime during the seven days of creation, before God made man?
2) sometime after the creation of man on the sixth day?
3) Sometime before the creation of the universe?

Many people quickly pick the third answer, thinking very little of it. But a fourth option seems possible in light of the early verses in Genesis. Satan may have rebelled sometime after the creation of the universe as recorded in Genesis 1:1 and then been cast out of heaven, down to earth—thus explaining all the chaos, emptiness, and darkness of God's judgment on the earth we read about in Genesis 1:2.

Isaiah records:

> "How you have fallen from heaven O morning star, son of the dawn! You have been cast down to the earth…You said in your heart, 'I will ascend to heaven…I will make myself like the Most High." Isaiah 14:12-14

Ezekiel 28:12-16 says:

> "You were the model of perfection, full of wisdom and perfect in beauty. You were in Eden, the garden of God; every precious stone adorned you."

Satan was a fantastic spiritual being—full of wisdom, perfect in beauty, and adorned with precious stones. Ezekiel lists nine of those precious stones, and they just so happen to be nine of the same stones worn by the High Priest of Israel.

> "You were anointed as a guardian cherub, for so I ordained you. You were on the holy mount of God; you walked among the fiery stones." Ezekiel 28:14

The cherubim class of angels is always associated with the presence of God. Lucifer was anointed as the guardian cherub and was allowed to move in and out of the presence of God (another mark of a high priest). This information was revealed about Lucifer before he fell:

1) He had access to God and was trusted in God's presence.
2) He served in a priestly function by representing the angels before God and representing God to the angels.
3) He had vast amounts of inside information, knowledge and wisdom.
4) He was created the perfect angelic model.

About Lucifer we read:

> "You were blameless in your ways from the day you were created until wickedness was found in you. Through your widespread trade, you were filled with violence, and you sinned. So I drove you in disgrace from the Mount of God, and I expelled you, O guardian cherub, from among the fiery stones."

Because of his sin, Satan was expelled from God's presence. According to Isaiah, he was "cast down to the earth." Jesus confirms these accounts when he says in Luke 10:18, "I saw Satan fall like lightning from heaven."

The result of Satan's sin was not just his expulsion from heaven, but also a judgment on everything he had administration over, including, possibly, the earth.

The Account of Creation

Genesis 1:2 says:

> "Now the earth was formless and empty, darkness was over the surface of the deep and the Spirit of God was hovering over the waters."

In the margin notes of the New International Version, it tells us that another way of reading this verse is, "Now the earth *became* formless and empty..." The Hebrew verb "hajah" translates in English as "had become" or "to become, come to pass." The verb, therefore, suggests that the chaotic condition of the earth was not its original state. It had *become* that way. Although this explanation is not universally accepted by Christians, most agree on these major points:

1) God created the universe.
2) There was an angelic rebellion.
3) God created mankind to live in a physical universe in the midst of an *already existing* conflict with evil.

The passage ends by noting that even in the earth's chaotic, empty state, the Spirit of God was hovering over its dark waters. God was making a move to restore life and dignity to the world.

In Genesis 1:3-25, God totally reforms the earth. John 1:3 tells us that through the Word "all things were made" and "without him nothing was made that has been made." Colossians 1:16 says that through Jesus, "all things were created; things in heaven and on earth, visible and invisible."

God the Father and God the Son worked together throughout the creation process. In Proverbs we read that "wisdom" or "the Word" says this about the first day of creation:

> "I was there when he set the heavens in place, when he marked out the horizon on the face of the deep, when he established the clouds above and fixed securely the fountains of the deep."

In reference to the second day of creation, he says:

> "[I was there] when he gave the sea its boundary so the waters would not overstep his command, and when he marked out the foundations of the earth."

In reference to the third day of creation, he says:

> "[I was there as a] craftsman at his side. I was filled with delight day after day, rejoicing always in his presence."

Throughout the creation process, "wisdom" or "the Word" was there with God. At the end of the sixth day, he "rejoiced in the whole world and delighted in mankind."

On the first day of creation, God said, "Let there be light." He was instructing the glory of God as manifested above (through "the Word") to finally move over the desolate earth.

On the second day of creation God said:

> "Let there be an expanse between the waters to separate water from water…and God called the expanse sky." Genesis 1:7, 8

God created the sky (or the atmosphere) of our planet to be surrounded with water both above and below. (At this time, no land had been drawn out of the earth's water.) The atmosphere held back a layer of water encircling the earth that helped protect the planet from the sun's radiation. The result was a green, tropical environment and a much longer, healthier lifespan.

On the third day of creation, God said:

> "Let the water under the sky be gathered to one place, and let dry ground appear." Genesis 1:9

This would indicate the appearance of land as God gathered the waters on earth into one place. The land that appeared was probably one single continental land mass, not the various continents as we know them today.

On the fourth day, God said:

> "Let there be lights in the expanse of the sky to separate the day from the night, and let them serve as signs to mark seasons and days and years." Genesis 1:14

The First Dispensation

On the fifth and sixth day, God made animals. And finally, when everything else was ready, God created man. Man was made in God's likeness and was put in charge of all things.

> "Let us make man in our image, in our likeness, and let them rule over the fish of the sea and the birds of the air, over the livestock, over all the earth and over all the creatures that move along the ground." Genesis 1:26

The creation of man put into motion the first dispensation (or age) of human history. There was no death, no sin, no sickness, no pain, no doubt. The earth, the climate, and everything God had created to live within it were perfect. The Lord himself walked with and spoke to mankind in the garden. The relationship between God and man was unhindered.

It was also during this time that God set the institution of marriage into place.

> "The man said, 'This is now bone of my bones and flesh of my flesh; she shall be called *woman* for she was taken out of man.' For this reason a man will leave his father and mother and be united to his wife, and they will become one flesh." Genesis 2:23, 24

Honoring of the institution of marriage is necessary for the well being of mankind.

During this first dispensation, man was told,

> "You are free to eat from any tree in the garden; but you must not eat from the tree of the knowledge of good and evil, for when you eat of it you will surely die." Genesis 2:16

That was the only rule man had to follow. There were no sacrifices to complete, no confession to make, no Law of Moses to follow, no Lord's Supper to partake of. There was simply one command to obey.

But obeying that command wasn't as easy as one might imagine. Because even as God was creating man, there was already an evil spiritual presence on earth. There was an enormous unresolved conflict between God and Satan.

Satan: The Courtroom Adversary

According to Matthew 25:41, an eternal fire has been prepared for Satan.

> "Depart from me, you who are cursed, into the eternal fire prepared for the devil and his angels."

For some reason, after Satan sinned against God, he was cast down to earth rather than thrown into the eternal fire already prepared for him. It is as though Satan, the great accuser (the word "Satan" comes from the Hebrew word for "accuser" or "adversary"), had defended himself in the courts of heaven and managed to get his sentence suspended. It may sound like a silly concept at first, but it is possible. The Bible often speaks of a "heavenly courtroom." (In Job and Zechariah, we learn about Satan accusing specific men in the courts of heaven.) Some scholars believe that Satan literally challenged God in this same heavenly courtroom, and I too think this likely happened.

Satan may have questioned God's character in court, trying to build a case against him. The great accuser may have said, "If God is really omniscient (all-knowing) and omnipotent (all-powerful), he would have known about my future sin when he created me. So I'm no more at fault in all this than God is. My sin is God's responsibility because he's the one who created me and made me capable of sinning." Satan may then have blasphemed God's character, asking, "How can God be love if he creates beings capable of sin but then requires them not to sin? Why did he make me and the other fallen angels if he knew we were all destined for the Lake of Fire? Is a God who will do something like that really worthy of our respect and worship?"

Satan may have made false accusations against God, slandering him in front of all the heavenly beings. Interestingly, the word "devil" is a translation of the Greek word "diabolos" which means "slanderer."

God could have responded to Satan's accusations in one of two ways:

1) He could demonstrate his absolute power in front of the angels and send Satan immediately to the Lake of Fire. This would forever solidify who was in charge.

Or:

2) He could call a recess in the trial and send Satan to earth during the interim. This way God could build his side of the case and set up a true demonstration of his character throughout the history of mankind. He would build evidence that he was more than just absolute power and justice; he was also love, mercy, and compassion. And he would display all this in our physical realm for the spiritual realm to behold.

God apparently chose #2 and suspended Lucifer's death sentence. He decided to demonstrate his character on earth so that, when the trial reconvened, he would be able to call earthly witnesses (mankind) to testify on his behalf, disproving Satan's accusations. Satan could then be given his original sentence and thrown into the Lake of Fire. Following the trial, all men who had served their purpose by living "for the glory of God" or to demonstrate the character of God would be richly rewarded for eternity.

Considering this courtroom scenario helps us better understand Paul's words in Ephesians 3:8-11:

> "This grace was given me: to preach to the Gentiles the unsearchable riches of Christ, and to make plain to everyone the administration of this mystery, which for ages past was kept hidden in God, who created all thing. His intent was that now, through the church, the manifold

31

wisdom of God should be made known to the rulers and authorities in the heavenly realms, according to his eternal purpose which he accomplished in Christ Jesus our Lord."

Paul says that God's intent was for his great wisdom to be made known to all the beings in the heavenly realm. In other words, perhaps our world has less to do with us and our individual lives on this small planet and more to do with an enormous battle that's been raging in the heavens long before humanity came on the scene.

Regarding our possible testimony in this ongoing court case, Paul says:

> "Do you not know that we will judge angels?" I Corinthians 6:3

Daniel also reveals the future court scene when he records this vision:

> "As I looked, thrones were set in place, and the Ancient of Days took his seat...Thousands upon thousands attended him; ten thousand times ten thousand stood before him. The court was seated, and the books were opened...I kept looking until the beast was slain and its body destroyed and thrown into the blazing fire." Daniel 7:9-11

The First Sacrifice

Adam was placed on earth to demonstrate the glory (or character) of God, as were all those who came after him. But, unfortunately, Adam joined the ranks of Satan's rebellion after he and Eve ate from the forbidden tree. The human race was thereby put under Satan's curse and also damned to eternal fire. But, this time, God promised a savior for all mankind. Satan was told that a child of a woman would crush his head and ultimately destroy his power. In the process of destroying Satan, the seed of the woman would himself be bruised and have to give his life in order for men to recover the glory of God.

God skinned an animal to cover Adam and Eve's nakedness as they hid shamefully in the garden. Their disobedience had caused them to lose their natural coverings—the physical manifestation of the glory of God. After God killed an animal to make new physical coverings for them, he taught them how to sacrifice animals themselves as a symbol of the future savior, the seed of the woman, who would cover their offspring in future days. The animal sacrifice was a portrayal of how one man would eventually pay the price for all of mankind's rebellion toward God. Through the one ultimate sacrifice of his son, God would demonstrate his deep love and mercy to both the earthly and the spiritual realm.

Adam and Eve were never allowed back into the garden because of their sin. The innocence of mankind was, for now, lost. The first dispensation came to an abrupt end, and the second dispensation began

The Second Dispensation

The second dispensation begins in Genesis 4 and ends in Genesis 9. This dispensation starts with the establishment of the institution of family. There is no government and there are no nations yet. Man is supposed to govern himself and his own family. It is during this time that Cain murders Abel and Lamech murders another man. Because there is no government, there is much vigilante justice. For instance, Lamech says:

> "I have killed (Hebrew "slay" or "slaughter") a man for wounding me, a young man for injuring me." Genesis 4:23

To compound the problems on earth, mankind had to endure one of Satan's greatest attacks on God's plan. In the Garden of Eden, God said to Satan:

> "I will put enmity between you and the woman and between your offspring ("seed") and hers; he will crush your head, and you will strike his heel." Genesis 3:15

Satan knows a man will eventually be born with the power to defeat him. Therefore, during the second dispensation, Satan attempted to corrupt the bloodline of humanity by infiltrating it with evil seed. If seed from fallen angels could mix with the bloodline of the human race, mankind would be rendered incapable of producing a savior as promised in the garden. In order to prevent his head from being crushed, Satan may have tried to corrupt the woman's seed so the Messiah could not be born. This might explain what we read in Genesis 6:

> "When men began to increase in number on the earth and daughters were born to them, the sons of God saw that the daughters of men were beautiful, and they married any of them they chose." Genesis 6:1, 2

The phrase "sons of God" is the same phrase we see in Job 1:6 and Job 38:7:

> "One day the angels (same Hebrew word that translates "sons of God") came to present themselves before the Lord, and Satan also came with them." Job 1:6

> "And all the angels (sons of God) shouted for joy." Job 38:7

The Nephilim

In Genesis 6:4, we read:

> "The Nephilim were on the earth in those days – and also afterward – when the sons of God went to the daughters of men and had children by them. They were the heroes of old, men of renown."

The Nephilim may have been the offspring of fallen angels and human women. The Bible says the Nephilim were legends; their abilities and accomplishments made them well-known heroes. Greek mythology is probably based on these historical events, recording stories of "gods" and "sons of gods."

I am not impressed when someone says Genesis 6:1-4 can't be talking about angels because Jesus later said angels don't marry. These people often cite Matthew 22:30 which says:

> "At the resurrection people will neither marry nor be given in marriage; they will be like the angels in heaven."

To use this verse to extrapolate too much information about angels is bad hermeneutics. It is using isogesis (reading your predetermined doctrine into scripture) rather than exegesis (letting the scriptures speak for themselves and determine your doctrine). This verse explicitly says there will be no marriage and no families in heaven. Marriage and families are institutions God has given mankind on earth for the well being of the human race.

The same debate is revisited in Luke 20:34-36 when Jesus says:

> "The people of this age marry and are given in marriage. But those who are considered worthy of taking part in that age and in the resurrection from the dead will neither marry nor be given in marriage, and they can no longer die; for they are like the angels. They are God's children, since they are children of the resurrection."

Is Jesus telling everyone here that when you go to heaven you cannot have children because you will be like angels who cannot reproduce? Not exactly— although we do know from scripture that angels don't give birth to baby angels. But that isn't the point here. The point is that men in the age to come are being compared to angels in that "they can no longer die."

There are three basic ways to interpret Genesis 6:1-4:

1) The Sons of God are the good boys from that time who attended Sunday school, wore nice clean clothes, and never got in trouble, while the daughters of men are bad girls—probably descendents of Cain— who liked to drink, cuss, and wear short skirts.
2) The Sons of God are the sons of kings and pharaohs. They are royal princes. The daughters of men are the daughters of common folk gathered up by the royal princes to form their harems.
3) The Sons of God are angelic creatures. The daughters of men are the daughters of men.

Genesis 1-11 covers 2,000 years of the history of man. The rest of Genesis (chapters 12-50) plus 38 additional Old Testament books cover only 1,600 years. So, whatever is happening in Genesis 6:1-4 is taking up some very valuable space. Are good boys marrying naughty girls worth recording? Maybe, but I doubt it.

If the Hebrew phrase "sons of God" is translated here the way it is in other Old Testament verses, it means "angels." And "daughters of men" just might mean "daughters of men." So this strange mixing of angelic and human beings would cause some mighty bizarre offspring—offspring much like the Nephilim—super-human in strength and stature. This would explain the references to incredible giants found in Genesis through Deuteronomy, and again in I Samuel. (Goliath wasn't the only giant in his family, he had four giant brothers.)

Why is the idea of the Nephilim often rejected today? Because we live in a secular, materialistic culture. Our society has a hard enough time believing in God, let alone the existence of demons and evil creatures we cannot see. We have been born into a spiritual war against a band of rebel angels whose destiny is the Lake of Fire. But with our vision limited to our physical universe, this concept often seems absurd. It's probably safe to say the spiritual realm takes this whole thing a lot more seriously than we do.

Josephus (70-90 AD) wrote concerning the Nephilim: "For which reason they removed their camp to Hebron; and when they had taken it, they slew all the inhabitants. There were til then left the race of giants, who had bodies so large, and countenances so entirely different from other men, that they were surprising to the sight, and terrible to the hearing. The bones of these men are still swhewn to this very day, unlike to any credible relations of other men." (Antiquities ch. II vs. 3)

Justin Martyr (100-165 AD) wrote: "The angels transgressed this appointment and were captivated by love of women. And they begat children, who are those who are called demons."

Iranaeus (130-202 AD) wrote: "In the days of Noah, He justly brought on the Deluge for the purpose of extinguishing that most infamous race of men then existent, who could not bring forth fruit to God. For the angels who sinned had commingled with them."

Tertullian (155-230 AD) wrote: "They are the same angels who rushed from heaven on the daughters of men."

New International Dictionary of the Old Testament (1997), page 678 says: "There have been skeletons excavated in Palestine that are 3.2 meters or 10 ½ feet."

I Enoch (recorded around 160 BC) which is quoted by Jude in Jude 14 and 15 says:

> "And it came to pass when the sons of men had increased, that in those days there were born to them fair and beautiful daughters. And the angels, the sons of heaven, saw them and desired them. And they said to one another, 'Come, let us choose for ourselves wives from the children of men, and let us beget for ourselves children.' And they took wives for themselves, and everyone chose for himself one each. And they began to go into them and were promiscuous with them...And they became pregnant and bore large giants, and their height was three thousand cubits. These devoured all the toil of men, until men were unable to sustain them. And the giants turned against them in order to devour men. And they began to

sin against birds, and against animals, and against reptiles and against fish, and they devoured one another's flesh and drank the blood from it. Then the earth complained about the lawless ones." I Enoch 7:6-7

The Worldwide Flood

There was clearly much wickedness during the time of the Nephilim:

> "The Lord saw how great man's wickedness on the earth had become and that every inclination of the thoughts of his heart was only evil all the time…So the Lord said, 'I will wipe mankind, whom I have created, from the face of the earth.'" Genesis 6:5, 6

It is at this time that God speaks to Noah and asks him to build an ark so he can preserve the human race and the promised seed, while destroying everything that had become corrupt on earth. -

All these events are detailed in Genesis 6-9. The dimensions of the ark are given, and journal entries are recorded with the precision of an eye witness like Noah himself. These records include the date of entry and a vivid description of the geological occurrences resulting from the flood. One entry dated the 17th day of the 2nd month of the 600th year says:

> "On that day all the springs of the great deep burst forth, and the floodgates of the heavens were opened. And rain fell on the earth forty days and forty nights."

The flood wasn't just an enormous rainstorm. What happened during the flood could never be duplicated because the pressurized water under the continental plates and above the atmosphere was released once and for all. When the "great deep burst forth" the continental plates cracked and water erupted. At the same time, (maybe as a result of atmospheric changes created by the blasts of water), the canopy of water above the atmosphere broke, causing the "floodgates of the heavens to open." The fallout of this cataclysmic event lasted forty days and forty nights. All life on earth perished while the ark maintained buoyancy—an enormous barge riding on top of the water.

The Third Dispensation

When Noah and his family emerged from the ark, they reentered a world very different from the one they'd left. There was no longer a protective layer of water above the earth's atmosphere. Due to this loss, man's life expectancy was greatly reduced.

It was at this time that God introduced the new institution of social rule we now call government. In the previous dispensation, anarchy had become a way of life. This new system of authority would help preserve peace and dispense justice on the earth.

Government

God told Noah:

> "For your lifeblood I will surely demand an accounting…from each man, too, I will demand an accounting for the life of his fellow man. Whoever sheds the blood of man by man shall his blood be shed." Genesis 9:5, 6

God gave the government the authority to take a man's life for the crime of murder. He also gave governing men permission to prosecute lesser crimes deserving lesser punishment. Failure to enforce laws and punish crimes would indicate rebellion toward God and injustice toward men.

Noah had three sons: Shem, Ham and Japheth. Ham had a son named Cush who had a son named Nimrod who became a powerful world leader in this new governmental system. The name "Nimrod" means "rebel" or "we will rebel." Nimrod is described as being a "mighty hunter" (Genesis 10:9) and "a mighty warrior" (I Chronicles 1:10). Just because someone is a good warrior, however, doesn't make him a great leader, a just king, or a shepherd to his people. Government was designed to provide peace for mankind, but Nimrod used it as a tool to oppress people, promote himself, and lash out against God. Just three generations after the flood, the system of world government fell into the hands of one evil man. The government under Nimrod corrupted the entire earth…again.

The Fourth Dispensation

The Tower of Babel

The Tower of Babel was God's antidote to the corruption he saw on earth. God confused the language of what was previously one unified, but evil, culture. This diffused the unity of mankind and drove people apart to form new groups where they could better understand each other. Each language group then developed its own culture and government. This was the way God established the institution of nations.

It was also during this time, just one hundred years after the fountains of the deep burst open through the continental plates causing the flood, that the single land mass formed in Genesis 1 was divided. It broke apart to form several land masses separated by water. In this way, cultures were able to separate themselves entirely from other cultures. Shem, one of Noah's sons, had a son named Arphaxad who had a son named Eber who had a son named Peleg. The Hebrew word "peleg" means "divided" or "split" and refers to divisions caused by water-channels. Peleg was named after this great event—when the land masses were divided by water.

> "One was named Peleg, because in his time the earth was divided."
> Genesis 10:25; I Chronicles 1:19

Nations

Only four generations after the flood, people were already divided into different cultures with various languages living in separate lands. Each of these nations developed its own form of government. Genesis 10 lists the original seventy nations that came about as a result of God creating this new institution.

Nationalism remains a safe guard for the world today. It stops us from having a corrupt one-world government. Now, when one nation goes astray, God can deal with that nation directly through a cycle of discipline over a period of generations. If that nation is unwilling to repent, God can eliminate it from human history without wiping out everyone else, as he was forced to do in the worldwide flood.

A Review of Institutions Established by God

At this point in time, God has established five institutions for mankind to function within:

1) Individual volition
2) Marriage
3) Family
4) Government
5) Nations

These institutions correlate to the dispensations we've seen so far:

1) Age of the Individual in the Garden of Eden
2) Age of Families between the fall of man and the flood
3) Age of Government between the flood and the Tower of Babel
4) Age of Nations after the Tower of Babel

A timeline from eternity past until the Tower of Babel might then look something like this:

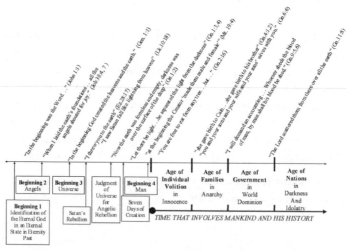

The five institutions needed to preserve life on earth have been successfully established, and now it is up to mankind to honor the institutions and live within their guidelines. God's next step will be creating Israel as a means of communicating his revelation to all nations because, unfortunately, many of the newly formed nations quickly returned to idol worship and rebellion (Joshua 24:2).

The Fifth Dispensation

In Genesis 12:1, the Lord appears to Abraham (Acts 7:2; John 8:56) and tells him to leave his family, his nation, and his government. God is going to use him to build a separate nation where he will establish his own government so his law can be passed down from generation to generation. This culture of people will all stem from Abraham and his offspring. God said to Abraham:

> "Leave your country, your people and your father's household and go to the land I will show you. I will make you into a great nation…." Genesis 12:1, 2

Israel

The purpose of the formation and preservation of Israel on the earth was so that God might communicate with and bless all nations. God told Abraham, "You will be a blessing…all peoples on earth will be blessed through you."

Israel would bring other nations information that would help them better understand God and walk in his light. And through Israel would come the foretold "seed of the woman"—the one who would have the power to crush Satan's head.

During the years 2000 to 1750 BC, Abraham had a son named Isaac who had a son named Jacob who had twelve sons. These twelve sons and their families were oppressed as slaves in Egypt for 400 years. At the end of that time, the twelve sons of Jacob had become twelve tribes of people. In total, they numbered 603,550 men twenty years of age or older, plus women and children. Moses led these men and their families to Mt. Sinai to receive instructions from God.

Those instructions included:

1) God's standards for morality and righteousness
2) A sacrificial system by which they would learn spiritual truths about obtaining forgiveness
3) A governmental code they should live by

God then led the people to the land promised to Abraham, Isaac, and Jacob more than 400 years earlier. It was in this land that Israel was to set up their nation. It was from this land that Israel would become a blessing to all other nations. It was also from this land that the seed of the woman would one day rule as King of Israel and lead all men into a prosperous and righteous age known as the Kingdom of God.

During the years 1400 to 586 BC, Israel lived in the land promised to Abraham. But when the ten northern tribes of Israel became corrupt and started worshipping idols again, God used another people group (the Assyrians) to remove the wicked tribes from the land of Israel. This happened in 721 BC, and those ten tribes have never returned to the land.

In 605 BC, God also temporarily removed Israel's southern kingdom of Judah by allowing the Babylonians to take them into captivity. After seventy years in captivity, what was left of Israel returned to the Promised Land and rebuilt the capital city of Jerusalem. They stayed in the land throughout the Persian and Greek empires. Then, during the days of the Roman Empire, the seed of the woman as promised in the garden, came through the family of Abraham to the people of Israel. He was a man named Jesus.

The leaders of Israel rejected Jesus and his "crazy" talk about the Kingdom of God. Jesus warned them that if they didn't listen to him and believe, the kingdom would be taken from them. After several months of trying to talk to them, Jesus said:

> "I tell you that the kingdom of God will be taken away from you and given to a people who will produce its fruit." Matthew 21:43

The Jewish nation was going to be rejected by God and set aside, no longer to be his representative to the world. The group of people that was supposed to represent the Kingdom of God had rejected its king. That king would now call upon a new group of people to proclaim his message of truth to the world.

The Sixth Dispensation

In Matthew 16:18, Jesus identifies the new group he will use to take his message to the nations:

> "I will build my church, and the gates of Hades will not overcome it. I will give you the keys of the kingdom of heaven."

The church will be made up of people from every nation (including Israel) who believe that Jesus is the one true king.

The Church

Today, we are in this sixth dispensation—the church age. Jesus will one day return to reestablish Israel, set up his throne in Jerusalem, and govern the world. In other words, there is a day coming when Israel will be restored as God's mouthpiece to all nations. Until that day, however, the Jewish people are unable to proclaim something they don't believe. It is the church's responsibility to pick up where they left off. In Jesus' final words before he left earth, he asked the church to fulfill Israel's mission until the day he restores them to their rightful position.

Jesus said:

> "All authority in heaven and on earth has been given to me. Therefore go and make disciples of all nations…and surely I am with you always, <u>to the very end of the age.</u>" Matthew 28:18-20

God needs the truth about Jesus proclaimed to the world, and it is the church's job to do so. Part of the church's ministry is to proclaim the message to Israel. God said:

> "Say to the Daughter of Zion, 'See, your Savior comes! See, his reward is with him, and his recompense accompanies him.'" Isaiah 62:11

The church began in approximately 30 AD in Jerusalem. Jesus told those first church members:

> "You will receive power when the Holy Spirit comes on you; and you will be my witnesses in Jerusalem, and in all Judea and Samaria, and to the ends of the earth." Acts 1:8

"The ends of the earth" includes all Gentile nations. The nations that hear the gospel message will be the ones that, according to Isaiah, will say to Israel, "Look, your Messiah is coming back! He has with him a reward for the service you are about to fulfill of blessing the nations."

Rapture

The Bible explains that when the church age is over and it is time for the keys of the kingdom to be returned to Israel, the dead will rise. The first phase of this resurrection will include believers who died during the church age. Then all believers still living on earth will be caught up with the resurrected and will have their physical bodies transformed into spiritual bodies (similar to how Jesus looked after his resurrection from the dead). Believers in Christ will finally become part of the heavenly realm. Paul talks about this event in I Thessalonians 4:16:

> "The Lord himself will come down from heaven, with a loud command, with the voice of the archangel and with the trumpet call of God, and the dead in Christ will rise first. After that, we who are still alive and are left will be caught up together with them in the clouds to meet the Lord in the air."

The phrase "caught up" here comes from the Greek word "harpazo," and it means "to snatch, to carry off by force." The word means an unexpected, sudden approach and capture that cannot be avoided. (The same word is used in Acts 8:39 and II Corinthians 12:2-4.) This is where we get the concept of "the rapture." With the removal of the church, the sixth dispensation comes to an end. It's now time for

God to finalize his 4,000 years of work with Israel and fulfill his ultimate purpose for them.

Dispensations - The Ages God Used to Lead Man Through History

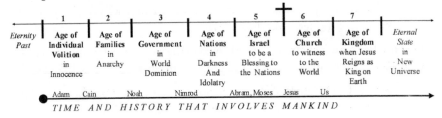

The Tribulation

Next comes a seven year period of time (Daniel 9:27) that Jesus says will be full of "great distress, unequaled from the beginning of the world until now and never equaled again" (Matthew 24:21). This distressful time will begin when a world ruler signs a seven year peace treaty with Israel. The people of Israel will reoccupy the temple mount and resume their sacrifical system according the Law of Moses. Israel will rejoice, thinking they have entered an age of peace, but Daniel says:

> "In the middle of the 'seven [years]' he (the world ruler who signed the treaty) will put an end to sacrifice and offering." Daniel 9:27

The breaking of the treaty will send Israel into 42 months (3 ½ years) of testing from which multitudes will emerge as believers in the one true Messiah. In these days of world tribulation, Zechariah records what will happen between Israel and God:

> "I will pour out on the house of David and the inhabitants of Jerusalem a spirit of grace and supplication. They will look on me, the one they have pierced, and they will mourn for him as one mourns for an only child...On that day a fountain will be opened to the house of David and the inhabitants of Jerusalem to cleanse them from sin and impurity." Zechariah 12:10 and 13:1

The Return of Jesus

God will again give Israel an opportunity to respond positively to Jesus. It's a true second chance. Multitudes will accept the invitation and mourn the way they previously rejected Christ. Anti-Semitism will reach an all-time high during this time period as all nations on earth organize to attack Jerusalem. When the attack begins, the nations will seem to be on the verge of destroying Jerusalem again, but then Christ himself will return to engage all the nations in war and defend Israel.

"I will gather all the nations to Jerusalem to fight against it; the city will be captured, the houses ransacked, and the women raped. Half the city will go into exile, but the rest of the people will not be taken from the city. Then the Lord will go out and fight against those nations, as he fights in the day of battle. On that day his feet will stand on the Mount of Olives, east of Jerusalem..." Zechariah 14:1-4

Jesus will then establish his throne in Jerusalem and call all the nations on earth to him for judgment. Matthew 25 says:

"When the Son of Man (used throughout the Bible as a reference to Jesus) comes in his glory, and all the angels with him, he will sit on his throne in heavenly glory. All the nations will be gathered before him, and he will separate the people one from another as a shepherd separates the sheep from the goats. He will put the sheep on his right and the goats on his left. Then the King will say to those on his right, 'Come, you who are blessed by my Father; take your inheritance, the kingdom prepared for you since the creation of the world'... Then he will say to those on his left, 'Depart from me, you who are cursed, into the eternal fire prepared for the devil and his angels... Then they will go away to eternal punishment, but the righteous to eternal life.'" Matthew 25:31-46

With this judgment, the Lord will establish his reign over the Kingdom of God on earth. He will tell the righteous, "Take your inheritance, the kingdom prepared for you since the creation of the world."

The Seventh Dispensation

At this time, there will be a resurrection of believers who died before the church age (anytime during the first five dispensations) as well as those who died during the seven year tribulation. They will return to live in the Kingdom of God on earth while Jesus reigns. This kingdom age is the seventh and final dispensation on earth and will last for a thousand years.

"I saw thrones on which were seated those who had been given authority to judge. And I saw the souls of those who had been beheaded because of their testimony for Jesus and because of the word of God. They came to life and reigned with Christ a thousand years." Revelation 20:4

After the thousand year reign of Christ on earth, God's purpose for the universe is complete. The heavens and the earth will then be consumed by fire (or perhaps some form of nuclear fission), and the created universe will cease to exist:

"The present heavens and earth are reserved for fire, being kept for the day of judgment and destruction of ungodly men. The heavens will disappear with a roar; the elements will be destroyed by fire, and the earth and everything in it will be burned up...That day will bring about the destruction of the heavens by fire, and the elements will melt in the heat. But in keeping with his promise, we are looking forward to a new heaven and a new earth, the home of righteousness." II Peter 3:8-13

Eternity

Isaiah and Revelation both tell us there will be a new universe ("a new heaven and a new earth") created after the old universe is destroyed. The new universe will contain the full presence of God, including all the spiritual realities we are blind to today.

"Then I saw a new heaven and a new earth, for the first heaven and the first earth had passed away, and there was no longer any sea...There will be no more night. They will not need the light of a lamp or the light of the sun, for the Lord God will give them light. And they will reign forever and ever." Revelation 21:1 and 22:5

This new universe will be an eternal state where all men who trusted in Jesus Christ as the promised seed of the woman (the Messiah of Israel) will live forever.

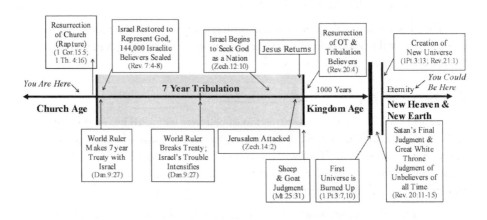

Chapter 7: Ten Times Revealed by God

Know Where You Are in the Race

My wife and I both ran track and cross country in high school and college. She was a three time state champ in the open half mile and was inducted into the Iowa Girls Track Hall of Fame. We both coached cross country teams, and we still frequently run races with our six boys. After all these years of running, there's one thing we know for certain. A runner must know how to set a pace. He or she must also know which pace is needed at different points throughout the race. If a runner begins a race too slow, he will fall behind and never catch up; but if he goes out too fast, he may end up like one of my runners did at his first 3.1 mile cross country race. He took off like a rabbit and was out in front with a huge lead at the half mile mark. But, when I saw him at the mile mark, he looked at me, staggered a bit, and collapsed. He had won the mile run. Unfortunately, however, it was a 3.1 mile race. He didn't finish, but he learned lesson number one about running—set a pace and know where you are on the race course at all times.

Even marathon runners sprint when they know they are near the finish line.

My wife Toni and I regularly run 5k, 10k, and half marathons. (I once ran a full marathon but I'm not sure if I'll ever do that again.) In each race, no matter what the distance, we have to set a pace so we can run our fastest time and still finish the entire course.

Also, as Toni and I run, we always make sure we know where the finish line is so we know at which point in the race we should change our pace for a strong finish. I have seen runners lead a race only to get passed at the very end because they were not sure how close they were to the finish line. In every long distance race, whether three miles or twenty-six, the good runners always pick up the pace and sprint near the end.

The same is true concerning God's plan for time. There is a certain amount of information that God wants us to know so we can turn in our best performance. Understanding where we're at in time is as essential to believers as knowing the race course is for runners.

Jesus criticized the people of his generation because although they knew great amounts of information concerning natural things, they didn't know where they were in time.

> "When evening comes, you say, 'It will be fair weather, for the sky is red,' and in the morning, 'Today it will be stormy, for the sky is red and overcast.' You know how to interpret the appearance of the sky, but you cannot interpret the signs of the times." Matthew 16:2, 3

Things were happening in Jesus' generation that had been prophesied about for years, but the people hadn't bothered to study those prophecies and, therefore, had no idea where they were on the timeline. The appearance of Jesus required that the world, especially the Jewish world, change pace. But they didn't understand this so they didn't adjust. In the end, they lost much more than a race.

The Old Testament scriptures refer to a group of men from the Jewish tribe of Issachar. They were "men who understood the times and knew what Israel should do" (I Chronicles 12:32). By paying close attention to what has happened in the past and where God's word says we're headed, we should be able to identify exactly where we're at on the race course Once we establish our location, we will be like the men of Issachar—we will understand the times and know what to do.

Throughout scripture, God has revealed his plan to people and predicted the future through prophets. Part of the reason he does this is to prove he is God. No other spiritual force, either demonic or angelic, has foreknowledge of all that will happen. Everyone but the Creator of the universe has a limited view of the future. In Isaiah it says:

> "Remember this, fix it in mind, take it to heart, you rebels.
> Remember the former things, those of long ago;
> I am God, and there is no other; I am God, and there is none like me. I make known the end from the beginning, from ancient times, what is still to come.
> I say: My purpose will stand, and I will do all that I please…
> What I have said, that will I bring about; what I have planned, that will I do." Isaiah 46:8-10

There have been at least ten times in history that God revealed to men what exactly was going on, hoping they would listen and choose the correct course of action.

	Ten Times Revealed By God	Scripture Reference
1	Day of the Fall of Man	Genesis 2:17, ". . .in the day you eat it you will surely die."

2	Year of the Flood	Genesis 6:3, "... his days will be 120..." Genesis 5:27, "Methuselah lived 969 years."
3	Year of the Exodus	Genesis 15:13-16, they will be enslaved 400 years and return in the fourth generation
4	Year of Entering Canaan	Exodus 14:34, for forty years they wandered in the wilderness
5	Year of Return From Babylon	Jeremiah 25:11, 12; 29:10; Daniel 9:2, Seventy Years
6	Year of the Messiah	Daniel 9:25, 483 years from the issuing of the decree to restore
7	Days Messiah Would be in Grave	Matthew 12:40; 27:63; Mk. 8:31; 14:58; Jn. 2:19, 20
8	Year of Jerusalem's Fall	Luke 23:28; 13:6-9, "in forty more years"—which is 70 AD
9	Length of Tribulation	Daniel 9:27 and other verses say it will last seven years
10	Length of Millennium	Revelation 20:4, a thousand years

1. Day of the Fall of Man

While Adam was still in the garden, the Lord spoke to him and said "You are free to eat from any tree in the garden; but you must not eat from the tree of the knowledge of good and evil, for when you eat of it you will surely die." God made it clear that conditions would change if man ate from this particular tree.

2. Year of the Flood

When the earth became too full of violence ("hamas"), God decided to destroy all life and start over with Noah and his ark full of animals. Even then, the men of Noah's generation who didn't see the flood coming had no excuse. In Genesis 6:3 God says, "My Spirit will not contend with man forever, for he is mortal, his days will be a hundred and twenty years." The Hebrew word translated as "contend" has three meanings:

1) to judge or strive – God will not strive forever trying to get man to obey, but will only try for 120 more years

2) to remain or dwell with –God will not remain in this present state with man forever, but will limit his time with man to 120 years

3) to be depressed or humbled –God's spirit had been depressed by man's continuous rejection, so man's "blaspheme" will only be allowed 120 more years

God was going to remain with man, urging him to change his ways, for just 120 more years. If after that time man continued to reject the Spirit's call—everything would be destroyed. These words where spoken during Noah's lifetime, 120 years before the catastrophic world-ending flood. Yet 849 years before that, God had spoken to Enoch, Noah's great-grandfather, and had given him a vision of the coming judgment of the flood *and* the second coming of the Messiah. Jude quotes part of what Enoch said referring to the second coming of Christ:

> "Enoch, the seventh from Adam, prophesied about these men: 'See, the Lord is coming with thousands upon thousands of his holy ones to judge everyone and to convict all the ungodly acts they have done in the ungodly way, and all the harsh words ungodly sinners have spoken against him.'"
> Jude 14, 15

Enoch prophesied concerning the day of the Lord's judgment after he was given a vision. This same vision also revealed a much closer day of judgment that would come upon the earth—the judgment of the flood. The year that Enoch had the vision of the flood, his wife gave birth to a son. Enoch named that son Methuselah which means "his death shall bring" and is made of two root words:

- *muth*, which means "death"
- *shalach*, which means "to bring," or "to send forth."

God told Enoch to name his son Methuselah just like he told Abraham to name his son Isaac because the very name Methuselah would itself be a sign for the next three generations. The sign indicated that whenever Methuselah died—the judgment of the flood would finally come to the earth.

Interestingly, Methuselah is the oldest man recorded in scripture, which is a tribute to the grace and long-suffering of God. The timeline below shows the first ten generations on earth from Adam to Noah. It also shows that Methuselah did, in fact, die the very same year of the flood. Just as his name foretold, his death "brought it."

Genesis 5 records each of the fathers from Adam to Lamech along with their age when their first son was born. Genesis 6 tells us how old Noah was when the Flood came to earth. By comparing the ages of the fathers when their first sons were born from Adam to Enoch, then adding Methuselah's age to the total, you can see the scriptural accuracy proving that Methusaleah died the same year the Flood came.

Age when son was born:	Father	Age when son was born:
130	Adam	130
105	Seth	105
90	Enosh	90
70	Kenan	70
65	Mahalalel	65
162	Jared	162
65	Enoch	65
969 at his death	Methuselah	187
	Lamech	182
	Noah	600 at the time of the flood (Gen.7:6)
TOTAL YEARS FROM Adam until Methuselah dies: **1,656 years**		*TOTAL YEARS FROM* Adam until the flood: **1,656 years**

3. Year of the Exodus

God spoke to Abraham concerning his family's future in Egypt while Israel was being formed into a nation. God told Abraham exactly how long they would have to remain in Egypt.

> "Know for certain that your descendants will be strangers in a country not their own, and they will be enslaved and mistreated four hundred years... in the fourth generation your descendants will come back here." Genesis 15:13, 16

Exodus 6:13-25 records the four generations from Jacob's twelve sons to the Exodus from Egypt. The four generations of Jacob to Moses are listed as: Jacob to Levi to Kohath to Amram to Moses

Exodus records the time the Hebrews left Egypt:

> "Now the length of time the Israelite people lived in Egypt was 430 years. At the end of the 430 years, to the very day, all the Lord's divisions left Egypt." Exodus 12:40

Since Jacob and his family arrived in Egypt while Joseph was the second most powerful ruler in the land, the 400 years of slavery did not begin until that ruling dynasty was overthrown. Thus, the Hebrews were in the land for 430 years (also seen in Galatians 3:17) but where only enslaved for 400 of those years (Genesis 15:13, 16; Acts 7:6).

Once again, God had revealed the exact time that Abraham and his family would leave Egypt. The people of the Exodus generation should not have been surprised that God sent Moses to deliver them from Pharaoh during the fourth generation.

4. Year of Entering Canaan

The Exodus generation left Egypt hoping to enter the Promised Land. But they had rebelled against God and were told that their generation would not see the Promised Land.

> "But you – your bodies will fall in this desert. Your children will be shepherds here for forty years, suffering for your unfaithfulness, until the last of your bodies lies in the desert. For forty years – one year for each of the forty days you explored the land – you will suffer for your sins and know what it is like to have me against you."

Forty years later, Joshua led the second generation into the Promised Land.

5. Year of the Return from Babylon

Later, during the days of the kings, Israel became a very rebellious culture, so God sent the prophet Jeremiah to warn them that they were going to be taken captive to the land of Babylon for seventy years.

> "This whole country will become a desolate wasteland, and these nations will serve the king of Babylon seventy years. But when the seventy years are fulfilled, I will punish the king of Babylon…When the seventy years are completed for Babylon, I will come to you and fulfill my gracious promise to bring you back to this place." Jeremiah 25:11,12; 29:10

God's discipline of Israel took place through three deportations. The people were taken away from the land of Judah and forced to live in Babylon under the reign of Nebuchadnezzar.

1) The first deportation was in 605.

> Nebuchadnezzar, who was then a general in his father's Babylonian army, defeated the ruling Assyrian empire in a battle north of Israel at Carchemish. Egypt had joined their military with Assyria's to fight against the Babylonians and defend the Assyrian Empire. After Assyrian forces were defeated, the Egyptians retreated south through Israel back into Egypt. General Nebuchadnezzar pursued the Egyptians back to their borders and would have entered Egypt itself but received word from Babylon that his father, Nabopolassar, had

died. His death left the royal throne of Babylon unoccupied and thereby undefended. Nebuchadnezzar stopped his pursuit of the Egyptians to return home to claim the throne. This left all lands occupied by the Assyrians under Babylonian rule. To secure the loyalty of Judah, Nebuchadnezzar ordered that the royal children of the Jews be brought to Babylon with him. Royal children like Daniel, Shadrach, Meshach, and Abednego were taken to Babylon to ensure that Nebuchadnezzar would have no fear of his newly acquired lands revolting against him. These royal children were placed in a Babylonian education system for training. They were to become useful ambassadors someday—as royal representatives of Babylon back in their homelands. Nebuchadnezzar spent a little over a year establishing his position as the King of Babylon before he asked for the royal children to appear before him, which is where the book of Daniel begins.

2) The second deportation of Jews occurred in 597.

In 601, Nebuchadnezzar returned to finish off the Egyptians but was instead defeated by them. The defeat of Nebuchadnezzar encouraged Judah and their king, Jehoiakim, to rebel against Babylon. While Nebuchadnezzar was rebuilding his forces over the next three years, Jehoiakim refused to pay the annual monetary tribute to Nebuchadnezzar. (The book of Jeremiah records Jeremiah's warnings to Jehoiakim telling him not to rebel against Babylon.) By 597, Nebuchadnezzar had rebuilt his military and returned to Judah to collect his overdue tribute and punish the king. Jehoiakim died before Nebuchadnezzar arrived and his son Jehoiachin became king. Jehoiachin had only been reigning for three months and ten days when Nebuchadnezzar and his rebuilt army arrived. The young 18-year-old king Jehoiachin was taken captive along with 10,000 people from Jerusalem, including all craftsmen and artisans— whom Nebuchadnezzar would use to help build and beautify his famous city of Babylon. One particular 25-year-old craftsman who was also training for the priesthood was taken away during this captivity. His name was named Ezekiel.

3) The third deportation and destruction of Jerusalem occurred in 586. After the deportation of Jehoiachin, Nebuchadnezzar placed Zedekiah on the throne in Jerusalem. During Zedekiah's eleven-year reign he entered into a covenant with Egypt against Nebuchadnezzar (even though Jeremiah constantly warned him not to). Nebuchadnezzar's forces arrived again on January 15, 588 and began a siege against the walls of Jerusalem. On July 18, 586, after the city had completely run out of food, the Babylonians finally broke through the city walls and the Jewish army fled. Nebuchadnezzar himself came to the city

to inspect it on August 14, 586. At this time, the temple, palaces, and homes had all been burnt down. The Babylonian army tore down the walls of Jerusalem and sent all surviving Jews to Babylon. Nebuchadnezzar later destroyed the Egyptians in 568.

We see Jeremiah's prophecy of a seventy-year captivity in Babylon fulfilled as:

1) The length of time between the first deportation in 605 until the Jews were allowed to return in 536 (70 years)
2) The length of time between the year Nebuchadnezzar destroyed the temple in 586 until a new temple was finally reconstructed in 516 (70 years)

According to Ezra 3:8, the Jews began rebuilding the temple around April/May of 536—70 years after the first captivity in 605. The temple was completed on March 12, 516—70 years after the original destruction of the temple in 586.

Once again, believers should understand God's plan so they know what they're supposed to do. Daniel, for example, read Jeremiah's writings and understood that the time had come for the Jews to prepare to return to Jerusalem. In 538 BC, Daniel is about 82-years-old and has been absent from Jerusalem for 67 years. He writes:

> "In the first year of Darius…I, Daniel, understood from the Scriptures, according to the word of the Lord given to Jeremiah the prophet that the desolation of Jerusalem would last seventy years. So I turned to the Lord God and pleaded with him in prayer and petition, in fasting, and in sackcloth and ashes." Daniel 9:1-3

	Dates of the 70-year captivity
605 BC	First Babylonian captives taken including Daniel (Daniel 1:1)
597	Second Babylonian captives taken including Ezekiel (II Chronicles 36:10)
586	Third captivity after Jerusalem and the temple are destroyed (II Chronicles 36:15-21)
538	Cyrus, the Persian, conquerors Babylon Daniel reads in Jeremiah about the 70 years of captivity (Daniel 9:1-3) Cyrus tells Jews to prepare to return to Jerusalem (Ezra 1:1-8)
536	**70 years after the first captivity in 605** Foundations are laid to rebuild the temple in Jerusalem (Ezra 3:8)
516	**70 years after the temple was destroyed in 586** The temple is completed on March 12, 516 (Ezra 6:15)

6. Year of the Messiah

In Daniel 9, God reveals the history of Israel from the time of the Jews' return from the Babylonian captivity through the time of the coming Messiah. The angel Gabriel communicates the following to an 82-year-old Daniel in 538 BC:

> "Know and understand this: From the issuing of the decree to restore and rebuild Jerusalem until the Anointed One, the ruler, comes, there will be seven 'sevens' and sixty-two 'sevens.' It will be rebuilt with streets and a trench...After the sixty-two 'sevens,' the Anointed One will be cut off and will have nothing. The people of the ruler who will come will destroy the city and the sanctuary. The end will come like a flood. War will continue until the end, and desolations have been decreed. He will confirm a covenant with many for one 'seven.' In the middle of the 'seven' he will put an end to sacrifice and offering. And on a wing *of the temple* he will set up an abomination that causes desolation, until the end that is decreed is poured out on him." Daniel 9:25-27

This is the most important announcement of time regarding the fulfillment of events in the scripture. These words pinpoint the time that the Messiah will come to his people (as promised in Genesis 3 as the "seed of the woman" and in Isaiah 53 as the "suffering servant"). He is referred to twice in this passage as "the Anointed One" which is the Hebrew word "mashiyach" (maw-shee'-akh) and translates "Messiah." The Greek word for "anointed one" is "christos" or Christ. The Anointed One or Messiah/Christ will come after "seven 'sevens,' and sixty-two 'sevens'"—after the "issuing of the decree to restore and rebuild Jerusalem."

The Hebrew word "sevens" translates "shabu'im" (shaw-boo'-im), and it is similar to the English word for "weeks." Whenever the Hebrew word "shabu'im" is translated, it is put into quotes because the word 'sevens' is being used in a special way that doesn't translate perfectly into English. The Hebrew word can refer to a period of seven days *or* a period of seven years,[1] but the context here leads us to believe each 'sevens' is a period of seven years rather than days. We know this because:

1) It is not reasonable to believe all the events described in Daniel 9:25-27 could transpire in 483 days.
2) There is no person known as "a Messiah" that comes into history 483 days after this was written.
3) Daniel has already been referring to periods of time in God's plan by years (Daniel 1:1 and 1:2).
4) References to one half of the time period known as the "seventieth seven" is described other places in scripture as being 1,260 days, 42 months or 3 ½ years.

This prophecy given to Daniel refers to the issuing of a decree to rebuild the city of Jerusalem. Jeremiah had already spoken about the restoration of the people to the land (which occurred in 536) and the rebuilding of the temple (516). Here in Daniel 9:25, Daniel is not referring to the release of people from Babylon or the actual rebuilding of the temple. He's talking about the issue of a decree to rebuild the whole city. He is saying that the decree to rebuild Jerusalem will be issued 483 years before the Messiah will come to his people, the Jews.

The Persian emperor issued the command "to restore and rebuild Jerusalem" in 458 BC, just 58 years after the temple was completed. The issuing of the decree occurred when the Persian King Artaxerxes sent Ezra, a Jewish teacher of scripture (Ezra 7:6, 10), back to Jerusalem with an "official proclamation" in the form of a letter. This letter begins by saying: "Now I *decree*..." (Ezra 7:12-26).

In the decree, the Persian king Artaxerxes says he will supply Ezra and the Jewish people with whatever they need to get the Jewish system (temple offerings, governmental positions, etc.) up and running again. Possessing this letter from the Persian Emperor gave the Jews a green light to completely restore their city. They could command cooperation from surrounding nations and could charge supplies to the empire's royal treasury. Below is a copy of the document in its entirety:

> From: Artaxerxes, king of kings,
> To: Ezra the priest, a teacher of the law of the God of heaven:
>
> Greetings.
>
> Now I decree that any of the Israelites in my kingdom, including priests and Levites, who wish to go to Jerusalem with you may go. You are sent by the king and his seven advisers to inquire about Judah and Jerusalem with regard to the Law of your God, which is in your hand. Moreover, you are to take with you the silver and gold that the king and his advisers have freely given to the God of Israel, whose dwelling is in Jerusalem, together with all the silver and gold you may obtain from the province of Babylon, as well as the freewill offerings of the people and priests for the temple of their God in Jerusalem. With this money be sure to buy bulls, rams, and male lambs, together with their grain offerings and drink offerings, and sacrifice them on the altar of the temple of your God in Jerusalem.
>
> You and your brother Jews may then do whatever seems best with the rest of the silver and gold, in accordance with the will of your God. Deliver to the God of Jerusalem all the articles entrusted to you for worship in the temple of your God. And anything else needed for the temple of your God that you may have occasion to supply, you may provide from the royal treasury.
>
> Now I, King Artaxerxes, order all the treasurers of Trans-Euphrates to provide with diligence whatever Ezra the priest, a teacher of the law of the

God of heaven, may ask of you up to a hundred talents of silver, a hundred cors of wheat, a hundred baths of wine, a hundred baths of olive oil, and salt without limit. Whatever the God of heaven has prescribed, let it be done with diligence for the temple of the God of heaven. Why should there be wrath against the realm of the king and of his sons? You are also to know that you have no authority to impose taxes, tribute, or duty on any of the priests, Levites, singers, gatekeepers, temple servants, or other workers at this house of God.

And you, Ezra, in accordance with the wisdom of your God, which you possess, appoint magistrates and judges to administer justice to all the people of Trans-Euphrates—all who know the laws of your God. And you are to teach any who do not know them. Whoever does not obey the law of your God and the law of the king must surely be punished by death, banishment, confiscation of property, or imprisonment." Ezra 7:12-26

Ezra left Babylon on April 8, 458 and arrived in Jerusalem August 4, 458. So the time between the issuing of the above letter until the time Christ came was going to be "seven 'sevens' and sixty-two 'sevens'" or a total of 69 'sevens'. The 69 'sevens' would then be 69 periods of seven years. Thus, a total of 483 years would pass between the issuing of Artaxerxes letter in 458 BC and the coming of the Christ.

If we count 483 years from the year 458 BC, we end up at the year 26 AD. According to the book "The Timetables of History" published by Simon & Schuster, this would put us right in the middle of John the Baptist's ministry.[2] John the Baptist's primary purpose was to prepare the people for the Messiah. John baptized and introduced Jesus to the Jewish nation around 26/27 AD. No matter how you count the years of Daniel's prophecy you always end up within a few months of Jesus' baptism and crucifixion.

No one should have been surprised when John the Baptist announced the Messiah was coming. Nor should they have questioned the arrival of a man like Jesus and the incredible things he did to verify that he was the prophesied one from Genesis 3, Isaiah 53, and Daniel 9.

7. Days Messiah Would be in Grave

The prophecy in Daniel 9 said that "the Anointed One will be cut off and will have nothing." The Messiah was the coming king, but when he arrived after 69 'sevens' he would be:

1) "Cut off" – means "to destroy, to consume." The Messiah, ruler of all, will be killed so as to "cut off" his ability to rule.
2) "Will have nothing" – is a reference to the fact that he won't receive his rightful claim to the kingdom.

When Jesus Christ came, he mentioned several times that he would be killed, lie dead in the grave for three days and three nights, only to return later, resurrected.

> "For as Jonah was three days and thee nights in the belly of a huge fish, so the Son of Man will be three days and three nights in the heart of the earth." Matthew 12:40

> "He then began to teach them that the Son of Man must suffer many things and be rejected by the elders, chief priests and teachers of the law, and that he must be killed and after three days rise again." Mark 8:31

> "The chief priests and the Pharisees went to Pilate. 'Sir,' they said, 'we remember that while he was still alive that deceiver said, 'After three days I will rise again.'" Matthew 27:62, 62

The gospels and other early church liturgy record Jesus' resurrection on the third day. Paul is clarifying church doctrine to the Corinthians when he says:

> "For what I received I passed on to you as of first importance: that Christ died for our sins according to the Scriptures, that he was buried, that he was raised on the third day according to the Scriptures and that he appeared to Peter and then to the Twelve." I Corinthians 15:3-5

8. Year of Jerusalem's Fall

Jesus taught that his generation would perish at the hands of the Romans. He spoke about these things in 30 AD. A generation is measured as 40 years (ever since the days of the Exodus generation and the 40 years they spent wandering in the wilderness). Sure enough, forty years after Jesus began his ministry (around 27 AD), the Romans invaded Israel (67 AD). And 40 years from Jesus' final warnings and crucifixion (30 AD), the Romans burnt Jerusalem, destroyed the temple, and took all remaining Jews captive (70 AD).

The same prophecy in Daniel mentions how the Roman military will destroy both the city of Jerusalem and the Jewish temple.

> "After the sixty-two 'sevens,' the Anointed One will be cut off and will have nothing. <u>The people of the ruler who will come will destroy the city and the sanctuary.</u> The end will come like a flood. War will continue until the end, and desolations have been decreed. He will confirm a covenant with many for one 'seven.'" Daniel 9:26

9. Length of the Tribulation

If we were to continue reading the prophecy given to Daniel concerning the time of the Messiah's coming, we would see that there is yet another 'seven' after the seven 'sevens' and the 62 'sevens' (which together equal 69 'sevens'). In other words, the ruler of the empire that is to come will make a treaty or "confirm a covenant" with Israel and other nations for "one 'seven.'" This last seven year period occurs some time *after* the Messiah has been cut off, Jerusalem and the temple destroyed, and the Jewish nation dispersed in 70 AD.

Daniel says the Jewish nation is going to be involved in a seven-year treaty with a world leader. This treaty involves a return to temple worship in Jerusalem. Since 70 AD, the Jewish people have been dispersed throughout the world and have been unable to sign such a treaty, let alone rebuild the temple in Jerusalem. Not until after World War II in 1948 did the Jews reassemble as a nation. Since 1948, the Jews have not made any kind of seven-year treaty with a world leader. Nor has there been any temple worship in Jerusalem. The world is still waiting for the final 'seven' in Daniel's prophecy.

Daniel 9:27 goes on to say that this ruler who is yet to come and is as of now unidentified will break the covenant "in the middle of the 'seven.'" This means that around the three-and-a-half-year mark, the seven-year covenant with Israel will be ignored. The world leader will break the treaty. This will usher in the most dreadful days the earth has seen, as described by Jesus:

> "For then there will be great distress, unequaled from the beginning of the world until now – and never to be equaled again." Matthew 24:21

This period of time is described several ways in Revelation, all of which equal three-and-a-half years:

1) **42 months** (12 months +12 months + 12 months + 6 months = 3 ½ years—Revelation 11:2;13:5)
2) **1,260 days** (1,260 days divided by 30 days = 42 months = 3 ½ years—Revelation 11:2)
3) **A time, times and half a time** (a "time" is a single year, a "times" is a plural year as in two years, and a "half a time" is a half a year, so, 1 + 2 + ½ = 3 ½ years—Daniel 7:25; 12:7; Revelation 12:6, 14)

10. Length of the Millennium

The promise of the Messiah's reign on earth is seen throughout the Old Testament. Daniel referred to the coming of a great ruler (Daniel 9). Isaiah was talking about the "seed of the woman" when he spoke of someone who'd establish a government that would never end. He said:

> "For unto us a child is born, a son is given, and the government will be on his shoulders. And he will be called Wonderful Counselor, Mighty God, Everlasting Father, Prince of Peace. Of the increase of his government and peace there will be no end. He will reign on David's throne and over his kingdom, establishing and upholding it with justice and righteousness from that time on and forever." Isaiah 9:6, 7

This verse and other verses speak of a man who will reign as God on the earth. This has not yet happened. It is described as happening at the end of the tribulation (Revelation 20).

Many believers will be executed in the last 3 ½ years of the Tribulation. After Jesus returns to earth (Revelation 19), these martyred believers, along with believers from all of time passed, will be resurrected. Revelation 20:4, 5 says, "They came to life and reigned with Christ a thousand years."

Revelation 20:1-6 also talks about a period of time lasting "a thousand years." After the thousand years comes to an end, the universe will be consumed by fire (II Peter 3:10, 12; Revelation 20:11; 21:1). We will then enter the eternal state described in Revelation 21 and 22.

Since God gave us this information shouldn't we assume he planned on us finding it useful?

Conclusion

If God has bothered to give us these details concerning time, its limits, and what he will be actively doing during each period, he must want us to *use* the information to plan our activities and determine how to spend our limited days.

We can conclude that we are living between the Messiah's first coming and his second coming. This means we are still waiting for the age of the Kingdom of God on earth. We are not living in paradise but in a fallen world that is headed for the worst days humanity has seen. We should not concentrate on building our personal kingdoms here, we should instead work to build the eternal kingdom to come.

We are living in the days that the prophets of the Old Testament longed to understand. Peter says:

> "Concerning this salvation, the prophets, who spoke of the grace that was to come to you, searched intently and with the greatest care, trying to find out the time and circumstances to which the Spirit of Christ in them was pointing when he predicted the sufferings of Christ and the glories that would follow." I Peter 1:10, 11

The next prophetic period of time on the horizon is the tribulation. We cannot just ignore the details of the coming ages revealed in scripture, as many have done in the past. The following people were not ready with an understanding of God's plan and thus reacted incorrectly when particular events occurred:

a) Adam
b) the people of Noah's day
c) the Exodus generation
d) the Jews who stayed behind in Babylon during the Persian Empire (e.g. Esther's family)
d) the generation that Jesus came to in 30 AD
e) the disciples (concerning Jesus' resurrection after three days)
f) the Jews who waited for God's deliverance from the Romans in 70 AD (it never came)

The people who will live to see the tribulation will also be caught off guard if they ignore God's clear revelation. If they decide "eschatology is just too confusing" for them, they will make the wrong choices when critical times come.

Attention to the word of God on these matters will empower us to be like the men of Issachar. We will be "men who understood the times and knew what to do."

The Four Generation Cycle

Chapter 8: Punishing the Sins of the Fathers

GOD ADDRESSES IDOL worship in the Ten Commandments. In the second commandment, he says:

> "You shall not make for yourself an idol in the form of anything in heaven above or on the earth beneath or in the waters below. You shall not bow down to them or worship them; for I, the Lord your God, am a jealous God, <u>punishing the children for the sin of their fathers to the third and fourth generation of those who hate me</u>, but showing love to a thousand generations of those who love me and keep my commandments." Exodus 20:4

Included in this command is a description of God's character and what we can expect from him based on our actions. Those of us who honor God and his word can expect to be shown love and grace generation after generation. On the other hand, those of us who "hate" God and "love" other gods (philosophies or world views that are not God's) can expect discipline and punishment for generations to come. A culture that receives discipline must change its ways or risk being removed by the fifth generation.

In the second commandment, God warns Israel not to look anywhere but to him for answers to questions like:

1) Where did I come from?
2) What is the purpose of life?
3) How should I act?
4) What is my future?

The punishment for turning away from God as we seek to discover our origin, purpose, ethics, and future will not be immediate judgment. Instead God says he will "punish the children for the sin of their fathers to the third and fourth generation."

The protest that often arises with this verse is that it doesn't seem fair for God to punish younger generations for sins that older generations committed. I believe those protesters have a very valid point. What hope would there be for us if we were subject to God's wrath simply because our great-grandfather whom we never met led a life of sin?

Israel apparently misunderstood this verse also. After they were taken into Babylonian captivity, some of the Jewish captives claimed the judgment was a result of the previous generation's sin. Ezekiel addresses this in chapter 18:

> "The word of the Lord came to me: 'What do you people mean by quoting this proverb about the land of Israel: 'The fathers eat sour grapes, and the

children's teeth are set on edge.'?" Ezekiel 18:2

The Lord was upset because the generation going into captivity was touting this trendy little slogan to justify an untrue idea—the idea that their fathers had eaten sour grapes (committed sin), and the result of tasting that bitterness had fallen upon on the next generation. Ezekiel explains that this is not a correct analysis of the judgment of God. He says:

> "Suppose this son has a son who sees all the sins his father commits, and though he sees them, he does not do such things…He will not die for his father's sin; he will surely live." Ezekiel 18:14-17

The second commandment is not teaching an unjust code of punishment where children have to pay for the sins of their parents and grandparents. The only way the son would be responsible for the sins of his father would be if he observed his father sin, learned how to behave like his father, and then began to practice the same sin himself.

God says he "punishes children for the sin of their fathers to the third and fourth generation of those who hate him." The word "punish" is the Hebrew word paqad (paw-kad') which means "to visit with friendly or hostile intent." The word indicates that God is "overseeing, looking after, inspecting, or examining." So God is inspecting and examining the sin of the fathers to see if it carried into the third and fourth generation. Why does he stop at the fourth generation? Why not go on to the fifth and sixth? We will see that by the fifth generation a father's sin has been dealt with in one of two ways. Either the fourth generation has made the necessary corrections, as mentioned in Ezekiel 18:14-17, or God has destroyed the society. There would be no fifth generation for that culture.

This is a principle of divine judgment—it is a called the four generation cycle of judgment, and it is used by God to control history by judging specific cultures that have become corrupt and sinful. He no longer has to destroy the whole world as he did in Noah's day or disperse the earth's population as he did in Nimrod's day in order to preserve his plan in the earth. Instead he can just discipline the cultures that threaten to destroy his work.

The Four Generation Cycle

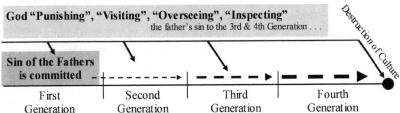

The first example of this cycle involves Abraham around 2000 BC, shortly after the Tower of Babel fell and many separate nations were created. God's covenant with Abraham has just been confirmed in a covenant ceremony when the Lord speaks to him in Genesis 15 about:

1) the future of his family
2) the rest of his own years on earth
3) a coming time when Israel will posses the Promised Land that Abraham now resides in as a temporary resident

> "Then the Lord said to him, 'Know for certain that your descendants will be strangers in a country not their own, and they will be enslaved and mistreated four hundred years. But I will punish the nation they serve as slaves, and afterward they will come out with great possessions. You, however, will go to your fathers in peace and be buried at a good old age. <u>In the fourth generation your descendants will come back here, for the sin of the Amorites has not yet reached its full measure.</u>'" Genesis 15:13-16

Abraham was given this prophecy around 2000 BC. He lived among the Amorites (also, called Canaanites) and entered into covenants with men like Mamre, Eshcol, and Aner—Amorite believers (Genesis 14:13). The king of Salem (the ancient city that is now Jerusalem) was Melchizek who was also a believer and mature enough in his faith to serve as the priest of God in his city (Genesis 14:18). Shem, one of Noah's sons, was still alive at this time and may have settled in the land of Canaan before Abraham arrived. During Abraham's lifetime, there were many believers living and ministering among the Amorites in Canaan.

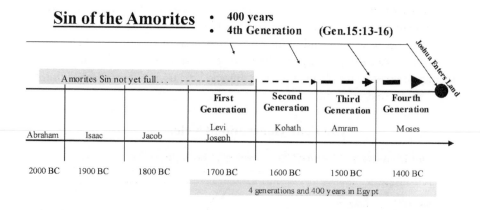

Noah's Son Shem and Abraham

"Two years after the flood, when Shem was 100 years old, he became the father of Arphaxad. And after he became the father of Arphaxad, Shem lived 500 years and had other sons and daughters." Genesis 11:10

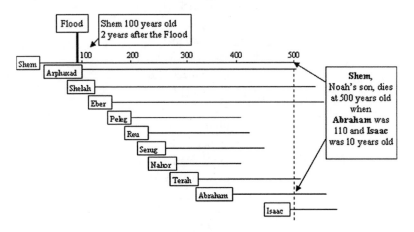

Note: Shem lived until Isaac's generation. There would have been a *first-hand* account of the entire flood story for ten generations after the flood. Noah himself was the tenth generation from Adam.

The land of Canaan included Lebanon, Israel, Jordan, and the Sinai. The people that occupied this land were a melting pot of nations—Canaanites, Amorites, Hittites, Hivites, Perizzites, Girgashites, and Jebusites (Exodus 3:8; Deuteronomy 7:1; Joshua 3:10). The group in its entirety can also be called the "Amorites" or the "Canaanites." Before cultural corruption set in, the Canaanites made several lasting contributions to both ancient and modern societies:[1]

1) Storage jars for the transportation of oil and wine
2) Musical instruments like the castanet (two small, concave, spoon-shaped shells of ivory or hard wood fastened to the thumb and beaten together with the middle finger)
3) The use of ivory
4) Vineyard production
5) Development of an alphabet that became the script for the Greek and Roman worlds—and later became the English alphabet we use today

†ω ᕤ 8 Υ ᔕ ᗞ ᖆ m C ω Ϟ ᛒ = ᕼ Ψ ⇒ ∟ ㅂ ㅿ

(read right to left ■)

'alp "ox" (A)

bet "house" (B)

gaml "throwstick" (C, G)

digg "fish" (D)

haw "jubilation" (E)

waw "hook" (F, U, V, W, Y)

zen "manacle" (Z)

het (H)

tet "wheel"

yad "arm" (I, J)

kap "hand" (K)

lamd "goad" (L)

mem "water" (M)

nahs "snake" (N)

samek "fish"

'en "eye" (O)

pit "corner" (P)

sad "plant"

qup (Q)

ras "head" (R)

šimš "sun, the Uraeus" (S)

taw "signature" (T)

During the days of Abraham's grandson Jacob, the four generation cycle in Canaan began with a terrible famine. Jacob, who was by this time an old man, along with his twelve sons and their families, moved to Egypt, and they stayed there throughout the decline of Canaan.

The demise of the great culture of Canaan would soon end in total collapse because the people had chosen to follow false philosophies.

Sins of Canaanites:

1) Homosexuality and other sexual corruptions (Leviticus 18:24; 18:6-23)
2) Bestiality (Leviticus 18:23)
    a. A cult that involved the cohabitation of women and goats existed.
    b. Hittite Laws legislated against certain forms of bestiality but allowed other forms.

3) Child sacrifices (Leviticus 18:21)
   a. Charred bones of children have been found in a temple near Amman.
   b. The worship of the god Molech involved placing children on the hands and arms of this god's large bronze image. Inside the bronze idol was a fire that would consume the baby when it rolled down the arms into the flames. The mother would dance and sing to make the sacrifice valid.
   c. The excavation of a temple of Baal and Ashtoreth found it to be 150 by 120 feet, surrounded by a wall. Buried within the temple were numerous jars containing the remains of children sacrificed to Baal.[2] This temple had been a place of torture, death, and burial for Canaanite children (at the hand of the Canaanites themselves).
   d. Children were sacrificed so that their dead bodies could be built into the walls of homes or gates of cities—thus bringing "blessings." Examples of this have been found in Gezer, Megiddo, Jericho, and many other Canaanite locations. This explains Joshua's curse on the one who would rebuild Jericho:

   > "At the cost of his firstborn son will he lay its foundations; at the cost of his youngest will he set up its gates." Joshua 6:26

   This curse came to pass in I Kings 16:34 when a man by the name of Hiel rebuilt Jericho in the days of King Ahab (after Israel had turned to the Canaanite practice of Baal worship):

   > "In Ahab's time, Hiel of Bethel rebuilt Jericho. He laid its foundations at the cost of his firstborn son Abiram, and he set up its gates at the cost of his youngest son Segub, in accordance with the word of the Lord spoken by Joshua son of Nun."

4) The temples of the fertility cults had numerous "in-house" prostitutes. Religious prostitution was used to encourage the gods Baal and Ashtoreth to mate and produce rain and fertile crops. This led to extreme abuse as women were turned into sexual objects and their children were sacrificed in the fire. These people's false philosophies led them to seek material prosperity at any cost.

Ugaritic[3] literature reveals the utter depravity of Canaanites. Their lack of morality had a destructive effect on every aspect of their culture. It corrupted their homes and business, as well as their industry, education, military, and judicial systems. The total destruction of the Canaanite culture had to happen to protect the world from being corrupted by them. The loss of the Canaanite culture was no real loss to the rest of the world.

By the end of the fourth generation, God warns the Israelites against learning the practices of Canaanite culture:

> "You must not do as they do in the land of Canaan, where I am bringing you. Do not follow their practices." Leviticus 18:3

The word "practices" (or "ordinances" in the King James and "statutes" in the New American Standard) is a translation of the Hebrew word "hoq" which refers to the laws in the Pentateuch. The very same Hebrew word is used in Jeremiah 5:22 to refer to a boundary line that the sea cannot cross. The word indicates a rule or standard set in place by God or by men. In Leviticus 18:3, "practices" refers to the boundaries established by men for their own societies. God tells the Israelites "do not follow" the boundaries that the Canaanites have established for their culture. At the end of chapter 18, God warns that if they do choose to follow the boundaries set by the Canaanites, the land will vomit them out.

"Follow" translates the word "halak" and literally means "to walk." This word is referencing a lifestyle or way of life. The Israelites were not to use the *boundaries* of the Canaanite culture as a *way of life*. The holiness of God is not just about a religious or spiritual experience. When God asks us to be holy, he wants us to be holy in the way we live our daily lives. For the Christian to separate their religious experiences from the way they live each day means they have separated the spiritual realm from reality. The result of such hypocrisy is a meaningless religion.

Guidelines for Israel's life of holiness (in contrast to the nations in the land of Canaan) are found in Leviticus 18-19. In Leviticus 19:2, God says to Moses:

> "Speak to the entire assembly of Israel and say to them: 'Be holy because I, the Lord your God, am holy.'"

What comes before this verse in chapter 18 and what follows in chapter 19 is not a list of religious rituals, but rather, standards for living. In these two chapters, (Leviticus 18 and 19), we find a moral code that if everyone in the United States— both pagans and believers—could ascribe to would cause a dramatic reversal of fate. We would no longer face impending disaster if we started adhering to this code.

Holiness in light of these chapters can be simply described as "doing things in the way that God intended them to be done." This applies to every area of life: family, business, education, relationships, sexuality, and so on. Let's look briefly at what we find in Leviticus 18-19 (a book that many consider to be the most boring book of the Bible).

A Break Down of Leviticus Chapter 18

After God begins by saying, "You must not do as they do in the land of Canaan...Do not follow their practices," he gives an extensive, almost ridiculous, list of ways Israel is not to have sex. This list takes up seventeen verses. If you read through the list of forbidden sexual encounters, you will find many things you already instinctively know. Men are forbidden to have sex with their mothers, sisters, grand-daughters, aunts, daughters-in-law, sisters-in-law, neighbor's wives, etc. Men are also forbidden from having sex with other men.

God did not need sex to be part of the human experience. He didn't have to use sex as a mode for human reproduction; he could have made humans reproduce like amebas that simply split apart and form another ameba. But God instead designed sex as a pleasurable experience that people desire. The joy of sex was all God's idea, and all the restrictions God has put on sex don't change the fact that it is right, fun, and holy within the proper context.

Remember, holiness means doing things the way God intended. God intended that societies be based on families, and families are built on marriages. Sex is part of a marriage relationship, and through sex, families are perpetuated. God's point is simple: if you pervert sex, you will have perverted marriage, which then messes up the family. If families fall apart, the society will eventually fall apart.

Holiness can be defined as simply doing things the way they were supposed to be done.

Holiness is the theme of Leviticus, but it is not a mystical holiness that can only be found in heaven. As I said before, it is a holiness that comes from doing things the way God intended them to be done. God intended sex to occur only within the context of marriage. If you do not have sex the way God intended it, you are not holy. If you follow God's intentions for marriage, families, and nations, you are holy. Sex is not the only thing God restricts, but it is the most important thing he restricts. Why? Because it is such an integral part of marriage, which is the foundation of well-being for mankind.

Leviticus 19

Some other instructions crucial for the well-being of society are also mentioned in this chapter in Leviticus:

1) Respect your mother and father (19:3) because societies are built on families.
2) Do not turn to idols (19:4) because they will give you incorrect boundaries and will eventually destroy you and your society.

3) Leave part of your fields for the poor to harvest (19:9, 10) because each society should take care of those who are less fortunate.
4) Do not steal, lie, or deceive (19:11-13) because a society is based in trust.
5) Do not withhold wages (19:13) because when the working class prospers, society will prosper (more than just financially).
6) Do not offend the handicapped, but help make their lives easier (19:14) because they are part of society and you are responsible for all men.
7) Do not pervert justice or show partiality but judge fairly (19:15) because by justice is a nation established.
8) Do not spread slander or endanger your neighbor's life (19:16) because by doing so you seek to benefit yourself at another person's expense.
9) Rebuke your neighbor openly if he is wrong (19:17) because if you do not, you share the guilt of his wrong action.
10) Love your neighbor as yourself.

The civil code found in Leviticus 18 and 19 is the foundation for social morality. Israel is told seven times not to behave like nations before them (Leviticus 18: 3, 24, 26, 27, 29, 30). According to historical records, archeology, and scriptural accounts, the Canaanites were not following the civil code of Leviticus. The Lord tells Israel:

> "It is on account of the wickedness of these nations that the Lord is going to drive them out before you. It is not because of your righteousness or your integrity that you are going in to take possession of their land; but on account of the wickedness of these nations, the Lord your God will drive them out before you." Deuteronomy 9:5

Israel is not being rewarded; the Canaanites are being punished. Israel is then warned that the same fate might befall them if they do not keep the common civil code:

> "And if you defile the land, it will vomit you out as it vomited out the nations that were before you." Leviticus 18:28

Israel is warned that they must destroy this culture and not adopt any of their ways:

> "Do not bow down before their gods or worship them or follow their practices. You must demolish them and break their sacred stones to pieces. Worship the Lord your God, and his blessing will be on your food and water." Exodus 23:24

"Otherwise, they will teach you to follow all the detestable things they do."
Deuteronomy 20:18

<u>"When you enter the land the Lord your God is giving you, do not learn
to imitate the detestable ways of the nations there.</u> Let no one be found
among you who sacrifices his son or daughter in the fire, who practices
divination or sorcery, interprets omens, engages in witchcraft, or casts
spells, or who is a medium or spiritist, or who consults the dead. Anyone
who does these things is detestable to the Lord, and because of these
detestable practices, the Lord your God will drive out those nations before
you." Deuteronomy 18:9-14

After four generations, Moses leads Israel back to the borders of Canaan and
Joshua eventually takes them all the way into the land to conqueror the Amorites
(Canaanites). By the end of its fourth generation, the Canaanite culture had
reached its end.

Because Israel disobeyed the Lord in the wilderness on the way to Canaan, the
people had to wait forty more years to enter the land. This meant the Canaanites
had forty more years to consider what the Lord was going to do to them after
hearing about what the Lord did to the Egyptians at the Red Sea. There was still
time to repent as Rahab, the Canaanite prostitute, would. Rahab understood what
the Lord had done and what he was going to do. She told the two spies:

> "I know that the Lord has given this land to you and that a great fear of
> you has fallen on us, so that all who live in this country are melting in fear
> because of you. We have heard how the Lord dried up the water of the
> Red Sea for you when you came out of Egypt…When we heard of it, our
> hearts melted and everyone's courage failed because of you, for the Lord
> your God is God in heaven above and on the earth below." Joshua 2:8-11

When Israel finally approached Jericho, they alerted the city six times in six
days by marching around the city walls. Why? Because there was still time for the
Canaanites to repent and flee the city. Any families who hadn't fled Canaan while
the Israelites spent forty years in the wilderness were being given an additional
six days to leave. Israel was there to overthrow the Canaanite culture, not hunt
down and kill individual Canaanites. In fact, the Bible talks about Canaanites who
escaped and later became believers. Two of them, Rahab and Bathsheba, are in the
genealogical records of Jesus (Matthew 1:5, 6).

After 400 years in Egypt, plus forty more years in the wilderness, and then six
days of warning laps around the city—God finally commanded Israel to begin
the destruction of the city. There would be no fifth generation for the Canaanite
culture. It took a five-year war for Joshua and the Israelites to conquer the land
completely, eliminating the Canaanites from history, and occupying their territory.

Concerning the United States today, there are many nations currently calling for our death and destruction. If we, for just a moment, could see ourselves in the place of the Canaanites and consider what we've learned from their overthrow, we might grasp what's going to happen. Our problem is not the fact that other nations are calling for our demise; our problem is our own stubborn hearts and our own sinful, selfish behavior. As surely as the God of heaven is just, he is also merciful. The entire Canaanite culture could have responded to the Lord as Rahab did and been spared. Unfortunately, they did not, so only Rahab and her family survived.

Our national existence will be determined by the state of our national soul.

Today we must defend against our enemies and fight off those who want to overthrow us, but if we really want to understand why we're having so many problems, we should consider the historical account of the fall of Canaan. They were an immoral people, but God gave them many years to repent and change. Like the Canaanites, God has given us more time. If we start living the way God intended us to live, we will become a holy nation again and our culture will continue.

"The man who obeys them (the laws of the common moral code) will live by them. I am the Lord." Leviticus 18:5

Chapter 9: The Five Cycles of Discipline

IN THE SPRING of 1983, my wife Toni and I finished college and moved to a small Iowa town where I took a job as the head coach of my first varsity baseball team. My new position was very important to me because I had been studying the game of baseball, along with various coaching techniques, since 1977. When our season was over, we had reason to rejoice. We were the official conference champions, which was a big deal to me and the whole community. I figured that if I'd won my first conference championship at age 23, I was on track for decades of coaching that would include many more victories. But no sooner had my coaching career begun than a new road for my life emerged.

Even now on long road trips and over late-night dinners, Toni and I speculate about how different life might have been if we'd stayed the course with my original dream to coach high school sports until retirement. There have been times we wished we hadn't decided to change direction. How different life might have been if we'd simply kept going down the road we were headed. But we had veered off that road long ago.

It all began on a Sunday morning in June when we decided to attend one of the local churches in our new town. The pastor used the entire sermon to rail about how all kids should be in Christian schools. We didn't go back to that church the next week; instead, we tried another one nearby. At the second church, the pastor spent most of the sermon reading anecdotes from that month's *Reader's Digest*. Holy smokes, I remember thinking, I could be spending this time on team statistics, practice plans, and game strategy.

I knew that, as a Christian couple, Toni and I needed to find a place where we could hear the word of God preached, but so far, we were 0-2. The next Sunday morning, we didn't dress up and go to church. We instead got up and turned on the TV. We watched a very intense preacher speak for about an hour. He quoted a lot of scripture and had an air of authority when he spoke. The next week, we watched him again. I was mesmerized. I loved the way he presented himself, and I envied his confidence. Toni said she thought he was arrogant. I agreed, but I still liked him. I recognized that he was teaching the Bible with the same traits I'd observed in successful coaches. He had a kind of poise and self-assurance I'd never seen in a pastor before.

The third time I listened to him, I realized the hour I'd spent sitting in front of our little black and white twelve-inch had flown by. It felt like just a few minutes had passed. I sat stunned as the closing song started to play, and I wished I didn't have to wait a full week to hear him preach again. Toni was sitting on the floor beside me, also staring at the little $64 TV we bought at Target on our honeymoon. I remember looking over at her and saying, *"We have to do something."* I doubt she was clear as to what I meant at the time, but I remember her nodding in agreement. From that point on, we had a mutual understanding that there was more out there for us spiritually.

The next few years we spent coaching and teaching in that little town, we also became consumed with Bible teaching. We listened to every sermon on tape we could get our hands on. We got up two hours early every day to read the Bible. As we did this, our dreams for our lives slowly started to change.

Two years later, we put our house up for sale and gave everything away that wouldn't fit into a U-haul trailer. We were now both 25 and had two boys under the age of two. We were quitting our jobs and stepping out in faith to follow our dream of going to Bible school. When we arrived in our new town, I took a job in a dumpy factory that paid me $4 an hour. That was where seminary began for me. There were no theology classes or Bible tests, but working in that factory refined my character through daily tests of perseverance.

Coaching became a distant memory from another life in which I called the plays. That first year chasing our dream, we lived below the poverty line. We had never experienced hopelessness like we felt then. We wanted to quit and we thought about going back, but we just couldn't. Something in our souls had changed. We had a desire that we didn't understand, and it was burning inside us, pushing us forward. Like the lyrics in Bob Seger's song "The Fire Inside," our dreams were slipping away, being eroded daily by the realities of life…but there was still something driving us. Seger calls it "The Fire."

> Then it comes to you how it all slips away
>
> Youth and beauty are gone one day
> No matter what you dream or feel or say
> It ends in dust and disarray
>
> Like wind on the plains, sand through the glass
> Waves rolling in with the tide
> Dreams die hard and we watch them erode
> But we cannot be denied
> The fire inside

Looking back now, I know that fire was the Spirit of God. He had dropped a plan into our souls, and we couldn't look back. While we worked, scrounged, and studied, God prepared us for a new direction in life. I didn't realize this at the time, however, and I became more and more frustrated each day. God had to discipline me through hardships, but those painful times were essential to refining my attitude. They were especially key in developing my sincerity and willingness to respond to the dream he had given me.

"Endure hardship as discipline; God is treating you as sons…<u>No discipline seems pleasant at the time</u>, but painful. <u>Later on, however, it</u>

<u>produces a harvest of righteousness and peace</u> for those who have been trained by it." Hebrews 12:7, 11

Hardships *can* be discipline from God, a way he trains us to produce righteousness and peace. We can refuse to be guided by God. We can become bitter, resentful, and fearful. We can quit altogether. But the factor that will determine our success in life will be whether or not we allow God to form us into something he can use. Paul addresses this when he writes to Timothy, a young man he had helped train for the ministry:

> "In a large house there are articles not only of gold and silver, but also of wood and clay; some are for noble purposes and some for ignoble. <u>If a man cleanses himself from the latter, he will be an instrument for noble purposes</u>, made holy, useful to the Master and prepared to do any good work." II Timothy 2:20, 21

Hebrews 12:6 quotes the wisdom book of Proverbs 3:12:

> "The Lord disciplines those he loves, and he punishes everyone he accepts as a son."

This is true for each of us as individuals, but it's even more valid for entire cultures and nations. God is not just going to let a nation wander away from his standards and embrace sin, darkness, and destruction without first disciplining the people and trying to grab their attention. Individuals and nations alike have free will and can choose to respond to God's discipline and repent or scoff at his discipline, and refuse to change. But any nation that continues to sin is setting itself up for the wrath of God.

God loves our nation, as he does all nations. But unfortunately, we are living below the standard of general revelation (basic right and wrong) he set in place long ago (Romans 2:15). Common sense tells us that the United States has set itself up to face continued cycles of divine discipline. Will our nation have enough sense to respond to these warnings? Or, are we too weak to change after so many years of secularism, materialism, and hedonism? Have we lost the desire to fight for our lives? If we are too far gone, we will march right through God's warnings to meet his ultimate judgment and our ultimate end.

We could march right past God's discipline only to meet his judgment.

Leviticus 26:14-33 describes the five cycles of discipline God promises to take Israel through them if they continue to rebel against him.

> "But if you will not listen to me and carry out all these commands, and if you reject my decrees and abhor my laws and fail to carry out all my commands and so violate my covenant, then I will do this to you."

Cycle Number One Comes to the First Generation (the first 40 years):

> "I will bring upon you sudden terror, wasting diseases and fever that will destroy your sight and drain away your life. You will plant seed in vain, because your enemies will eat it. I will set my face against you so that you will be defeated by your enemies; those who hate you will rule over you, and you will flee even when no one is pursuing you. If after all this you will not listen to me, I will punish you for your sins seven times over..."

Cycle Number Two Comes to the Second Generation (years 41-80):

> "I will break down your stubborn pride and make the sky above you like iron and the ground beneath you like bronze. Your strength will be spent in vain, because your soil will not yield its crops, nor will the trees of the land yield their fruit. If you remain hostile toward me and refuse to listen to me, I will multiply your afflictions seven times over, as your sins deserve."

Cycle Number Comes to the Third Generation (years 81-120)

> "I will send wild animals against you, and they will rob you of your children, destroy your cattle and make you so few in number that your roads will be deserted. If in spite of these things you do not accept my correction but continue to be hostile toward me, I myself will be hostile toward you and will afflict you for your sins seven times over."

Cycle Number Four Comes to the Fourth Generation (years 121-160)

> "And I will bring the sword upon you to avenge the breaking of the covenant. When you withdraw into your cities, I will send a plague among you, and you will be given into enemy hands. When I cut off your supply of bread, ten women will be able to bake your bread in one oven, and they will dole out the bread by weight. You will eat, but you will not be satisfied. If in spite of this you still do not listen to me but continue to be hostile toward me, then in my anger I will be hostile toward you, and I myself will punish you for your sins seven times over."

The Ultimate End of the Society

"You will eat the flesh of your sons and the flesh of your daughters. I will destroy your high places, cut down your incense altars and pile your dead bodies on the lifeless forms of your idols, and I will abhor you. I will turn your cities into ruins and lay waste your sanctuaries, and I will take no delight in the pleasing aroma of your offerings. I will lay waste the land, so that your enemies who live there will be appalled. I will scatter you among the nations and will draw out my sword and pursue you. Your land will be laid waste, and your cities will lie in ruins."

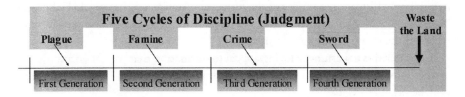

We can see from these verses that as nations move into the first generation of rebellion toward God, he sends out a warning, such as the plague seen here. The purpose is to remind men of their humble condition before an all-powerful God. During this time, many people will cry out to God and start to make better choices. Others will become hopeless, and, consumed in their self-pity, they will curse God.

Nations that, on a whole, repent and change their ways *will* recover. But if a nation continues in sin and that depravity is picked up by the second generation, God will step up his warnings out of love for mankind. If men were allowed to live as they please, the world would be a miserable place of sin. This is why God put laws into place. He gave us free will from the very beginning when he told Adam, "You are free to eat from any tree in the garden." He also warned Adam that eating from one tree in particular would kill him. God wants us to follow our desires, which is why he gave us free will. But we must bring our desires subject to his limits. God has standards already set in place, and because he is love, he will try to stop us in every way he can from acting against his word.

If the first generation does not repent, the second generation will experience a great famine. This should again cause them to realize how weak they are, (they can't do something as simple as gathering food). They will be given forty more years to reconsider the path they're on and decide whether or not to change course.

The third generation will face a dramatic increase in crime. God says this crime will rob them of their children and possessions and create deserted streets. Anarchy will begin to set in. The very corruptness of the culture has become a punishment in itself.

The <u>fourth generation</u> will experience some type of military attack on their land, giving them a taste of what is coming if their disobedience continues into the next generation. This fourth generation will deal with mounting discipline as they draw closer and closer to the end of God's patience.

At the end of the fourth generation, God will remove the disobedient nation from his plan. After 160 years of loving discipline, the nation will finally experience the wrath of God. Since the people of that nation rebelled, living in an unnatural state of immorality, so their punishment will be unnatural. Portrayals of the fifth cycle of judgment are some of the most hideous descriptions in history. You can see the details of the fifth cycle in the scripture list below. In a few chapters, we will look at some historical examples of the fifth cycle—examples that would be beyond belief, were not for the fact that God told us to expect it in Leviticus and historians recorded the events when they occurred.

Consider this a warning, a loving appeal to our nation that we not go any further. All God asks is that we return to what is right and good. We must change now, before it's too late.

Cycle of Judgment	Generation it Strikes	Characteristics Described in Leviticus 26
1 **Leviticus 26:16-17**	First Generation 1-40 years	a. Sudden terror b. Wasting diseases c. Fever destroys sight d. Drain away life e. Plant seed in vain f. Enemies eat produce g. Defeated by enemies h. Ruled by those who hate you i. Flee when no one pursues you.
2 **Leviticus 26:19-20**	Second Generation 41-80 years	a. Break down stubborn pride b. Sky like iron (no rain) c. Ground like bronze (famine) d. Strength spent in vain e. No crops from soil f. No fruit from trees
3 **Leviticus 26:22**	Third Generation 81-120 years	a. Send wild animals (crime) b. Robbed of children c. Destroy cattle d. Reduce population e. Deserted roads

4 **Leviticus 26:25-26**	Fourth Generation 121-160 years	a. Sword upon you (war comes to your land) b. Seek shelter from attacks c. Plagues d. Given into enemies hands e. Cut of supply of food f. Poor living conditions g. Food rationed h. Hunger
5 **Leviticus 26:29-39**	*No Fifth Generation* *The End of Society*	a. Eat flesh of sons & daughters b. Destroy high places, altars, sanctuaries c. Pile dead bodies on idols d. Ruin cities e. Lay waste sanctuaries f. Not listen to your prayers g. Lay waste the land h. Disperse the citizens among nations
		"But if they will confess their sins and the sins of their fathers...I will remember..." Leviticus 26:40

Chapter 10: The Character of Each Generation

THERE IS A passage in Proverbs that has intrigued me for years. Its verses seem to form an ancient mirror reflecting back the mistakes of past generations. That mirror is now angled at us.

> "There is a generation that curseth their father, and doth not bless their mother.
>
> There is a generation that are pure in their own eyes, and yet is not washed from their filthiness.
>
> There is a generation, O how lofty are their eyes! And their eyelids are lifted up.
>
> There is a generation, whose teeth are as swords, and their jaw teeth as knives, to devour the poor from off the earth, and the needy from among men." Proverbs 30:11-14 (KJV)

In these verses, God describes the heart and attitude of four generations of people. The generations are consecutive, and, unfortunately, all are perpetuating a culture full of rebellion toward God. By the fourth generation, the cycle is complete. The sin of the first generation has reached its fullness, and God promises to eliminate the society from history. This is his way of preserving the earth until his plan for mankind is complete. Since the establishment of the institution of nations, this four generation cycle has been used to preserve godly standards on earth.

Essentially, the first generation has rejected a divine viewpoint of life and developed a human-centered worldview that is not correct. Their worldview is then passed on to the next generation. By the time the second generation reaches an age where they can engage in critical thought, they have already been positioned to evaluate their world from their parents' wrong perspective. The third generation doesn't stand a chance and naturally turns all their attention to themselves. As the fourth generation comes of age, the culture is full of morally unrestrained people who will use violence to accomplish their personal agendas. This fourth generation will be the nation's last.

Types of Nations

These verses can be applied to generations found in every nation on earth. There are two distinct types of nations in the world:

1) Nations with access to the Bible (special revelation)
   a. Israel has always possessed the written law of Moses.
   b. Believing Gentile nations have a knowledge of scripture.

2) Pagan nations that have access to God's truth (general revelation)
   a. This would include all other nations that don't have access to the written word of God. The Lord said his absolute standards have been written on men's hearts. Everyone has a conscience to delineate right from wrong. Just like a bird knows to migrate south for the winter, if people follow natural laws they intuitively understand, they will be blessed by God.

A verse regarding this type of nation is found in Romans:

> "When Gentiles, who do not have the law, do by nature things required by the law, <u>they are a law for themselves</u>, even though they do not have the law, since they show that the requirements of the law are written on their hearts." (Romans 2:14, 15)

Generation Number One: A Generation That Curses Their Fathers

> "There is a generation that curseth their father, and doth not bless their mothers." Proverbs 30:11 (KJV)

In Deuteronomy 11:18-21, Hebrew parents are told to:

> "Fix these words of mine in your hearts and minds; tie them as symbols on your hands and bind them on your foreheads. Teach them to your children, talking about them when you sit at home and when you walk along the road, when you lie down and when you get up. Write them on the doorframes of your houses and on your gates, so that your days and the days of your children may be many in the land that the Lord swore to give your forefathers, as many as the days that the heavens are above the earth."

Parents have a responsibility to introduce their children to the creator. The command in Deuteronomy explains that if each generation strives toward righteousness, they will continue to enjoy the land promised them by God. If offspring are righteous, the nation has the potential to continue forever.

Proverbs 30:11 is about the beginning of a spiritual and moral decline that will eventually span four generations. The decline begins when one generation curses the righteous ways their fathers taught them, also refusing to show gratitude for their mother's moral teaching.

The first generation curses the very men who instructed them in the ways of the Lord—their fathers. The Hebrew word for "curse" is "qalal" which means "trifling, small, to bring contempt, to despise." This generation considers their righteous heritage a trivial, insignificant thing. This is what Esau did when he decided that a bowl of stew was more valuable than his father's blessing. Genesis 25:34 says, "So Esau despised his birthright."

Esau was heir to Abraham and Isaac's estate, which included the covenant with God. Yet Esau "cursed" it all in the name of his immediate need for food.

The verses in Proverbs aren't just talking about one immature teenager; they're talking about an entire generation. The parents of this generation have tried to pass down the knowledge of God and his eternal plan, but the response from the next generation was like that of Esau. They choose to sell eternity for a moment in time.

This same generation "did not bless their mothers." The word "bless" comes from the Hebrew word "barak" which means "to kneel." The association between kneeling and blessing comes from the old custom of taking a child on one's knee to pronounce a blessing on him.

The Jewish mother was instrumental in passing down knowledge of God and scripture to her children. We see this in Proverbs 1:8:

> "Listen, my son, to your father's instruction and do not forsake your mother's teaching. They will be a garland to grace your head and a chain to adorn your neck."

A generation that "does not bless their mothers" doesn't thank their mothers for the good teaching they received. They simply aren't grateful for their godly heritage.

Generation Number Two: A Generation Who Are Pure In Their Own Eyes

> "There is a generation that are pure in their own eyes, and yet is not washed from their filthiness." Proverbs 30:12"

The second generation rejects a universal code of right and wrong. They don't believe in a holy and righteous God, so they don't have an ultimate standard to compare themselves to. They are "pure in their own eyes" even though they are full of sin.

This generation creates its own rules and establishes its own value system. They develop theories and philosophies that are logical to the human mind but contrary to the divine view. They are ready to accept anything that makes sense to them after they evaluate it according to a judgment system based solely on human reasoning.

Generation Number Three: A Generation Who Are Haughty and Disdainful

> "There is a generation, O how lofty are their eyes! And their eyelids are lifted up." Proverbs 30:13

The NIV says "There are those whose eyes are ever so haughty, whose glances are so disdainful." This is a description of the third generation. Their "eyes are so haughty" because they are filled with pride and arrogance. They have been raised by parents who failed to acknowledge the sin nature, so they established their own ethics according to personal preferences. Now they have a very high evaluation of themselves and believe they should get whatever they want. They only deserve the best. They are self-absorbed and spend all their time fulfilling personal goals and desires.

Their "glances are disdainful" because they rationalize that nothing is as important as their own happiness. The third generation is the "Me Generation." Children raised by this generation spend their formative years with extremely self-centered parents. Divorce is rampant because the "quest for happiness" is paramount. Doing whatever it takes to "find oneself" is most important. This generation is constantly searching for something better but they often die unfulfilled and alone thanks to selfish choices.

Generation Number Four: A Generation Whose Teeth Are As Swords

"There is a generation whose teeth are as swords, and their jaw teeth as knives, to devour the poor from off the earth, and the needy from among men." Proverbs 30:14

Essentially, the first generation rejects the divine viewpoint of life and develops a human worldview that is not correct. Their worldview is then passed on to the next generation. By the time the second generation reaches an age where they can engage in critical thought, they have already been positioned to evaluate their lives and their world from their parents' corrupt perspective. The third generation doesn't stand a chance and naturally turn all their attention to themselves. As the fourth generation comes of age culture begins to fill up with a morally unrestrained people who will use violence to accomplish their social, judicial, economic and personal agenda. This fourth generation will be the society's last.

The fourth generation is the most violent. They are oppressive and abusive, taking advantage of anyone who's weak. Their insatiable desires make them cruel. When this generation is old enough to gain control of the government, their tyranny can only be stopped through foreign invasion.

Israel had a generation like this, as described in Amos 8:4, "You trample the needy and do away with the poor of the land." This type of behavior indicates the fourth and final generation of a society. In reference to that generation in Israel, God said, "The time is ripe for my people Israel; I will spare them no longer."

Reflections on David's Fourteenth Psalm

The generational cycle is again hinted at in Psalm 14. The chapter begins with the fool saying, "There is no God," which is exactly what happens in the first generation. In verse 2, there is no one left with a correct understanding of God and his ways, like the second generation. God then sees that men have become corrupt and sinful, looking only to fulfill their own desires—just like the third generation. Next these men "devour people as men eat bread," which reminds us of the fourth generation.

Psalm 14

1 "The fool says in his heart
    there is no God.
    They are corrupt, their deeds are vile;
    there is no one who does good.
2 The Lord looks down from heaven
    on the sons of men
    to see if there are any who understand,
    any who seek God.
3 All have turned aside,
    they have together become corrupt;
    there is no one who does good,
    not even one.
4 Will evildoers never learn—
    those who devour my people as men eat bread
    and who do not call on the Lord?"

A Look at Ages in the Scripture

Before the flood, men lived much longer. Adam is recorded to have lived 930 years, and his son Seth lived to be 912. The earth's environment was perfect at the time. There were no diseases until after the fall of man, and, as we already discussed, the earth was encircled with a layer of water that protected mankind from dangerous radiation (Genesis 1:6-8). During the flood, this water fell to earth, exposing men to solar radiation for the first time. Scientists have learned that the sun's ultraviolet light speeds up the aging process and contributes to skin cancer and cataracts. (An example of this would be the Apollo astronauts who got cataracts an average of seven years earlier than most people.) Scientists also found that ultraviolet exposure alters the immune response by changing cell structure.

Immediately after the flood, men stopped living as long. Noah's son Shem lived to be 500, and the first generation born after the flood lived an average of 400 years. After the Tower of Babel, we see those numbers cut in half again. Abraham's father dies at 205, and the years of life continue to decrease with each generation: 209, 207, 200, 119.

Therefore, the length of a generation in Adam's day was longer than the length of a generation after the flood in Shem's day. And a generation in Abraham's day (about 100 years) was longer than a generation in David's day (40 years).

What is a Generation?

Ever since Israel was established as a nation at Mount Sinai, a "generation" was determined to be a period of time lasting forty years.

> "He made them wander in the desert for forty years, <u>until the whole generation of those who had done evil in his sight was gone</u>." Numbers 32:13

The Hebrew word for generation is "dor" which means "a revolution of time such as an age or generation, roughly the period of time from one's birth to one's maturity." In the Old Testament, a "dor" is a period of about forty years.[1] " When Moses turned eighty, Joshua was about forty. Together, the two men represented the leadership of the first and second generations.

Recognizing 160 Years of Decline

If a generation turns away from God, they begin a decline that will end with the annihilation of their great-grandchildren. This four generation process takes 160 years, beginning with the original sin of the great-grandparents then passing through three more generations (each forty years in length). In this way, God is merciful by withholding his final judgment. He grants a nation many years to repent and eradicate the evil in their midst.

This process has been repeated for hundreds of years through many generations. It can be very difficult for a family, culture, or nation to identify the sin of their forefathers—the reason the judgment process began in the first place. Later we will see that this was a problem for the northern ten tribes of Israel when they didn't repent of the sin of Jeroboam.

Our Generation

As we look at our own generation, it can be hard to honestly judge ourselves in light of God's standards. It's hard because our society has suffered such an erosion of absolute truth. This is combined with the fact that most churches in our nation consider "an understanding of the Bible" just one of many optional activities for churchgoers. I have seen many full color brochures from churches that look like this:

Wednesday night activities:
a) Fishers of Men Basketball League – bring your unsaved friends!
b) Financial Planning for Families – learn to be a good steward even if you're in debt
c) The Maker's Diet – how to improve your temple God's way
d) Overview of the Gospels – for anyone ready get serious about the Bible
e) Children's Church – games, snacks, contests, videos, and more!!!

f) Martha's Kitchen – home decorating techniques for busy moms ($30 supplies fee)

g) Solitary Living – surviving as a Christian single in a postmodern world

h) Building Committee Meeting

Now don't get me wrong, these activities aren't bad. But the problem with this list is that studying the Bible is just *one* of many options. It's for the Christian whose "ready to get serious." This list gives us insight into many churches today.

Studying the Bible should be the main focus of every Christian, with additional church activities as the icing on the cake. But unfortunately, to get the traditional stamp of Christian approval today, you must be able to say, "I help in the nursery," or "I'm on worship team," or "I lead an outreach ministry." The underlying assumption is that if you are involved in *any* church activity, you must be walking the straight and narrow.

This assumption has worked wonders for church leaders who know that anytime you get people involved in church activities, they'll feel compelled to attend Sunday service, thus adding to church attendance numbers. While everyone would agree that Christians should be in some type of community, it's not good if the only reason they're attending church is because they're involved with church-related programs and, therefore, feel obligated to go on Sundays.

The Vanity Cycle of Church Activities

Yet another error in this system comes when people wrongly assume that anyone involved in "church ministry" must already know and understand the Bible. We don't have to look far in our churches today to see how false that assumption is. The purpose of the church is supposed to be: communicating the revelation of scripture to believers. But that purpose has been lost along the way. There simply isn't time to hear in-depth teaching on scripture between all the small group socials and marriage classes and outreach events.

Yet we know that only through hearing the word can people truly change:

"Faith comes from hearing the message, and the message is heard through the word of Christ." Romans 10:17

"Do not conform any longer to the pattern of this world, but be transformed by the renewing of your mind. Then you will be able to test and approve what God's will is." Romans 12:2

Paul tells Timothy:

> "Until I come, devote yourself to the public reading of Scripture, to preaching and to teaching." I Timothy 4:13

Timothy is told to read, preach, and teach the scriptures (I Timothy 4:13) because "faith comes from hearing the message" (Romans 10:17). When people gain an understanding of scripture, they grow in faith as their minds are renewed. They no longer conform to the pattern of the world but are transformed as they start to understand God's plan for mankind and the standards he's set into place (Romans 12:1). Only when people have a good grasp on scripture are local churches fulfilling their purpose. It is then that congregants can go out into the world and be salt to their generation.

Salt in the ancient world did three things:

1) Preserved – salt was added to meat before refrigeration to keep it from rotting
2) Prevented – enemies poured salt on cities after they destroyed them to prevent anything from growing on the land ever again
3) Added flavor – in the same way we use it today, salt has been used for ages to season food and draw out distinct flavors

Jesus told his disciples that they were the salt of the earth (Matthew 5:13). This means that those who believe in Jesus are supposed to help *preserve* their culture from moral decay, *prevent* the sins of their fathers from spreading to their generation, and add *flavor* to life by enjoying a happy and meaningful existence as part of God's plan. This is the purpose of the church as it relates to society, but this "saltiness" only comes after Christians first hear and understand the word of God.

Programs, activities, and social events have, sadly, replaced Bible teaching in our churches. Jesus says that once a church's saltiness is lost it can never be made salty again. The church is worthless to society if it's just a building full of people who have busy schedules (full of church-related activities) but still think and act exactly like everyone else in their generation. Jesus promised that pagan men will see the worthlessness of such a church and despise it.

> "You are the salt of the earth. But if the salt loses its saltiness, how can it be made salty again? It is no longer good for anything, except to be thrown out and trampled by men." Matthew 5:13

A few years ago, I was asked to teach a Sunday school class for young adults ages 20-30. I decided to teach on apologetics. The theme verse I used was I Peter 3:15, "Always be prepared to give an answer to everyone who asks you to give the reason for the hope that you have." (The word "answer" is the Greek word "apologia" which refers to someone giving a defense in court. It's where we get the words "apologize" and "apologetics.") Apologetics is all about providing evidence. I told the class how we knew there must be a God based on logic and science. I defended the authenticity of the scriptures and showed them that the Bible was consistent with ancient manuscripts written during the apostles' generation.

Even though the class was very interested in the teaching, I got called into one of the pastor's offices—clearly in trouble. The pastor casually flipped through my teaching notes and he asked, "So is *this* what you're teaching?" I nodded. Then the pastor asked, "Don't you think it's a little deep?" Out of respect for the position, I responded by asking, "What would you like me to teach?" The answer I received was, "Something simple…something basic."

"Something basic" seems to sum up most of our churches today. Being "seeker-friendly" is the new key to getting more people through the door, (and getting more people through the door is, after all, the ultimate goal). "Basic" sermons are required for seekers—sermons that shed light on "How to be a good parent," or "What to do with work-related stress." But trite mildly-motivational messages are not fulfilling the purpose of the church. Believers today *desperately need* an actual understanding of the Bible.

The Sunday school class I'd been teaching was full of college graduates who'd been raised in our ultra-secular society. Their schools, and in many cases, their churches, had promoted humanism at some level. The government and the media had taken that promotion a step further. These young adults had spent their entire lives dealing with doubts and questions from skeptics concerning the existence of God, the authenticity of scripture, the reality of hell, and the veracity of the Christian faith as a whole.

The purpose of the church is to communicate the revelation of scripture to believers.

Yet this pastor was telling me that giving the fourth generation some firm answers on why the Bible makes sense was not a good idea.

This type of thinking is the reason so many churches scrambled around in fear, trying save their congregations from the horrible deception of *The Da Vinci Code*. Hollywood releases some dumb fictional movie, and its premise confuses so many believers that most churches dedicate a six-week sermon series to refuting it. It's ridiculous, and it should have never happened. I would love to ask all those pastors what they've been doing the last few years. If their congregants had been consistently taught scripture, they wouldn't have had to do damage control over something so absurd. And perhaps if the body of Christ wasn't so bogged down by church-related activities and programs, they'd actually have more time to learn about the historical roots and theological foundation of their faith. Apologetics would obviously be a great place to start, but apparently it's just "too deep" for most modern churches.

More Examples from Bible History

Chapter 11: The Sin of Jeroboam

DAVID AND SOLOMON'S united kingdom of twelve tribes was split apart by God in 930 BC (I Kings 12). God divided them because Solomon had led the people astray and they'd begun to worship false gods (I Kings 11:33) including:

1) **Ashtoreth**, goddess of the Sidonians (also know as Ishtar to the Accadians, Assyrians, and Babylonians; Astarte to the Greeks; and Athtar to the Arabians) – Worship of Ashtoreth involved women cutting their long hair. Other women had to sacrifice their virginity. Herodutus records that every Babylonian woman had to offer herself up in the temple.

2) **Chemosh**, god of the Moabites – His name means destroyer or subduer. He could be appeased through human sacrifice.

3) **Molech**, god of the Ammonites – He was depicted as a man with the head of a bull (or an ox or calf). Children were supposed to "pass through the fire of Molech" by becoming human sacrifices. The first born from each family was offered up to appease the god.

As the Israelites drifted away from God's law, they started accepting more and more of these pagan practices. Although the Israelites maintained the use of the name Yahweh and the use of the temple building, the morality associated with Yahweh was replaced by immorality. This culminated when God spoke to the people through Jeremiah. God told them it was not acceptable for them to use his name and his temple while engaging in heathen behavior.

> "The people of Judah have done evil in my eyes, declares the Lord (Yahweh). They have set up their detestable idols in the house that bears my name and have defiled it. They have built the high places of Topheth in the Valley of Ben Hinnom to burn their sons and daughters in the fire – something I did not command, nor did it enter my mind." Jeremiah 7:30-31

God took Solomon's united kingdom (the twelve tribes of Israel) and split them into two separate nations. The ten northern tribes took the name Israel. Jeroboam, one of Solomon's officials who'd been promoted to Secretary of Labor (I Kings 11:28), became the northern kingdom's first ruler. Solomon's son Rehoboam was given the two southern tribes of Benjamin and Judah to rule. The combined southern tribes took the name Judah.

The prophet Ahijah promised that Jeroboam would have a successful dynasty as long as he obeyed God. Jeroboam did not obey God, however, and after four more generations, Israel was destroyed.

> "When he tore Israel away from the house of David, they made Jeroboam son of Nebat their king. Jeroboam enticed Israel away from following the Lord and caused them to commit a great sin. The Israelites persisted in all the sins of Jeroboam and did not turn away from them until the Lord removed them from his presence, as he had warned through all his servants the prophets. So the people of Israel were taken from their homeland into exile in Assyria, and they are still there." II Kings 17:21-23

Of the eighteen kings that followed Jeroboam, fourteen are said to have "remained in the sin of Jeroboam."

Generation in Cycle	First Year	King	Verse: Sin of Jeroboam	Events
1st 930-890	930	*Jeroboam*		Set up two golden calves
	909	Nadab	A* I Kg. 15:26	Jeroboam's only son; reigned for two years
	908	Baasha	B* I Kg. 15:34	Killed Nadab and Jeroboam's family
2nd 891-850				
	886	Elah	-	Reigned for two years
	885	Zimri	C* I Kg. 16:19	Reigned for seven days
	885	Omri	D* I Kg. 16:26	Ahab's Father; built Samaria
	874	Ahab	E* I Kg. 16:31	Started Baal worship; faced prophet Elijah; Omri's 2nd generation

Generation in Cycle	First Year	King	Verse: Sin of Jeroboam	Events
	853	Ahaziah	F* I Kg.22:52	Ahab's Son; Omri's 3rd generation
	852	Joram	G* II Kg. 3:2,3	Ahab's Son; Omri's 3rd generation
851-810				
(Cycle Stopped for one generation)	841	Jehu	H* II Kg. 10:29,31	Eliminated Baal worship and reversed the national decline that had occurred throughout the last forty years; kills all of Ahab's family, eliminating Omri's lineage in its fourth generation
	814	Jehoahaz	I* II Kg. 13:2	Oppressed by the nation of Aram (Syria)
3rd 809-770				
	798	Jehoash	J* II Kg.13:11	War with Judah
	782	Jeroboam II	K* II Kg. 14:24	Restored land lost to Aram; God spoke to him through the prophet Jonah; national prosperity briefly restored
4th 771-721				
	753	Zechariah		Jeroboam II's son; reigned for six months
	752	Shallum		Killed Zechariah; reigned for one month

Generation in Cycle	First Year	King	Verse: Sin of Jeroboam	Events
	752	Menahem	L* II Kg. 15:18	During his reign the Assyrian King Tiglath-pileser carted away 37 tons of silver
	742	Pekahiah	M* II Kg. 15:24	Assassinated by General Pekah
	740	Pekah	N* II Kg. 15:28	During his reign, Assyrian king Tiglath-pileser takes land in the north and east from Israel
	731	Hoshea	O* II Kg. 17:2	Assassinated Pekah; betrays Assyria and goes to Egypt for help; Assyrian king Shalmaneser imprisons Hoshea; Israel is invaded in 725; Samaria is besieged for three years and finally falls in 721

*A – "Walking in the ways of his father (Jeroboam) and in the sin which he had caused Israel to commit." (I Kings 15:26)

B – "He did evil in the eyes of the Lord, walking in the ways of Jeroboam and in his sin, which he caused Israel to commit." (I Kings 15:34)

C – "Because of the sins he had committed, doing evil in the eyes of the Lord and walking in the ways of Jeroboam and the sin he had committed and had caused Israel to commit." (I Kings 16:19)

D – "He walked in all the ways of Jeroboam son of Nebat and in his sin, which he had caused Israel to commit, so they provoked the Lord, the God of Israel, to anger by their worthless idols." (I Kings 16:26)

E – "He not only considered it trivial to commit the sins of Jeroboam son of Nebat, but he also married Jezebel...and began to serve Baal and worship him." (I Kings 16:31)

F – "He did evil in the eyes of the Lord because he walked in the ways of his father and mother (Ahab and Jezebel) and in the ways of Jeroboam son of Nebat who caused Israel to sin." (I Kings 22:52)

G – "He did evil in the eyes of the Lord, but not as his father and mother (Ahab and Jezebel) had done. He got rid of the sacred stone of Baal that his father had made. Nevertheless he clung to the sins of Jeroboam son of Nebat, which he had caused Israel to commit; he did not turn away from them."   (II Kings 3:2, 3)

H – "So Jehu destroyed Baal worship in Israel. However, he <u>did not turn away from the sins of Jeroboam</u> son of Nebat, which he had caused Israel to commit – the worship of the golden calves at Bethel and Dan." (II Kings 10:28, 29) "Yet Jehu was not careful to keep the law of the Lord, the God of   Israel, with all his heart. He <u>did not turn away from the sins of Jeroboam</u>, which he had caused Israel to commit." (II Kings 10:31)

I – "He did evil in the eyes of the Lord by <u>following the sins of Jeroboam</u> son of Nebat which he had caused Israel to commit, and he did not turn away from them." (II Kings 13:2)

J – "He did evil in the eyes of the Lord and <u>did not turn away from any of the sins of Jeroboam</u> son of Nebat, which he had caused Israel to commit; he continued in them." (II Kings 13:11)

K – "He did evil in the eyes of the Lord and <u>did not turn away from any of the sins of Jeroboam</u> son of Nebat, which he had caused Israel to commit." (II Kings 14:24)

L – "He did evil in the eyes of the Lord. During his entire reign <u>he did not turn away from the sins of   Jeroboam</u> son of Nebat, which he had caused Israel to commit." (II Kings 15:18)

M – "Pekahiah did evil in the eyes of the Lord. <u>He did not turn away from the sins of Jeroboam</u> son of Nebat, which he had caused Israel to commit." (II Kings 15:24)

N – "He did evil in the eyes of the Lord. <u>He did not turn away from the sins of Jeroboam</u> son of Nebat, which he had caused Israel to commit." (II Kings 15:28)

O – "He did evil in the eyes of the Lord, but not like the kings of Israel who preceded him." (II Kings 17:2)

The sin of Jeroboam is first reported in I Kings 12. After Jeroboam became king, he wanted to stop his people from returning to the temple in Jerusalem to worship God. He feared that if too many people returned to Jerusalem, they would want to rejoin Judah, which was under the reign of King David's dynasty (I Kings 12:27).

Jeroboam decided it would be best to create new gods for his new nation. These gods would be available for worship close by, thus preventing people from going to Jerusalem. Jeroboam even rewrote national history to better promote the worship of these gods.

> "After seeking advice, the king made two golden calves. He said to the people, 'It is too much for you to go up to Jerusalem. Here are your gods, O Israel, who brought you up out of Egypt.' One he set up in Bethel, and

the other in Dan. And this thing became a sin; the people went even as far as Dan to worship the one there." I Kings 12:28-30

I Kings 12:31-33 goes on to say:

1) Jeroboam built shrines
2) Jeroboam appointed priests
3) Jeroboam instituted a festival to replace the Feast of Tabernacles
4) Jeroboam offered sacrifices on the altar in Bethel to the golden calves

The first day that Jeroboam went to offer sacrifices in Bethel, a prophet of God appeared and warned that one day Israel would fall for the sin they were committing. It would take five generations (209 years) to move through the four cycles of judgment before their nation would meet its end. Leviticus 26:14-33 describes the cycles of judgment that God promised to take Israel through if they continued to rebel. (See page 74)

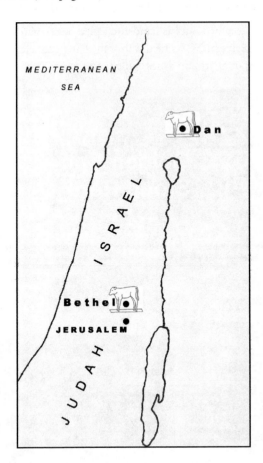

The First Cycle Begins

According to Leviticus 26:29-35, one of the God's final judgments on a nation includes piling up their dead bodies on the lifeless forms of their idols (Leviticus 26:30). As Jeroboam was conducting the opening ceremonies for a shrine to false gods in Israel, a prophet from the region stepped out and said:

> "O altar, altar! This is what the Lord says: 'A son named Josiah will be born to the house of David. On you he will sacrifice the priests of the high places who now make offerings here, and human bones will be burned on you.'" I Kings 13:2

The prophet continued, saying:

> 'This is the sign the Lord has declared: The altar will be split apart and the ashes on it will be poured out.' I Kings 13:3

Two signs followed this prophecy, confirming its authenticity:

1) Jeroboam stretched out his hand and called out (regarding the prophet), "Seize him!" As he did this, his hand shriveled up.
2) The altar split apart and ashes spilled out.

This is the excavated remains of Jeroboam's Golden Calf worship center in the city of Dan. The events at Bethel would have happened in a place similar if not identical to this location since they were built at the same time and originated from the same royal decree of Jeroboam. This picture was taken by Galyn Wiemers in June of 2007. Below are the steps that led up to the Golden Calf (left) and a detail photo of the stone work around the platform (right).

This proved that the first cycle of judgment had begun because two things that accompany the first cycle had already occurred:

a. Wasting disease (Jeroboam's hand shriveled up)
b. Sudden terror (Jeroboam was terrified when the altar split)

In fact, Jeroboam was so terrified at what he'd just seen that he begged the prophet:

"Intercede with the Lord your God and pray for me that my hand may be restored." I Kings 13:6

But, just like Pharaoh during the ten plagues in Exodus, Jeroboam had no real change of heart. Even though he'd seen the judgment God was capable of bringing upon his people, he didn't truly repent. Yes, he may have been terrified by his shriveled hand, but the incident simply wasn't enough to change him permanently.

"Even after this, Jeroboam did not change his evil ways, but once more appointed priests for the high places form all kinds of people." I Kings 13:33

The chapter ends by saying:

"This was the sin of the house of Jeroboam that led to its downfall and to its destruction from the face of the earth." I Kings 13:34

The original sin occurred in 930 BC. In 721 BC, the Assyrians dispersed Israel's ten tribes throughout the earth.

The Second Cycle and the Legacy of Ahab

During the second generation, King Ahab and Queen Jezebel sat in rebellion against God. Ahab was called the "worst of all rulers," according to I Kings:

"He not only considered it trivial to commit the sins of Jeroboam son of Nebat, but he also married Jezebel, daughter of Ethbaal king of the Sidonians, and began to serve Baal and worship him. He set up an altar for Baal in the temple of Baal that he built in Samaria. Ahab also made an Asherah pole and did more to provoke the Lord, the God of Israel, to anger than did all the kings of Israel before him." I Kings 16:31-33

During this second generation, God sent the prophet Elijah to Israel, and he correctly predicted there would be a three-and-a-half year famine. Leviticus 26:18-20 says God will "break down the stubborn pride" of the second generation by sending drought and famine to the land. And so he did.

Elijah walked into King Ahab's palace and said:

"As the Lord, the God of Israel, lives, whom I serve, there will be neither dew nor rain in the next few years except at my word." I Kings 17:1

The famine continued as promised until Elijah met for a showdown with Ahab and the prophets of Baal on the top of Mt. Carmel. It was there that Elijah challenged Baal's prophets to call fire down from heaven as a sign to the people that would identify the true God. Elijah ultimately won the showdown when God sent fire from the sky.

On that occasion God didn't let the false prophets produce fire and deceive the people. However, there will be a time in the future when the false prophets of the anti-christ will produce many deceptive signs and wonders. They will even call fire down from heaven.

"And he performed great and miraculous signs, even causing fire to come down from heaven to earth in full view of men." Revelation 13:3

"The coming of the lawless one will be in accordance with the work of Satan displayed in all kinds of counterfeit miracles, signs and wonders, and in every sort of evil that deceives those who are perishing. They perish because they refused to love the truth and so be saved. For this reason God sends them a powerful delusion so that they will believe the lie and so that all will be condemned who have not believed the truth but have delighted in wickedness." II Thessalonians 2:9-12

Ahab's son Ahaziah continued to rule Israel into the next generation. We know that Ahaziah "did evil in the eyes of the Lord, because he walked in the ways of his father and mother and in the ways of Jeroboam son of Nebat, who caused Israel to sin," (I Kings 22:52).

Ahaziah's sin was catorgorized as twofold:

a) He walked in the ways of his father and mother (the sin of the second generation)
b) He walked in the ways of Jerobaom (the sin of the first generation)

Ahaziah's brother Joram became Israel's next king. Regarding Joram, we know:

"He did evil in the eyes of the Lord, but not as his father and mother had. He got rid of the sacred stone of Baal that his father had made. Nevertheless he clung to the sins of Jeroboam." II Kings 3:2-3

It appears that Joram successfully reversed the sins of the second generation, but he made the mistake of clinging to the sin of the first generation.

In 841, nine years into the third generation, Elisha sent a prophet he had personally trained to anoint Israel's General Jehu to be the next king (II Kings 9:1). Jewish tradition says the prophet sent was Jonah. (Jonah was alive and ministering at this time, so it is quite possible.) After Jehu was anointed, he killed King Joram, queen mother Jezebel, and seventy other royal sons of Ahab including all the priests of Baal. Jehu was determined to purge Israel of Baal worship and reverse the damage caused by the second generation. Under Jehu's leadership, false gods were finally destroyed:

"So Jehu destroyed Baal worship in Israel." II Kings 10:28

Thanks to Jehu's efforts, Israel was given an extra forty years to undo the sin of Jeroboam. Thus, Israel's demise takes five generations rather than four (200 years rather than 160).

One statement stands out in II Kings' description of Jehu. After explaining how Jehu effectively removed Baal worship from Israel, we learn:

"...He <u>did not turn away from</u> the sins of Jeroboam son of Nebat, which he had caused Israel to commit the worship of the golden calves at Bethel and Dan." II Kings 10:28, 29

We also learn:

"Jehu was not careful to keep the law of the Lord, the God of Israel, with all his heart. He <u>did not turn away from the sins of Jeroboam</u>, which he had caused Israel to commit." II Kings 10:31

Jehu had managed to eliminate the sin of Baal worship from Israel, but had not yet dealt with the sins of his grandfather's generation.

In the Ten Commandments, God promises to observe the sins of fathers into the third and fourth generations. The nation of Judah was bothered by this promise and asked:

"Why has the Lord decreed such a great disaster against us? What wrong have we done? What sin have we committed against the Lord our God?" Jeremiah 16:10

God tells Judah:

"It is because your fathers forsook me and followed other gods and served and worshipped them. They forsook me and did not keep my law. But you have behaved more wickedly than your fathers...so I will throw you out of this land." Jeremiah 16:12-13

The fathers in the first generation had sinned, and this sin was taught to the next generation. The second generation became caught up in their fathers' sins to an even greater degree. That is why Jeremiah says:

a) "your fathers sinned"
b) "you have behaved more wickedly than your fathers"

Jehu and his generation were able to look back and see how Baal worship had developed in their nation's recent history. They knew in their hearts that Baal worship was a sin. What they could not do was draw from their memory regarding the sin of Jeroboam. That particular sin had become such a part of the foundation and fabric their culture that no one, including Jehu and those devoted to God, could identify it and repent of it. The penalty for Jeroboam's sin haunted Israel until the very end.

This is a sobering thought for us today. If we examine our culture by the standards of our culture, we too will miss what God expects from us. Our only hope is to examine our culture by the written revelation of God's word. It is here that God has preserved truth for every culture for all time. It should be our only means of examining ourselves and our society. Our problem is not that we don't have a list of standards to abide by but that we don't take them seriously enough to study them and honor them through our words and actions.

God's intention with the cycles of discipline is to draw people back to himself.

Jehu, his son, grandson, and great grandson (Jehoahaz in 814 BC, Jehoash in 798 BC and Jeroboam II in 793 BC) all had the same problem:

"He did evil in the eyes of the Lord by following the sins of Jeroboam." II Kings 13:2, 11; 14:24

Jehoahz, Jehoash and Jeroboam II took Israel through the third generation (811-770). Jeroboam II was the fourth and final king in the dynasty of Jehu. During this entire time, there was no repentance for continuing in the sins of the first generation.

The Fourth Cycle

The kings that ruled in the fourth generation (771-721) were also consistently described as men who "did not turn away from the sin of Jeroboam." (Manahem in II Kings 15:18, Pekahiah in 15:24, and Pekah in 15:28).

Under these leaders, the fourth generation experienced the fourth cycle of judgment just as God warned when he said, "I will bring the sword upon you...you will withdraw to your cities. I will send a plague...you will be given into enemy hands."

This very thing occurred in 743 during the reign of Menahem. Tiglath-Pilesesr III (Pul), king of Assyria, invaded Israel, and the Assyrians carted away 37 tons of sliver. Every wealthy man had to surrender more than a pound of silver to Tiglath-pileser (II Kings 15:19-20). Israel was then invaded and given over to the enemy. In 732, Tiglath-pileser returned to take over five cities and the land of Gilead, Galilee, and Naphtali (II Kings 15:29).

In 725 BC, the final move of God's wrath began when Assyrian King Shalmaneser V invaded Israel and laid siege to the capital city of Samaria. In 721, Samaria fell and the survivors were deported to other lands.

II Kings 17:22 sums it all up:

> "The Israelites persisted in all the sins of Jeroboam and did not turn away from them until the Lord removed them from his presence."

In 621, King Josiah tried to bring revival to the land of Judah and the remnant left in Israel. Josiah went to the original altar set up by Jeroboam in Bethel and completely demolished it. He first went to nearby tombs where Israel's priests had been buried. He removed all their bones so he could burn them on the altar (II Kings 23:15-20). This event fulfilled the prophecy given to Jeroboam on the day he introduced Israel to their new gods.

> "A son named Josiah will be born to the house of David. On you he will sacrifice the priests of the high places who now make offerings here, and human bones will be burned on you." I Kings 13:2

This scriptural account of 200 years of history in Israel shows the process of four generations and the cycles of judgment they went through. In the second commandment (Exodus 20:5), God says he will punish children for the sins of their fathers to the third and fourth generations of those who hate him. Jeroboam's sin (committed in 930 BC) remained part of Israel culture both in philosophy and practice for four generations. Israel did not identify this sin nor repent of it for four generations, which is why they were destroyed. Each generation had the opportunity to re-evaluate the worldview handed down to them by their parents, but instead they accepted the ways of Jeroboam up until their national end.

The sobering question we must ask ourselves is: if we are the fourth generation of the United States of America, can we even recognize the sins of our great-grandfathers? Do we know the sins of the first generation—the sins that set the cycle of judgment in motion? If we don't recognize those sins and repent of them, we are doomed to continue in them just like the Israelites continued in the sin of Jeroboam. Let's learn from their mistake and take time to understand where our nation went wrong.

Chapter 12: The Return of Elijah

BIBLE TEACHERS AND pastors know there are a few Bible subjects that always grab people's attention. Topics like angels, demons, spiritual gifts, heaven, and hell are always good for crowd interest. Teaching about events associated with end times also tends to fascinate people. I've heard it advised that if you want to start a church, your first sermon series should be on the last days.

I, on the other hand, just finished teaching verse-by-verse through the book of Isaiah. It took me well over a year. My method is not one people would generally recommend for building church attendance, yet I cannot stress how important it is that each Christian has a full understanding of the Old Testament prophets. Bible personalities like Enoch and Daniel may be shrouded in mystery, but we must dive in and dissect them if we hope to understand God and his plan for mankind.

The Prophet That Comes Before the Judgment

Malachi, the last book of the Old Testament, promises that God "will send the prophet Elijah before that great and dreadful day of the Lord comes" (Malachi 4:5). Malachi's promise applies to all "great and dreadful" days of judgment, like the day in 70 AD when Jerusalem was destroyed at the hands of the Romans.

The prophet God sent to fulfill the role of Elijah before that particular judgment day was none other than John the Baptist.

> "The disciples asked him (Jesus), 'Why then do the teachers of the law say that Elijah must come first?' Jesus replied, 'To be sure, Elijah comes and will restore all things. But I tell you, Elijah has already come, and they did not recognize him, but have done to him everything they wished. In the same way the Son of Man is going to suffer at their hands.' Then the disciples understood that he was talking to them about John the Baptist." Matthew 17:10-13

Jesus also says:

> "This is the one about whom it is written: 'I will send my messenger ahead of you who will prepare your way before you!' (from Malachi 3:1)…and if you are willing to accept it, he is the Elijah who was to come." Matthew 11:9, 10, 14

We should not make the mistake of thinking God is talking about sending Elijah himself back to earth over and over again to warn people. We know that when Elijah is spoken of in these verses, it's a reference to the "role of the ministry of Elijah." When John the Baptist is asked, "Who are you? Are you Elijah?" he replies, "I am not" (John 1:20, 21).

However, when John the Baptist came to Israel in 29 AD, he achieved the same results that Elijah achieved in 870 BC (thus fulfilling the role of Elijah's ministry). Multitudes flocked to hear John speak, and many people repented after hearing his message. John, the Elijah of his time, brought the people back to a correct understanding of God.

This is the essence of the "role of Elijah." The original prophet Elijah warned Israel about a soon-coming famine in the days of King Ahab's rebellion. Elijah was supposed to lead Israel out of Baal worship and help reverse the four generation cycle. The purpose of Elijah's ministry was to restore the nation's relationship with the Lord. He was to teach the people how to live righteously.

> "He (Elijah) will turn the hearts of the fathers to their children, and the hearts of the children to their fathers; or else I will come and strike the land with a curse." Malachi 4:6

A person fulfilling the ministry of Elijah is supposed to restore the foundational principles of God to a nation so they can avoid being overthrown. Doing this involves, first and foremost restoring the institutions established by God.

The Seven Institutions

There are seven institutions established by God for the welfare of mankind:

	Institutions	Scripture Found	Purpose
1	Individual Volition	Genesis 1:16-17	Individuals can respond to God's offer of salvation
2	Marriage	Genesis 2:24	Foundation for the family
3	Family	Genesis 4:1, 7:1	Foundation for society
4	Government	Genesis 9:5,6	Create and maintain a peaceful society
5	Nations	Genesis 10, 11	So societies can collectively respond to God
6	Israel	Genesis 12:2,3	Preserve the truth of God's revelation on the earth
7	Church	Matthew 13; 16:18; Acts 2	Communicate to the kingdoms of the world the truth about God's eternal kingdom

1. **Individual Volition** – is what each person the authority of his/her own soul. We all have the freedom to respond positively or negatively in all circumstances. This is what makes us susceptible to God's grace or his justice. Man is ultimately responsible for everything he does.

   > "And <u>the Lord God commanded the man, 'You are free</u> to eat from any tree in the garden; but you must not eat from the tree of the knowledge of good and evil, for when you eat of it you will surely die." Genesis 1:16, 17

   In this verse, we hear a command from God establishing the fact that man is free to choose which tree he eats from. Along with this freedom comes the responsibility to make the right choice. If a man makes the right choice, he will reap the benefits of his correct decision. If he uses his freedom to make the wrong choice, he will suffer.

   > "The righteousness of the righteous man will be credited to him, and the wickedness of the wicked will be charged against him." Ezekiel 18:20b

2. **Marriage** – is the foundation upon which the greatness of mankind can be developed and expressed in a society. Without marriage, mankind would do little beyond survive (much like an animal). Marriage is the bedrock of the family used to produce and train the next generation. If marriage fails, the family fails, and society will collapse.

3. **Family** – is the cornerstone of society. Animals only pass down instincts to their young, but mankind passes down a set of values. Parents are responsible for training the next generation, just as Israel was commanded to teach the word of God to their children.

   > "Fix these words of mine in your hearts and minds…<u>Teach them to your children</u>, talking about them when you sit…when you walk…when you lie down…when you get up." Deuteronomy 11:18, 19

4. **Government** – was established by God to maintain peace and justice on earth. Men are to hold each other accountable using this institution.

   > "He is God's servant to do you good. But if you do wrong, be afraid, for he does not bear the sword for nothing. <u>He is God's servant</u>, an agent of wrath to bring punishment on the wrongdoer." Romans 13:4

   > "I urge, then, first of all, that requests, prayers, intercession, and thanksgiving be made for everyone – for kings and all those in authority, <u>that we may live peaceful and quiet lives</u> in all godliness and holiness." I Timothy 2:1, 2

Governmental authorities are God's servants to establish order in our societies by punishing those who don't conform to a specific standard of conduct. It is the government's divine mandate to demand justice while ruling justly.

"By justice a king gives a country stability, but one who is greedy for bribes tears it down." Proverbs 29:4

5. **Nations** – were instituted to preserve the various earthly governments. God's plan to prevent absolute world domination involves separate nations. This concept was established after the one and only government of the ancient world was overthrown at the tower of Babel (Genesis 11:1-9) and, in its place, seventy individual nations were formed (Genesis 10).

"The Lord said, 'If as one people speaking the same language they have begun to do this, then nothing they plan to do will be impossible for them… From there the Lord scattered them over the face of the whole earth." Genesis 11:6, 9

6. Israel – is the nation chosen for the purpose of preserving the knowledge of God in a dark world of lost nations. God told Abraham, "I will make you into a great nation…and all peoples on earth will be blessed through you" (Genesis 12:2, 3).

It is through Israel that we have the recorded history of God's work on the earth and his plan for mankind. The savior of the world was promised by prophets who came from the nation of Israel. Jesus Christ himself was a product of Israel. The New Testament scriptures, which are the foundation of the church, were written by men from Israel. (Luke is the only Gentile writer in the entire Bible since before Abraham's time.) Only through Israel has God revealed future events leading up to the return of the Messiah and the establishment of his kingdom on earth. Israel will again represent God to all nations after the church age ends and the world enters a seven year tribulation period (Isaiah 60:1-22; 61:6).

7. **Church** – is the institution set in place by God to proclaim the finished worked of the Messiah and invite people from all nations to join his kingdom.

"Go and make disciples of all nations, baptizing them in the name of the Father and of the Son and of the Holy Spirit, and teaching them to obey everything I have commanded you." Matthew 28:19, 2

The church has received the completion of God's revelation to man. This revelation was first exposed by the apostles and now comes from people in every nation.

"The commission God gave me to present you—the word of God in its fullness—the mystery that has been kept hidden for ages and generations, but is now disclosed to the saints." Colossians 1:25

"The church of the living God, the pillar and foundation of the truth." I Timothy 3:15

"Guard the good deposit that was entrusted to you." II Timothy 1:14

We have seen in our own culture that there is a chain reaction when foundational institutions established by God start to collapse. When individuals fail to live with integrity, it affects marriages. When marriages fail, families break up, and thereby neglect to teach the next generation about morality and self-control. Because children from these families don't make the best citizens, the government must spend more effort on enforcing laws and creating social service programs. When these immoral children grow up and take over the government, the government becomes corrupt. A weak nation with bad leadership can be easily overtaken by its enemies.

More About the Institution of Marriage

When individuals misuse their volition and make selfish decisions, they become unfaithful covenant breakers. This sin deeply affects the institution of marriage. Whenever people are immoral or perverted, marriages will breakdown. Honoring the institution of marriage is necessary for the health of mankind.

Malachi addresses this:

> "So guard yourself in your spirit and do not break faith with the wife of your youth. 'I hate divorce,' says the Lord God of Israel, 'and I hate a man covering his wife with violence as well as with his garment,' says the Lord Almighty. So guard yourself in your spirit and do not break faith." Malachi 2:15, 16

Malachi points back to the first institution of individual volition as a means for strengthening the second institution of marriage. For a marriage to be strong and enduring, Malachi tells each partner to "guard yourself in your spirit." This admonition is stated twice in two verses. If a man fails to guard his spirit, he dishonors his individual volition—the first institution given to him by God to control his life and his eternal destiny.

This same warning is given by Solomon in Proverbs 4:23:

> "Above all else, guard your heart, for it is the wellspring of life."

My wife has often quoted these words to our six sons to prepare them for future life assaults that will challenge their character. Failure to properly guard the heart will end in the soul's corruption. Someone with a corrupt soul sees little harm in violating covenants and encourages others to do the same.

Malachi 2:13, 14 says:

> "Another thing you do: you flood the Lord's altar with tears. You weep and wail because he no longer pays attention to your offerings or accepts them with pleasure from your hands. You ask, 'Why?' It is because the Lord is acting as witness between you and the wife of your youth, because you have broken faith with her, though she is your partner, the wife of your marriage covenant."

Marriage is to be honored by all men, not just believers. Hebrews 13:4 says:

> "Marriage should be honored by all, and the marriage bed kept pure, for God will judge the adulterer and all the sexually immoral."

Failure to guard your heart will result in the corruption of your soul.

Marriage is not just an institution of the church. It greatly benefits the entire society. For a culture to be strong, marriage should be honored by all people. When a culture stops honoring marriage, they commit cultural suicide.

Malachi 4:6 closes by saying:

> "He (Elijah) will turn the hearts of the father's to their children and the hearts of the children to their fathers or else I will come and strike the land with a curse."

It was Elijah's duty to restore the family. Families can only be restored when marriages are restored. If individuals use their volition to act honorably, marriages will again thrive. But if a society doesn't respond to the ministry of "Elijah," God says he will strike the land with a curse. This refers to the fifth cycle of discipline—the overthrow of a nation.

Around 30 AD, John the Baptist came to Israel with the ministry of Elijah. His nation was entering the fourth generation and facing the fourth cycle of discipline. They did not turn from their sin and moved into the fifth cycle of judgment. Forty years later, in 70 AD, their society was overthrown.

The angel Gabriel announces the birth of John the Baptist to his father Zechariah in Luke 1:16, 17:

"Many of the people of Israel will he bring back to the Lord their God. And he will go on before the Lord, in the spirit and power of Elijah, to turn the hearts of the fathers to their children and the disobedient to the wisdom of the righteous – to make ready a people prepared for the Lord."

It's interesting to note a few things in this verse:

1) John will bring many back to the Lord.
2) John will successfully execute the ministry of "Elijah." Gabriel says John will go "in the spirit and power of Elijah," (not as Elijah himself).
3) The nation of Judah will be destroyed in forty years (70 AD) despite the fact that John will fulfill his ministry.
4) There is a clear connection to Malachi's prophecy when Gabriel quotes the phrase, "turn the hearts of the fathers to their children."
5) The ultimate purpose of Elijah's ministry is to prepare people to meet the Lord. This refers to the Lord's coming and the twofold results that will follow: salvation or damnation. Malachi 3:1 says, "See, I will send my messenger, who will prepare the way before me." The Lord's coming will be both a day of great joy and a day of great terror. The next verse asks, "But who can endure the day of his coming? Who can stand when he appears?" How the people responded to John the Baptist prepared them to meet the Lord either as their savior or as their enemy.

In 30 AD, Jesus Christ came to Israel. Jesus presented himself as a deliverer, and many responded. But even those who rejected him had been prepared beforehand through the ministry of John the Baptist.

John the Baptist and Jesus both came on the scene at the beginning of the fourth generation in Israel. Jerusalem was going to be destroyed by the Romans in just forty years.

In the middle of the first generation, (63 BC), Pompey, the Roman general stationed in the East, invaded the land of Palestine. The Romans set up their standard with the SPQR insignia and the golden Roman eagle—meaning Israel was officially under occupation from the rising Roman Empire. The SPQR insignia was a Latin phrase meaning "Senatus Populusque Romanus" or "The Senate and People of Rome." This referred to the government of the Roman Republic, and it appeared on all Roman coins, documents, monuments, and public works. The Roman occupation of Israel was a manifestation of the first cycle of judgment (Leviticus 26:17). The first generation had been issued a warning. Israel would be given four generations to respond to this warning. By 70 AD, their time would be up.

Chapter 13: Jesus, a Prophet to His Generation

JOHN THE BAPTIST prepared the way for the coming of the Lord. He introduces Jesus as the savior in John 1:29:

> "Look <u>the Lamb of God</u>, who takes away the sin of the world!"

John recognizes Jesus as the eternal God in John 1:15:

> "He who comes after me has surpassed me because <u>he was before me.</u>"

After the Spirit descends on Jesus at his baptism, John says in John 1:34:

> "I have seen and I testify that <u>this is the Son of God.</u>"

John also refers to Jesus as Lord in John 1:23 when he uses a quote from Isaiah 40:3 to identify himself and his ministry:

> "I am the voice of one calling in the desert, 'Make straight the way for the Lord.'"

Jesus is the eternal God. He is the son of God, the second member of the trinity. He is the Lord who took on flesh to die. Jesus was there at the creation of the world (John 1:3). He called out Abraham and formed the nation of Israel (John 8:56-58). He is now seated at the right hand of the father as our High Priest (John 16:23, 24, 28; 17:9, 20). He will judge all mankind at some point in the future (John 5:22). But we also must remember that, during his ministry on earth, Jesus was a prophet to his generation.

Jesus knew where Israel was in the judgment cycle. In the book of Luke, Jesus speaks directly to his generation in three sets of verses. In one set of verses, he connects current events in Israel to the nation's ultimate overthrow. In the second set of verses, he uses a parable to illustrate the process of the four generation cycle. And in the third set of verses, he speaks with the imagery and language of a prophet to reveal that they are indeed the fourth and final generation. God is about to pour out his wrath on their society and let their enemies overtake them.

The background for the first set of verses begins in Luke 11:14 where we see Jesus drive out a demon in front of a growing crowd. Jesus performed this miraculous sign to show them "the kingdom of God has come to you." Some people called him Satan after he performed this miracle. To this, Jesus replied:

> "If Satan is divided against himself, how can his kingdom stand?" Luke 11:18

Jesus explained to the people that he is actually much stronger than Satan. He used this illustration to demonstrate his point:

> "When someone stronger attacks and overpowers him, he takes away the armor in which the man trusted and divides up the spoils." Luke 11:22

According to Luke 11:29, the crowds continued to grow around Jesus as he taught. Jesus told these crowds they were part of a "wicked generation." He then compared himself to Jonah and compared the crowds to the Assyrians of Ninevah.

> "For as Jonah was a sign to the Ninevites, so also will the Son of Man be to this generation." Luke 11:30

Jonah went to Ninevah to preach to the fourth and final generation. Ninevah was a mere forty days away from total destruction when Jonah arrived (Jonah 3:4). When the people of Ninevah heard Jonah preach, they repented. Now it was up to Israel to decide how they would respond to the prophet placed before them.

The crowds asked Jesus for a miraculous sign so they could know he was telling the truth. Jesus said to them:

> "This is a wicked generation. It asks for a miraculous sign, but none will be given it except the sign of Jonah…The men of Nineveh will stand up at the judgment with this generation and condemn it; for they repented at the preaching of Jonah, and now one greater than Jonah is here." Luke 11:29, 32

When Jesus took a break from the crowds to get lunch, some Pharisees invited him to eat with them (Luke 11:37). The Pharisees began to criticize their guest for not closely adhering to religious traditions, including the ceremonial washing before the meal. Jesus responded to these charges with the same attitude he had had while speaking to the crowds just moments earlier. He said:

> "Now then, you Pharisees clean the outside of the cup and dish, but inside you are full of greed and wickedness. You foolish people!" Luke 11:39

Jesus then explained the "woes" of the Pharisees, including:

1) They gave away a tenth of everything they owned, (including their kitchen spices), but they neglected justice. (In the Bible, nations are never overthrown because they've failed to tithe, but they are overthrown if they aren't just.)
2) They love to be recognized by others. They love the feeling of being important and famous.
3) They defile people with their false teachings and their superior attitudes.

When Jesus finished his rebuke of the Pharisees over lunch, Luke records:

> "One of the experts in the law answered him, 'Teacher, when you say these things, you insult us also.'" Luke 11:45

You would think that after hearing Jesus rebuke the wicked crowd in the morning and the Pharisees at lunch, this "expert in the law" wouldn't rush to be the next in line for chastisement. But he spoke up nonetheless, again challenging Jesus. To this, Jesus replied:

> "And you experts in the law, <u>woe to you</u>, because you load people down with burdens they can hardly carry, and you yourselves will not lift one finger to help them." Luke 11:51

Jesus left the Pharisees to rejoin the crowd which had now grown to "many thousands" and was so large that people were "trampling on one another." Jesus spent the afternoon speaking to them. We read about it in Luke 11:52:

> "A crowd of many thousands had gathered, so that they were trampling on one another, Jesus began to speak first to his disciples, saying: 'Be on your guard against the yeast of the Pharisees, which is hypocrisy.'"

For the rest of the afternoon, Jesus alternated between speaking to the large crowd that had formed and speaking directly to his disciples. (In Luke 12:1, 22 he speaks to his disciples; in Luke 12:13, 16, 54 he speaks to the crowd; in Luke 12:41 the disciples are confused as to whom he's addressing.)

Jesus first criticizes the crowd and says they are hypocrites just like the Pharisees:

> "Hypocrites! You know how to interpret the appearance of the earth and sky. How is it that you don't know how to interpret the present time?" Luke 12:56

Some people from the crowd then inform Jesus about an event that had recently taken place in Jerusalem:

> "Now there were some present at that time who told Jesus about the Galileans whose blood Pilate had mixed with their sacrifices." Luke 13:1

Apparently, Pilate had had some Galilean Jews apprehended and killed in the temple during a sacrificial ritual. The people who brought up this event for discussion might have thought it was relevant because it involved people from Jesus' homeland of Galilee, although their reason for raising the issue is ultimately unclear. If we consider the story in context of the days' activities, however, we might guess what's going on. Earlier that afternoon, the Pharisees and "experts of the law" had unleashed an arsenal of questions, trying to trap Jesus in his words (Luke 11:53-54). Perhaps by bringing up the issue of the Galileans, people were hoping Jesus would make a public anti-Roman or anti-Pilate statement. We cannot know for sure.

Jesus instead used the tragic example of the Galileans as a teaching point. He explained that the Galileans who were killed were not worse sinners than their fellow Galileans. Therefore, if even they suffered in this way, then all sinners will perish in a similar manner.

"Do you think that these Galileans were worse sinners than all the other Galileans because they suffered this way? I tell you, no! But unless you repent, you too will all perish." Luke 13:2 , 3

Most Bible teachers do not put this situation into context of the day's events beginning in Luke 11:14. So they often define Jesus' call to "repent" or "you too will all perish" in the context of eternal salvation. They conclude that Jesus was telling the crowd to change their ways or risk spending eternity in hell. But that message doesn't make sense in the context of Jesus' day. He'd spent all morning talking to a generation that had rejected him and called him Satan. During lunch, the leaders of this generation had tried to trap Jesus in some way, hoping to bring the wrath of the Romans down on him.

The word "too" that Jesus uses when he says "unless you repent, you too will all perish" is the Greek word "hosautos." The Greek meaning for this word is "similarly" or "in the same way." Basically, Jesus is saying, "Unless you repent, you will all perish in the same way." In other words, the killing of the Jews in the temple around 30 AD was a mere precursor for what was to come. Jesus was warning the crowds about a future time when the Roman legions would kill the Jews (70 AD). History records that many Jews were slain in the temple courts, just as the Galileans had been killed.

Jesus then says:

"Or those eighteen who died when the tower in Siloam fell on them—do you think they were more guilty than all the others living in Jerusalem? I tell you, no! But unless you repent, you too will all perish." Luke 13:1-5

Here Jesus is talking about current events again as he brings up another recent tragedy. Eighteen people had recently died in Siloam when a tower fell on them. This event might have occurred on the eastern edge of Jerusalem near the water source called the Gihon Springs..

After the tower of Siloam fell and killed eighteen people in 30 AD, Jesus told his generation that, unless they changed, they would perish in the same way. Forty years later, thousands of Jews died when the buildings and towers of Jerusalem, including the temple and Fort Antonia fell on them.

To the left is a photo of the author and some of the stones the Romans pushed from the temple mound in 70 AD in fulfillment of Jesus' prophecy.

To the left is a photo of a road below the temple mound that still shows the impact of these stones. The indention the stones made from the collapsing temple structure remains after 2000 years.

Jesus draws attention to the collapsing tower as a warning about future disasters of greater intensity. At the end of the fourth generation, the Romans would knock over *all* towers and buildings in Jerusalem, including the temple and Fort Antonia.

Jesus then told this parable to conclude his day of teaching:

> "A man had a fig tree, planted in his vineyard, and he went to look for fruit on it, but did not find any. So he said to the man who took care of the vineyard, 'For three years now I've been coming to look for fruit on this fig tree and haven't found any. Cut it down! Why should it use up the soil?' 'Sir,' the man replied, 'leave it alone for one more year, and I'll dig around it and fertilize it. If it bears fruit next year, fine! If not, then cut it down.'" Luke 13:6-9

This parable is connected to the four generation cycle of judgment. Scholars, commentators, and Bible teachers often come at this parable from a variety of angles without considering its context. Jesus' words on that particular day were for a "wicked generation." In this parable, he was pointing out the punishment that would occur forty years from that time if the fourth generation refused to repent. The Old Testament had already explained the four generation cycle of judgment. Israel's covenant with God included the stipulations of the cycle. History had already confirmed the cycle. And now, not surprisingly, Jesus was also referencing the cycle.

In the ancient world, fig trees were planted in the corners of vineyards as a way to take full advantage of vineyard space. An unproductive tree was always cut down, not only because it was useless, but also because it was occupying space that could be more used more effectively. In this parable, the fig tree represents Israel, and the vineyard refers to the plan of God. Israel will be removed if the people don't change.

(They will eventually be replaced by the church for a period of about 2,000 years before they will be restored to their original place in the vineyard.)

The conversation in the parable is between the man who owns the vineyard and planted the tree and another man who works in the vineyard and tends to the tree. The owner has had enough with the unproductive fig tree and tells the worker to cut it down. The worker asks for one more year, or one more growing season, in which he will water and fertilize the tree. He says that if the fig tree remains unproductive next season, he will then cut it down.

The two men in the parable are God the Father and God the Son. They are discussing the nation of Israel and its future in God's plan for mankind. God wants to remove Israel from the vineyard of his kingdom now. Jesus intercedes on behalf of Israel and asks if he can have one more season to work with them. God has been seeking the fruit of righteousness and justice in Israel, but he hasn't found it. The generation in 30 AD was similar to the generation in 760 BC—a generation addressed in Amos:

> "You have turned justice into poison and the fruit of righteousness into bitterness." Amos 6:12

God's promise to the last generation of Israel in 760 was:

> "I will stir up a nation against you, O house of Israel, that will oppress you…" Amos 6:14

That generation ended forty years later in 721 BC.

Jesus asked his father for "one more season" to work with Israel. A "season" for a nation is a forty year generation. Israel will be given forty more years in which to produce good fruit. According to the parable, the nation was already given three seasons (or generations) in which to prove themselves. Each of those generations were disciplined by God, yet remained unproductive.

If 30-70 AD is the extra "season" Jesus has to work with Israel, then the previous 120 years (90 BC-30 AD) are the three combined previous seasons the vineyard owner is referring to when he says:

> "'For three years now I've been coming to look for fruit on this fig tree and haven't found any. Cut it down!'"

The first generation was 90-50 BC, and the first cycle of judgment that occurred during that time was prophesied in Leviticus 26:17, "Those who hate you will rule over you." This prophecy came to pass in 63 BC when Roman General Pompey invaded the land and forced Israel to become a client kingdom to Rome.

The second generation was 50-10 BC, and the second cycle of judgment included the great famine recorded by Josephus:

"Now on this very year, which was the thirteenth year of the reign of Herod, very great calamities came upon the country; whether they were derived from the anger of God… there were perpetual droughts, and for that reason the ground was barren, and did not bring forth the same quantity of fruits that it used to produce; and after this barrenness of the soil, that change of food which the want of corn occasioned produced distempers in the bodies of men, and a pestilential disease prevailed, one misery following upon the back of another… The destruction of men also after such a manner deprived those that survived of all their courage, because they had no way to provide remedies sufficient for the distresses they were in. When therefore the fruits of that year were spoiled, and whatsoever they had laid up beforehand was spent, there was no foundation of hope for relief remaining."

Josephus Antiquities of the Jews, Book XV, Chapter IX, verses 1, 2

The third generation was 10 BC-30 AD. John the Baptist appeared to Israel at the end of the third generation. The fourth generation began around 30 AD. Israel suffered under the fourth cycle of discipline for the next forty years, up until 70 AD.

Generation	Years	Events	Cycle of Judgment
1st	90-50 BC	63 BC Pompey invades Israel and Israel becomes a client kingdom of Rome	1st – "Those who hate you will rule over you." Leviticus 26:17
2nd	50-10 BC	25 BC a famine strikes and Herod saves the Jewish people by selling his possessions and buying grain from Egypt	2nd – "Make the sky…like iron and the ground…like bronze…" Leviticus 26:19
3rd	10 BC-30AD	29 AD John the Baptist preaches to the nation in the spirit of Elijah (Luke 1:17)	3rd – "Wild animals… rob you of your children…destroy cattle…so few in numbers that your roads will be deserted." Leviticus 26:22
4th	30-70 AD	46 AD a famine strikes (as predicted by Agabus in Acts 12:28 and recorded by Josephus) 66 AD Roman General Titus lays siege to Judea/Jerusalem	4th – Leviticus 26:25-26 • Sword upon the land • Seek shelter • Cut off supply of food • Food rationed

Generation	Years	Events	Cycle of Judgment
The End	70 AD	70 AD Romans burn Jerusalem and the temple	5th – Leviticus 26:29-33 • Destroy altars, sanctuaries • Pile up the dead bodies • Ruin cities/lay waste land • Dispersed among nations

Most people know about Palm Sunday when Jesus rode into the city of Jerusalem on the back of a donkey. This happened just six days before he was crucified. In Luke's account of Palm Sunday, he records Jesus' words and emotions as he approached the city crowds and the angry religious leaders. Luke writes:

> "As he approached Jerusalem and saw the city, he wept over it and said, 'If you, even you, had only known on this day what would bring you peace—but now it is hidden from your eyes. The days will come upon you when your enemies will build an embankment against you and encircle you and hem you in on every side. They will dash you to the ground, you and the children within your walls. They will not leave one stone on another, because you did not recognize the time of God's coming to you.'" Luke 19:41-44

The days of destruction for the fourth generation were just around the corner.

Six days later, Jesus was on his way to the cross after enduring a sleepless night on trial. He'd been beaten by Herod's guards and had received a flesh-tearing scourging from the Romans. Now he was collapsing from the weight of the cross beam he was forced to carry. Crowds lined the streets to watch. In his horrible physical condition on the way to the cross, Jesus' message was the same. He had not given up on his generation, and he wanted them to know what they would face if the fifth cycle of judgment was released. One final time Jesus warns his "wicked generation" to reconsider their ways and repent.

> "As they led him away, they seized Simon from Cyrene, who was on his way in from the country, and put the cross on him and made him carry it behind Jesus. A large number of people followed him, including women who mourned and wailed for him. Jesus turned and said to them, 'Daughters of Jerusalem, do not weep for me; weep for yourselves and for your children. For the time will come when you will say, blessed are the barren women, the wombs that never bore and the breasts that never nursed! Then they will say to the mountains, fall on us! And to the hills,

cover us! <u>For if men do these things when the tree is green, what will</u> <u>happen when it is dry?'"</u> Luke 23:26-31

Even in his broken, bloody condition, Jesus tells the women to cry for themselves and their children because they will have to live through the fifth cycle of judgment. In 70 AD, it will be better for these women and their children to die than to face the famine, crime, fires, foreign armies, slavery, and crucifixion they will face at the hands of the Romans.

Jesus then asks a question that connects back to his parable of the fig tree in the vineyard. After three seasons (or generations) the fig tree was given one final season to produce fruit. Jesus was about to be crucified, but because his death was part of this final season, the nation of Israel still had hope. The tree was still in the vineyard. The day would come, however, forty years in the future, when that same tree would be cut down and removed from God's plan. The dead, dry tree would be taken from the vineyard and cast aside.

Jesus was hinting to these women that if they found his crucifixion horrifying, they wouldn't want to see what was in store for them after 70 AD when they would be hauled out of the vineyard.

The young mothers Jesus spoke to at this time were about 18-30 years old. They would have children ranging from infants to 12-year-olds. When Jerusalem fell to Rome under the fifth cycle of judgment, these same mothers would be 58-70, and their children would be 40-52. These women and children are the same people Josephus writes about in his eye witness account of Jerusalem's fall.

Josephus (37-100 AD) was a Jew with a heritage from the royal line of Israel. He was a Pharisee and a general in the Jewish military. He defended Galilee and fought against the Romans in 67 AD. After being defeated, he surrendered and accompanied the Romans to Jerusalem. He pleaded with the Jews on many occasions, asking them to surrender and save themselves, their city, and their temple. Below are first-hand accounts of a few of the events that took place in Jerusalem around 70 AD under the fifth cycle of discipline.

Josephus' "Wars of the Jews" Book V Chapter XI verses 1

+ Jerusalem is surrounded by the Roman army and there is no food in the city.
+ The famine is so great that people risk leaving the city to find food.
+ When these people are captured they are whipped, tortured, and crucified on crosses encircling the city for everyone to see.
+ Josephus writes that 500 people a day were thus treated. So many where crucified "that room was wanting for the crosses, and crosses wanting for the bodies."

"So now Titus's banks were advanced a great way...He then sent a party of horsemen, and ordered they should lay ambushes for those that went out into the valleys to gather food...the severity of the famine made them bold in thus going out...so they were first whipped, and then tormented with all sorts of tortures, before they died, and were then crucified before the wall of the city. This miserable procedure made Titus greatly to pity them, while they caught every day five hundred Jews; nay, some days they caught more...The main reason why he did not forbid that cruelty was this, that he hoped the Jews might perhaps yield at that sight, out of fear lest they might themselves afterwards be liable to the same cruel treatment. So the soldiers...nailed those they caught, one after one way, and another after another, to the crosses, by way of jest, when their multitude was so great, that room was wanting for the crosses, and crosses wanting for the bodies."

Josephus' "Wars of the Jews" Book V Chapter XIII verses 4

+ The Jews would swallow gold and flee the city, hoping to escape and use the gold.
+ The Syrian and Arabian armies that had been assisting the Romans found out about this and began to cut open Jews to search for the gold they swallowed.

"...There was found among the Syrian deserters a certain person who was caught gathering pieces of gold out of the excrements of the Jews' bellies; for the deserters used to swallow such pieces of gold...when they came out, and for these did the seditious search them all; for there was a great quantity of gold in the city...when this contrivance was discovered in one instance, the fame of it filled their several camps, that the deserters came to them full of gold. So the multitude of the Arabians, with the Syrians, cut up those that came as supplicants, and searched their bellies. Nor does it seem to me that any misery befell the Jews that was more terrible than this, since in one night's time about two thousand of these deserters were thus dissected."

Josephus' "Wars of the Jews" Book VI Chapter III verses 4

+ The words of God are not idle and will be fulfilled to the smallest detail.
+ Jerusalem is suffering under the fifth cycle of judgment (66-70 AD).
+ Included in the fifth cycle of judgment are these words, "If in spite of this you still do not listen to me but continue to be hostile toward me...You will eat the flesh of your sons and the flesh of your daughters" (Leviticus 26:27-29).
+ Mary, a woman who fled to the city of Jerusalem for protection, roasted and ate her own son.

"There was a certain woman that dwelt beyond Jordan, her name was Mary...and had fled away to Jerusalem with the rest of the multitude, and was with them besieged therein at this time…what food she had contrived to save, had been also carried off by the rapacious guards, who came every day running into her house for that purpose. This put the poor woman into a very great passion…if she found any food, she perceived her labors were for others, and not for herself; and it was now become impossible for her any way to find any more food, while the famine pierced through her very bowels and marrow, when also her passion was fired to a degree beyond the famine itself…She then attempted a most unnatural thing; and snatching up her son, who was a child sucking at her breast, she said, 'O thou miserable infant! For whom shall I preserve thee in this war, this famine, and this sedition? As to the war with the Romans, if they preserve our lives, we must be slaves. This famine also will destroy us, even before that slavery comes upon us…Come on; be thou my food…which is all that is now wanting to complete the calamities of us Jews.' As soon as she had said this, she slew her son, and then roasted him, and eat the one half of him, and kept the other half by her concealed. Upon this the seditious came in presently, and smelling the horrid scent of this food, they threatened her that they would cut her throat immediately if she did not show them what food she had gotten ready. She replied that she had saved a very fine portion of it for them, and withal uncovered what was left of her son. Hereupon they were seized with a horror and amazement of mind, and stood astonished at the sight, when she said to them, "This is mine own son, and what hath been done was mine own doing! Come, eat of this food; for I have eaten of it myself! Do not you pretend to be either more tender than a woman, or more compassionate than a mother; but if you be so scrupulous, and do abominate this my sacrifice, as I have eaten the one half, let the rest be reserved for me also." After which those men went out trembling, being never so much frightened at anything as they were at this, and with some difficulty they left the rest of that meat to the mother. Upon which the whole city was full of this horrid action immediately; and while every body laid this miserable case before their own eyes, they trembled, as if this unheard of action had been done by themselves. So those that were thus distressed by the famine were very desirous to die, and those already dead were esteemed happy, because they had not lived long enough either to hear or to see such miseries."

Josephus' "Wars of the Jews" Book VI Chapter IX verses 1

+ General Titus speaks of the greatness of Jerusalem's fortification.
+ General Titus says that no man or machine could have removed the Jews from this city.

+ General Titus credits God by saying, "It was no other than God who ejected the Jews."

> "Now when Titus was come into this [upper] city, he admired not only some other places of strength in it...for when he saw their solid altitude, and the largeness of their several stones, and the exactness of their joints, as also how great was their breadth, and how extensive their length, he expressed himself after the manner following: 'We have certainly had God for our assistant in this war, and it was no other than God who ejected the Jews out of these fortifications; for what could the hands of men or any machines do towards overthrowing these towers?'...To conclude, when he entirely demolished the rest of the city, and overthrew its walls, he left these towers as a monument of his good fortune, which had proved his auxiliaries, and enabled him to take what could not otherwise have been taken by him."

The warnings and events during the fourth generation of Jerusalem have been preserved for us in historical documents. We have reviewed the writings of two first century writers: Luke and Josephus. Luke recorded Jesus' warnings from 30 AD and Josephus recorded the gruesome events that took place forty years later. The events of 70 AD happened because people refused to take the warnings seriously.

The United States today cannot continue to ignore God's standards for social and moral righteousness. God expects certain behaviors from every nation and society, regardless of their religious beliefs. Events in our country's recent history would suggest we're running a parallel course with the Jews from 30-70 AD. Over the last four generations, God has not been silent; he has given us numerous warnings and wake up calls. A change is necessary if we want our nation to see a fifth generation.

Modern Application To the United States

Chapter 14: Secular Humanism

MEN IN EVERY culture and every generation must answer these questions:

1) Where did I come from?
2) What is the purpose of life?
3) How should I act?
4) What happens when I die?

God answers these questions for mankind through general revelation in the created world and special revelation in scripture. But what about those who scoff at God's revelation? How do they answer these essential questions?

The Answer to Life's Questions

A man by the name of John Dewey was part of a movement of people who signed the Humanist Manifesto in 1933. Dewey wanted to create a profoundly humanistic institution in which to train younger generations. He eventually met this goal. John Dewey is the father of our modern public school system.

So what is secular humanism exactly? The definition of "secular" is: of or pertaining to the worldly or temporal as distinguished from the spiritual or eternal. *The Humanist* magazine defines "humanism" as "a rational philosophy informed by science, inspired by art, and motivated by compassion." It can also be defined as "a philosophy, world view, or life stance based on naturalism." A secular humanist is, then, one who rejects every form of religious faith that requires something beyond the physical senses. The Humanist Society of Western New York defines their organization as:

> "A joyous alternative to religions that believe in a supernatural god and life in a hereafter. Humanists believe that this is the only life of which we have certain knowledge and that we owe it to ourselves and others to make it the best life possible for ourselves and all with whom we share this fragile planet…when people are free to think for themselves, using reason and knowledge as their tools, they are best able to solve this world's problems."

The secular humanistic view of the world—the one that has been consistently taught in America's public school system—is a view devoid of God. It's a view that has created its own answers to essential life questions.

Secular Humanism as an Idol

When I was young, churches gave out pins to children who had good Sunday school attendance. I still have my pins from each year beginning in 1963 when I was a 3-year-old Presbyterian until 1975 when I was a 15-year-old Methodist. I have many memories from those years in Sunday school. I still recall the songs we sang and the books we used. I also remember being really bored and making other kids laugh during class. I remember wondering why anyone would want to learn so many confusing, pointless Bible stories. I can still feel the rush of freedom I felt every time Sunday school ended and we ran outside to play while our parents lingered inside for "fellowship" and coffee. Coffee, like organ music, still reminds me of those Sunday mornings. To this day, I hate the taste of coffee.

A strange tidbit of information I took away from my years in Sunday school was that idol worship is really, really bad. The problem was that I had never seen an idol. Whenever the Sunday school teacher would talk about idols, I would look around the classroom, trying to figure out if any of my peers were honestly struggling with the temptation to worship idols. I had a feeling nobody was. Why I needed to get up early on Sunday mornings just to be told not to worship idols was beyond me.

It was later explained to me that modern idol worship could include money, power, fame, or anything else we might put before God. But that didn't sound right to me because I knew the people of Israel weren't having trouble with money, power, or fame. They were worshipping actual stone idols. God was adamant that they not bow down to these graven images. So what would be the equivalent of an actual idol in our society today?

Idols worshipped in those days were very unique. Each idol represented a philosophy or worldview, and each one had specific character traits and supernatural powers. The idols carried with them legends explaining their past and their influence on the history of mankind. Idols were worshipped for specific purposes such as agricultural productivity, sexual fertility, military victory, etc. Idols held their followers to certain standards. Pleasing some idols was as easy as bringing a yearly offering; pleasing other idols involved extreme measures with regard to diet, dress, and sexual activity.

There were four things an idol did for its worshippers:

1) Explained origin
2) Identified purpose
3) Developed ethics
4) Determined future

Therefore, the equivalent of idol worship in today's society would have little to do with power or wealth, but would be some kind of worldview that's not biblical. It would be a philosophy that answers the essential questions of life without involving God. Secular humanism fits this definition perfectly. It is an idol that has been worshipped in our country for much of the last century.

Where did we come from?
How does secular humanism explain human origins?

The first and second theses in the Humanist Manifesto say that humanists must regard the universe as self-existing, not created. Man is a part of nature and has emerged as a result of a continuous process. Evolution explains our origins. Everything we see emerged from nothing, over billions of years.

What is the purpose of life?
What does secular humanism identify as the purpose of life?

Thesis eight of the Humanist Manifesto says that the complete realization of human personality is the purpose of life. If humanity is simply an oddity that sprung up randomly in a pointless universe, our lives have no real purpose. Thus, we should seek our own personal fulfillment right here right now.

How should I act?
How does secular humanism develop ethics?

To determine limits of behavior, a secular humanist will point to the legal system. Any behavior accepted by law is okay. Any behavior not accepted by law is harmful to the common good of society. But the legal system is created by people, and the ethics of those people determine their laws. Ethics tend to ebb and flow alongside popular opinion, and external forces like the media dictate public opinion. This means that the ethics of those who control society's means of communication will eventually become the ethics of the masses.

What happens when I die?
How does secular humanism determine the future?

Theses fourteen of the Humanist Manifesto says:

> "A socialized and cooperative economic order must be established to the end that the equitable distribution of the means of life be possible. The goal of humanism is a free and universal society in which people voluntarily and intelligently cooperate for the common good. Humanists demand a shared life in a shared world."

The future of a humanist society is connected to a global vision. They desire nothing more than world peace. Any intervention in world affairs should always promote peace.

The End Result of Secular Humanism

Whenever people get their answers to life's fundamental questions from secular humanism, their world becomes clouded by these eight things as their culture begins to define their beliefs and goals for them.

1) Evolution
2) Materialism
3) Pleasure
4) Legislature
5) Popular Opinion
6) Media
7) World Peace

Let's take a closer look at each item on the list.

1. **Evolution** involves the pursuit of scientific study. Scientific investigation is a good thing. It's what brought the world out of the dark ages. Every time an evolutionist discovers a truth in nature, he has discovered information about what God has made. Even scientific investigation into evolution is good. If there is a Creator, he will have left his mark on his work. Honest evolutionists and creationists alike will eventually see that mark. In fact, many former evolutionists now accept the idea of some kind of Creator because of what they've discovered through their studies. Mirosaw Orzechowski, Poland's deputy minister of education, recently told a local newspaper, "The theory of evolution is a lie. It is an error we have legalized as a common truth."[1]

2. **Materialism** is the theory that physical matter is the only reality and, therefore, worldly possessions are of great significance. Secular humanism has seeped into the cracks of our national subconscious, and we find ourselves always wanting more. We are a materialistic culture that's never satisfied.

3. **Pleasure** is defined as the state or feeling of being pleased or gratified. God wants us to have pleasure, but not in a realm that doesn't include him. Jesus talked about a man who surrounded himself with good things apart from God. He called the man a fool. He said God would demand his life from him and all his pleasures would eventually prove useless (Luke 12:19, 20).

4. **Legislature** is the application of the institution of government. It's the body of people responsible for creating laws. God wants men to maintain order through their own regulations; however, he is not pleased when the legislature enacts laws that disregard his standards.

6. **Popular Opinion** is not always bad; in fact, it is something we should be mindful of. Solomon's son, Rehoboam, rejected the voice of public opinion concerning taxation, and he lost most of his father's kingdom. In his case, rejecting popular opinion was foolish. But in many other instances, especially when popular opinion goes against a rule that God has set forth for mankind, we should reject it.

7. **Media** is comprised of those who control the avenues of communication. The power of the media is clear. When a company must pay $2.5 million for 30 seconds of air time during the Super Bowl, it's obvious that the media possesses the capability to manipulate us and determine our behavior. If it didn't, advertisers wouldn't pay $73,333 a second to control what we see.

Remember, God does not call us "sheep" because we're fluffy. God refers to us as sheep because sheep follow whomever or whatever is placed in front of them. If the first sheep in a group jumps over a log, the next sheep will jump over the same log and so on. However, if the log is taken away after the first sheep jumps, the second sheep will jump anyway. Why would he jump over nothing? Because his brain is too small to analyze the situation and realize the log is gone. Likewise, men have an inherent desire to follow and imitate those in front of them. This can be good, (it sure makes raising children a lot easier), but it can also be bad because, like sheep, we jump only because we saw the sheep in front of us jumping.

8. **World Peace** will be the end result of Jesus' return to earth, after his victory in history's greatest battle. But before Jesus returns, the world will be in a continual state of war, poverty, and large-scale social injustice. The travesties we see across the globe will not go away. The world is getting worse, not better. The best thing we can do to promote peace in our lifetime is to uphold the institutions God has given us—marriage, family, government, and nationalism.

God does not call us 'sheep' because we're fluffy.

Who's Winning?

Although we've willingly bowed to the idol of secular humanism for the last eighty years, the worldview hasn't our total allegiance. There has always been a philosophical tug-of-war against secular humanism in our country because of our distinctly Christian heritage. In a tug-of-war that pits two evenly matched teams against each other, there will be a lot of effort and straining. Both sides will pull to the point of exhaustion, and the results will show little movement or progress. Not until one side wears the other down will a victor be named.

We are fortunate to be living at this time in our nation's history. I believe the eighty year tug-of-war between people who believe in God and people who embrace secular humanism is nearing an end. Thankfully, it is the other side that is showing signs of exhaustion. The secular humanist view of mankind has pulled long and hard on the soul of our society with doubt, unbelief, and skepticism. Yet our interest in the spiritual has not gone away. It cannot and will not go away because it's true.

Doubt and skepticism could not even exist if truth wasn't out there somewhere. Without truth, there would be no logic or reasoning at all. It would be like a tug-of-war with no one pulling on the other side of the rope. Doubt can only exist if a person is willing to admit they are searching for truth but don't think they've found it yet.

How can I suggest that we may actually be winning the tug-of-war in our culture? See for yourself.

Christians believe in creation. Secular humanists believe the world is a cosmic accident. (Yes, we're literal freaks of nature.) If we check polls in America over the last twenty-five years, we find that our culture is holding a firm grip on the idea of creation despite all the effort that's been put into promoting evolution. A *Newsweek* poll from March 2007 found that:

- 48% of all Americans believe "God created humans pretty much in the present form at one time within the last 10,000 years or so."
- 30% believe "Humans developed over millions of years from less advanced forms of life, but God guided this process."
- 13% believe "Humans developed over millions of years from less advanced forms of life, but God had no part in this process."[2]

On December 14, 2006, a Gallup poll was released that said:

"The public has not notably changed its opinion on the question [of creation] since Gallup started asking it in 1982."[3]

Some evolutionists fear we are headed back to the dark ages because public opinion no longer supports evolutionary theory. They are equally frustrated because public support for teaching creationism is also on the rise.

"A recent survey by the Pew Forum on Religion and Science found that 64% of respondents support teaching creationism side-by-side with evolution in the science curriculum of public schools. A near majority of 48% do not believe that Darwin's theory of evolution is proven by fossil discoveries, and 33% believe that a general agreement does not exist among scientists that humans developed over time."[4]

This evidence means the glory days for atheists and evolutionists are over. And although many scholars and scientists will continue to believe in a godless world until they die, it seems that our culture as a whole is taking a turn toward the spiritual.

Paul and John write that, in the final days before Christ returns, the world will be full of people who will be spiritual to the extent that they will worship a god in the temple and demand that others do the same. In fact, people will have such religious fervor that they will actually crown a man as god.

"He will oppose and will exalt himself over everything that is called God or is worshiped, so that he sets himself up in God's temple, <u>proclaiming himself to be God</u>." II Thessalonians 2:4

"<u>All inhabitants of the earth will worship the beast</u>...He (the false prophet) was given power to give breath to the image of the first beast so that it could speak and cause all who refused to worship the image to be killed." Revelation 13:8, 15

Christianity is winning the battle with secular humanism regarding the origins of existence. Scientific study cannot undermine God because, "God's invisible qualities have been clearly seen, being understood from what has been made" (Romans 1:20). We should worry less about proving our side scientifically and turn our attention to what's coming on the horizon—a so-called "new spiritual dimension."

The pendulum is swinging from denying the existence of God to embracing some kind of spirituality. This poses great danger for those who've failed to grow in their knowledge of the Bible. Without a full understanding of God's truth, people won't be able to face this new enemy. This enemy that won't just deny the existence of God, but will be a spiritual, demonic force claiming to be the one true God.

The pendulum is swinging from denying the existence of God to embracing some kind of spirituality.

Although 91.8% of the people in the United States say they believe in the existence of God,[5] only 11% say our American society closely reflects Christianity.[6] Our real problem, then, is not that we don't believe in God, but that we don't live in a way that reflects our belief. As a nation we are still holding onto the concept of God, the spiritual realm, and eternity, but we are not embracing the holy character of God or his righteous requirements for our personal lives. In this way we are very similar to the Israelites who where dispersed by the Assyrians in 721 BC and the people of Judah who where taken captive by the Babylonians in 586 BC. The people of this time continued to use the name Yahweh in their worship but they had also redefined his character by placing pagan deities along side of the true God. These pagan deities not only brought corrupt worship practices but also mixed false philosophies and corrupt standards of living with the truth of God. The people of Israel and Judah practiced their religion at the "high places" outside the true temple and then lived their lives according to these false standards.

In this photo Galyn stands inside a high place set up as a community temple in the ancient city of Arad near Beer Sheba. This picture shows the remains of the room that would have been the Holy of Holies. There are two incense altars instead of one because setting in the Most Holy Place were two deity stones : one for Jehovah and one for Asherah (Ashtaroth). (Jeremiah 7:30-31; Second Chronicles 24:18) This is similar to our culture in that we name the name of Christ but follow the philosophies of secular humanism.

Likewise, we name the name of God but we replace his standards with the standards of our cultural idols. We call ourselves Christians but make our decisions like secular humanists.

A majority of Americans embrace some distinctly Christian beliefs, as shown below:

Percentage of Americans Who Believe These Statements (*Newsweek* 12/10/04)[7]
82% Believe that Jesus lived
55% Believe that every word of the Bible is literally true
79% Believe that Jesus was born of a virgin
67% Believe the details of the Christmas story are true
52% Believe that Jesus will return to earth
62% Believe creation should be taught in schools

Although these core Christian values are espoused by many, they're lived out by few, as other recent studies have shown. One such study by the Barna Research Group showed that divorce rates among conservative Christians were significantly higher than those of other faith groups, including atheists and agnostics. George Barna first commented on these statistics, saying, "While it may be alarming to discover that born-again Christians are more likely than others to experience a divorce, that pattern has been in place for quite some time." When Barna came under criticism for his findings, he wrote a letter to his supporters stating: "we rarely find substantial differences" between the moral behavior of Christians and non-Christians.[8]

In an article by the Barna Research Group entitled *"Practical Outcomes Replace Biblical Principles as the Moral Standard"* adults were asked for the basis they used to make moral choices. The outcome was that 44% of adults said "whatever will bring me the most pleasing or satisfying results," while only 24% claimed to use religious principles to guide them with moral decisions.

Of all church-going adults polled, 33% said it was okay to break the speed limit, 15% said it was fine to smoke marijuana, 23% said it was all right to get drunk, 13% believed homosexuality was an honorable lifestyle, 42% believed cohabitation was an acceptable moral choice, and 33% believed watching pornography was okay.

Saying "I'm a Christian" is encouraged in our culture. When political figures do it, their image is improved and their ratings go up. But actually *living* like a Christian is a very different story. Although people who live like Christians in the United States today don't have to worry about being stoned in the public square, they do have to worry about being ridiculed. They are labeled judgmental, intolerant, conservative, narrow-minded, old-fashioned, backwards. A college boy must be gay if he isn't having sex. A teenage girl must be a "Jesus freak" if she doesn't party on the weekends. Even though we say we're a Christian nation, few of us live as Christ would because to do so would be too radical given our culture's current conditions.

In conclusion, what the secular humanist movement has tried to accomplish over the last century has damaged the soul of our country but still hasn't conquered us. We have suffered spiritual casualties in the secular humanist battles and lost some of our warriors to doubt and disbelief, but we haven't lost the war. Unfortunately, a greater and even more threatening adversary is on its way. Secular humanism was just that—secular. It's wasn't spiritual in any way; it was merely devoid of God. The new idol will be far worse because it will be spiritual. And it will be evil.

The Humanist's Manifesto

Below is a word for word copy of the Humanist Manifesto I from 1933. By definition, a "manifesto" is a public declaration of intentions, principles, information, and motives. The secular humanists planned to remove religious thinking from our nation and replace it with this new way of thinking in order to create a better world. Below is the game plan for how they would accomplish this. The document below is the sin of our fathers. It appears to be our "sin of Jeroboam."

Humanist Manifesto I

(Humanist Manifesto I first appeared in The New Humanist, May/June 1933 Vol. VI, No. 3)

"The time has come for widespread recognition of the radical changes in religious beliefs throughout the modern world. The time is past for mere revision of traditional attitudes. Science and economic change have disrupted the old beliefs. Religions the world over are under the necessity of coming to terms with new conditions created by a vastly increased knowledge and experience. In every field of human activity, the vital movement is now in the direction of a candid and explicit humanism. In order that religious humanism may be better understood we, the undersigned, desire to make certain affirmations which we believe the facts of our contemporary life demonstrate.

"There is great danger of a final, and we believe fatal, identification of the word religion with doctrines and methods which have lost their significance and which are powerless to solve the problem of human living in the Twentieth Century. Religions have always been means for realizing the highest values of life. Their end has been accomplished through the interpretation of the total environing situation (theology or world view), the sense of values resulting therefrom (goal or ideal), and the technique (cult), established for realizing the satisfactory life. A change in any of these factors results in alteration of the outward forms of religion. This fact explains the changefulness of religions through the centuries. But through all changes religion itself remains constant in its quest for abiding values, an inseparable feature of human life.

"Today man's larger understanding of the universe, his scientific achievements,

and deeper appreciation of brotherhood, have created a situation which requires a new statement of the means and purposes of religion. Such a vital, fearless, and frank religion capable of furnishing adequate social goals and personal satisfactions may appear to many people as a complete break with the past. While this age does owe a vast debt to the traditional religions, it is none the less obvious that any religion that can hope to be a synthesizing and dynamic force for today must be shaped for the needs of this age. To establish such a religion is a major necessity of the present. It is a responsibility which rests upon this generation. We therefore affirm the following:

First: Religious humanists regard the universe as self-existing and not created.

Second: Humanism believes that man is a part of nature and that he has emerged as a result of a continuous process.

Third: Holding an organic view of life, humanists find that the traditional dualism of mind and body must be rejected.

Fourth: Humanism recognizes that man's religious culture and civilization, as clearly depicted by anthropology and history, are the product of a gradual development due to his interaction with his natural environment and with his social heritage. The individual born into a particular culture is largely molded by that culture.

Fifth: Humanism asserts that the nature of the universe depicted by modern science makes unacceptable any supernatural or cosmic guarantees of human values. Obviously humanism does not deny the possibility of realities as yet undiscovered, but it does insist that the way to determine the existence and value of any and all realities is by means of intelligent inquiry and by the assessment of their relations to human needs. Religion must formulate its hopes and plans in the light of the scientific spirit and method.

Sixth: We are convinced that the time has passed for theism, deism, modernism, and the several varieties of "new thought."

Seventh: Religion consists of those actions, purposes, and experiences which are humanly significant. Nothing human is alien to the religious. It includes labor, art, science, philosophy, love, friendship, recreation -- all that is in its degree expressive of intelligently satisfying human living. The distinction between the sacred and the secular can no longer be maintained.

Eighth: Religious Humanism considers the complete realization of human personality to be the end of man's life and seeks its development and fulfillment in the here and now. This is the explanation of the humanist's social passion.

Ninth: In the place of the old attitudes involved in worship and prayer the humanist finds his religious emotions expressed in a heightened sense of personal life and in a cooperative effort to promote social well-being.

Tenth: *It follows that there will be no uniquely religious emotions and attitudes of the kind hitherto associated with belief in the supernatural.*

Eleventh: *Man will learn to face the crises of life in terms of his knowledge of their naturalness and probability. Reasonable and manly attitudes will be fostered by education and supported by custom. We assume that humanism will take the path of social and mental hygiene and discourage sentimental and unreal hopes and wishful thinking.*

Twelfth: *Believing that religion must work increasingly for joy in living, religious humanists aim to foster the creative in man and to encourage achievements that add to the satisfactions of life.*

Thirteenth: *Religious humanism maintains that all associations and institutions exist for the fulfillment of human life. The intelligent evaluation, transformation, control, and direction of such associations and institutions with a view to the enhancement of human life is the purpose and program of humanism. Certainly religious institutions, their ritualistic forms, ecclesiastical methods, and communal activities must be reconstituted as rapidly as experience allows, in order to function effectively in the modern world.*

Fourteenth: *The humanists are firmly convinced that existing acquisitive and profit-motivated society has shown itself to be inadequate and that a radical change in methods, controls, and motives must be instituted. A socialized and cooperative economic order must be established to the end that the equitable distribution of the means of life be possible. The goal of humanism is a free and universal society in which people voluntarily and intelligently cooperate for the common good. Humanists demand a shared life in a shared world.*

Fifteenth and last: *We assert that humanism will: (a) affirm life rather than deny it; (b) seek to elicit the possibilities of life, not flee from them; and (c) endeavor to establish the conditions of a satisfactory life for all, not merely for the few. By this positive morale and intention humanism will be guided, and from this perspective and alignment the techniques and efforts of humanism will flow.*

"So stand the theses of religious humanism. Though we consider the religious forms and ideas of our fathers no longer adequate, the quest for the good life is still the central task for mankind. Man is at last becoming aware that he alone is responsible for the realization of the world of his dreams, that he has within himself the power for its achievement. He must set intelligence and will to the task."

34 Signers of the 1933 Humanist Manifesto I:

J. A. C. Fagginger Auer
E. Burdette Backus
Harry Elmer Barnes
L. M. Birkhead
Raymond B. Bragg
Edwin Arthur Burtt
Ernest Caldecott
A.J. Carlson
John Dewey
Albert C. Dieffenbach
John H. Dietrich
Bernard Fantus
William Floyd
F. H. Hankins
A. Eustace Haydon
Llewllyn Jones
Robert Morse Lovett

Harold P. Marley
R. Lester Mondale
Charles Francis Potter
John Herman Randall, Jr
Curtis W. Reese
Oliver L. Reiser
Roy Wood Sellars
Clinton Lee Scott
Maynard Shipley
W. Frank Swift
V. T. Thayer
Eldred C. Vanderlaan
Joseph Walker
Jacob J. Weinstein
Frank S. C. Wicks
David Rhys Williams
Edwin H. Wilson

Chapter 15: The Four Generation Cycle in the United States

1880-1920: The Generation that Cursed Their Parents

> "There is a generation that curseth their father, and doth not bless their mother." Proverbs 30: 11 KJV

This first generation above appears to have unfolded in America between the years 1880-1920. When we read documents from this time, we find the generation in a continual process of questioning and rejecting the validity of Christianity. Criticism of Christian ideas grew strong during these years, bolstered by arguments from science, education, industry, and philosophy. The arguments against Christianity even found a way into the church itself.

Between 1880 and 1920, the citizens of the United States became a generation that "cursed their father and did not bless their mother." People began thinking that the way their fathers always sought to honor God was strange. Communication with the divine was deemed silly and worshipping God unnecessary. Thanks to the teaching of some key figures during this time, an entire generation began to break away from the Christian worldview altogether.

Robert G. Ingersoll

This first generation brought us Robert G. Ingersoll, "the great agnostic." Although Ingersoll is rarely talked about today, he was once the leading orator and political speaker in the United States. (One of main streets in the city where I live is Ingersoll Avenue.) Ingersoll was a Republican attorney with distinguished military service in the Civil War. He also served as the first attorney general of Illinois.

Because Ingersoll had such a brilliant mind and eloquent way of communicating, the public continually demanded to hear him speak. He ended up touring the country, taking numerous speaking engagements. Between 1865 and 1899, he packed out the largest theaters that big cities could provide. People paid a one dollar admission fee to hear him speak, (a price roughly equivalent to twenty dollars today). He memorized all his speeches ahead of time, even though some of them were up to three and four hours long.

Since the television had not yet been invented, it can be said with certainty that Robert G. Ingersoll was the one person seen and heard by the most people in the country during this time. He could have gone on to become a great political figure, (the *Chicago Tribune* said as much in 1899). But Ingersoll instead chose to enlighten the world on the "Mistakes of Moses."

In his much repeated lecture "Mistakes of Moses," Ingersoll challenges his generation to reject the religious superstition of their parents. He suggests they need only accept what can be proven. In the following excerpt from the lecture, Ingersoll explains that he doesn't believe Moses wrote the first five books of the Bible (the Pentateuch).

> "Every good father and every good mother wish their children to find out more than they know; every good father wants his son to overcome some obstacle that he could not grapple with; and if you wish to reflect credit on your father and mother, do it by accomplishing more than they did, because you live in a better time. Every nation has had what you call a sacred record, and the older the more sacred, the more contradictory and the more inspired the record. We, of course, are not an exception, and I propose to talk a little about what is called the Pentateuch, a book or a collection of books, said to have been written by Moses. And right here in the commencement let me say that Moses never wrote one word of the Pentateuch—not one word was written until he had been dust and ashes for hundreds of years."[9]

Ingersoll then begins to attack scripture itself:

> "Now, they say that book is inspired. I do not care whether it is or not; the question is, is it true? If it is true it doesn't need to be inspired. Nothing needs inspiration except a falsehood or a mistake. A fact never went into partnership with a miracle. Truth scorns the assistance of wonders. A fact will fit every other fact in the universe, and that is how you can tell whether it is or is not a fact. A lie will not fit anything except another lie made for the express purpose and, finally someone gets tired of lying, and the last lie will not fit the next fact, and then there is a chance for inspiration. Right then and there a miracle is needed. The real question is: In the light of science, in the light of the brain and heart of the nineteenth century, is this book true? The gentleman who wrote it begins by telling us that God made the universe out of nothing. That I cannot conceive; it may be so, but I cannot conceive it. Nothing, regarded in the light of raw material, is to my mind, a decided and disastrous failure, I cannot imagine of nothing being made into something, any more than I can of something being changed back into nothing. I cannot conceive of force aside from matter, because force to be force must be active, and unless there is matter there is nothing for force to act upon, and consequently it cannot be active. So I simply say I cannot comprehend it. I cannot believe it. I may roast for this, but it is my honest opinion."[10]

The "Mistakes of Moses" is entertaining reading with good logic, and it actually gives us justifiable suspicion of the religious system; however, Ingersoll goes on to attack and demean the scriptures as a whole. His goal is to undermine the foundation of the Christian faith. (You can read "Mistakes of Moses" at http://www.edwardtbabinski.us/lectures/mistakes_moses.html.)

Ingersoll also wrote and published an article concerning the absurdity of religion entitled "Why I am an Agnostic." In it, Ingersoll asks:

> "Has a man the right to examine, to investigate the religion of his own country—the religion of his father and mother?"

Although Ingersoll presented a noble challenge by encouraging people to investigate the religion of their parents and society, he had no intention of letting Christianity pass the scrutiny. And Ingersoll's attitude of disgust toward the most religion of his culture was eventually embraced by many in his generation.

In "Why I am an Agnostic," Ingersoll describes his early experiences with the Bible:

> "From my childhood I had heard read and read the Bible myself. Morning and evening the sacred volume was opened and prayers were said. The Bible was my first history, the Jews were the first people, and the events narrated by Moses and the other inspired writers, and those predicted by prophets were the all important things. In other books were found the thoughts and dreams of men, but in the Bible were the sacred truths of God. Yet in spite of my surroundings, of my education, I had no love for God. He was so saving of mercy, so extravagant in murder, so anxious to kill, so ready to assassinate, that I hated him with all my heart." [11]

Ingersoll describes his response to a sermon he heard about the suffering of a rich man who had cried out as he was torment, dying in flames of fire:

"For the first time I understood the dogma of eternal pain—appreciated 'the glad tidings of great joy.' For the first time my imagination grasped the height and depth of the Christian horror. Then I said: 'It is a lie, and I hate your religion. If it is true, I hate your God.' From that day I have had no fear, no doubt. For me, on that day, the flames of hell were quenched. From that day I have passionately hated every orthodox creed. That sermon did some good."[12]

Ingersoll goes on to say:

> "We find now that the prosperity of nations has depended, not upon their religion, not upon the goodness or providence of some god, but on soil and climate and commerce, upon the ingenuity, industry, and courage of the people, upon the development of the mind, on the spread of education, on the liberty of thought and action; and that in this mighty panorama of national life, reason has built and superstition has destroyed."

Ingersoll ended "Why I am an Agnostic" with these words:

> "The foundation of Christianity has crumbled, has disappeared, and the entire fabric must fall."

Charles Darwin

Charles Darwin (1809-1882) was the founder of the modern theory of evolution. By the time he died, his teachings had already captured the academic world. Darwin collected fossils, animal and plant specimens, and notes from his expeditions that took him around the world between 1831-1836. From his studies, he arrived at several theories:

1) Evolution did occur.
2) Evolutionary change occurred gradually over millions of years.
3) Natural selection was the primary driving force of evolution.
4) All the species on the earth today came from a single original life form.

On November 24, 1859, Darwin's findings were published in a book called *The Origin of Species*. The 1,250 copies of the first edition were sold the day they were published. Darwin's theories found instant inroads to religious thought and all aspects of sociology.

The first generation of the United States' decline (1880-1920) considered and discussed these revolutionary ideas continually. Darwin's theories gave this first generation a reason to fosake the God of their fathers and ponder the possibilities of new, godless philosophies.

Karl Marx

Karl Marx (1818-1883) gained American attention by teaching specific ways to implement the concept of evolution into human society. The great influence of Marx is revealed by what two American newspapers had to say about him at his death. The *Boston Daily Advertiser* called him "one of the most remarkable men of our time," while the *Chicago Tribune* labeled him "a man of high intelligence, a scholar, and a thinker."

Julius Wellhausen

German historian Julius Wellhausen (1844-1918) took the principals of evolution a step further, applying them to the interpretation of the Bible. In his book about the history of Israel, Wellhausen writes:

"According to the historical and prophetical books of the Old Testament, the priestly legislation of the middle books of the Pentateuch was unknown in pre-exilic time, and this legislation must, therefore, be a late development."

Wellhausen is saying that the priesthood of Israel and the concept of temple worship did not exist until after the Israelites returned from Babylon in 536 BC. He is wrong in this because the books of Exodus, Numbers, and Leviticus all indicate that the Israel's priesthood and religious traditions were established by God at Mt. Sinai around 1400 BC.

Wellhausen would have us believe that much of Old Testament history is a fabrication, something a group of influential men made up after 536 BC in an attempt to unite the fractured Jewish people. Wellhausen actually believed that a group of Israeli leaders came up with names like Abraham, Moses, and David—then constructed elaborate stories about them. This way the leadership could develop a strong national history in order to manipulate the Jews who were returning from captivity and had no social unity. Wellhausen insisted the leaders forged documents to convince the people of these lies, and those documents eventually became the Old Testament. This plan apparently worked so well that all Jews and Christians still believe the lies today.

Wellhausen abandoned the view that the Bible had been divinely inspired; he instead claimed the Bible was created by a group of people who eventually became the nation of Israel. His writings were published, and academia devoured them, including many seminaries throughout America. Wellhausen's views are still deeply entrenched in many church denominations and religious universities today.

Sigmund Freud

Sigmund Freud (1856-1939) presented his pioneering work on psychoanalysis during this first generation. Freud called religion a pointless delusion and said that all phenomenon of religious experience could be explained. He believed society would be much more productive and pleasant if Christianity was abandoned completely and, in its place, his own theories embraced.

Ingersoll, Darwin, Marx, Wellhausen, and Freud were key leaders from many fields of study during this time who consistently spoke out against God. They exalted mankind as the end of all things. These men became leaders, not because they were right, but because an entire generation of Americans listened to them and followed them. The belief that all men evolve physically, mentally, and socially laid the foundation for the rise of secular humanism.

With the rise of evolutionary thinking in America, many people also began to believe that scripture had evolved over time. Therefore, if Christianity hoped to remain relevant, it needed to forget its outdated truths and evolve into something new and better.

These teachings from this first generation were passed down to the second generation. The "sins of the fathers" were handed down to the children who naturally adopted the same erroneous worldview.

1921-1960: The Generation That Was Pure in Their Own Eyes

"There is a generation that are pure in their own eyes, and yet is not washed from their filthiness." Proverbs 30:12 KJV

The second generation felt a void left to them by the first generation as they drifted further into sin. This was keenly observed by a great man of God who lived during the generation. On November 3, 1921, J. Gresham Machen, a New Testament professor at Westminster Theological Seminary in Philadelphia, said,

"Modern liberalism has lost all sense of the gulf that separates the creature from the Creator...According to the Bible, man is a sinner under the just condemnation of God; according to modern liberalism, there is really no such thing as sin. At the very root of the modern liberal movement is the loss of the consciousness of sin."

Of course, this second generation had been raised to question and doubt. They'd been taught to consider traditional Christian doctrine as ancient myth and pre-scientific thinking. They believed the concept of a God who would judge all mankind was nothing more than an age-old ploy used to intimidate people into socially acceptable behavior. They decided that the concept of "the sinfulness of man" was merely a stumbling block to human potential.

In 1908, the Federal Council of Churches adopted the "Social Creed of the Churches." By the 1920s, the promotion of this new liberal gospel was in full swing in the second generation. Churches stopped teaching of the word of God and focused instead on social reform. Below is what the church embraced as their new gospel. As you can see, their goals were not necessarily wrong, but the problem was that they *all* begin and end with man. The church was caught up in the wave of secular humanism that was sweeping society. They may have called themselves the "churches of Christ," but they had become institutions of men seeking only to meet the goals and needs of men.

The Social Creed of the Federal Council of Churches 1908
(Now the National Council of Churches of Christ)

We deem it the duty of all Christian people to concern themselves directly with certain practical industrial problems.
To us, it seems that the Churches must stand—

1. For equal rights and complete justice for all men in all stations of life.
2. For the right of all men to the opportunity for self-maintenance, a right ever to be wisely and strongly safeguarded against encroachments of every kind.
3. For the right of workers to some protection against the hardships often resulting from the swift crisis of industrial change.
4. For the principle of conciliation and arbitration in industrial dissensions.
5. For the protection of the worker from dangerous machinery, occupational disease, injuries and mortality.
6. For the abolition of child labor.
7. For such regulation of the conditions of toil for women as shall safeguard the physical and moral health of the community.
8. For the suppression of the "sweating system."
9. For the gradual and reasonable reduction of the hours of labor to the lowest practical point, and for that degree of leisure for all which is a condition of the highest human life.
10. For a release from employment one day in seven.
11. For a living wage as a minimum in every industry, and for the highest wage that each industry can afford.
12. For the most equitable division of the products of industry that can ultimately be devised.
13. For suitable provision for the old age of the workers and for those incapacitated by injury.
14. For the abatement of poverty.

To the toilers of America and to those who by organized effort are seeking to lift the crushing burdens of the poor and to reduce the hardships and uphold the dignity of labor, this council sends the greeting of human brotherhood and the pledge of sympathy and of help in a cause which belongs to all who follow Christ.

The 1920s marked the beginning of a new movement toward "user friendly faith." The divorce rate in the United States increased five-fold from the beginning of the first generation to the middle of the second generation (1870-1930). Well-known authors attacked religion and mocked the concept of revival (e.g. F. Scott Fitzgerald's *The Great Gatsby*, Sinclair Lewis's *Elemer Gantry*, Ernest Hemingway's *The Sun Also Rises*).

The mood of the country became restless and wild. During prohibition, Chicago gang warfare left hundreds of people dead. Women known as "flappers" bobbed their hair and wore short skirts while they smoked, danced, and drank their way across town. More than 40,000 members of the Ku Klux Klan gathered to march down Pennsylvania Avenue in Washington, D.C.

The Court Case Heard Around the Nation

In 1925, the Tennessee legislature passed a bill that said: "It shall be unlawful for any teacher in any of the universities, normals, and all other public schools of the State to teach any theory that denies the story of the Divine Creation of man as taught in the Bible, and to teach instead that man has descended from a lower order of animals." After this law passed, many people became angry. A national showdown was about to happen between the modern thinkers of the second generation and those who were still trying desperately to hold onto America's traditional values.

The American Civil Liberties Union (ACLU) paid the fees necessary to challenge this latest education statute. On July 10, 1925, the issue of creation verses evolution got its first day in court in Dayton, Tennessee. It was the *State of Tennessee v. John Thomas Scopes*. Scopes had admitted to teaching evolution in a public school classroom, thus violating the new statute. The ACLU brought in a man named Clarence Darrow to defend the science teacher. Darrow was a lawyer and a well-known leader in the ACLU. On the other side of the courtroom, defending both the statute and creationism as a whole, stood William Jennings Bryan, a three-time Democratic candidate for president. He had previously led a vigorous campaign against evolution, which had kept him in the public spotlight.

People across the country listened to the trial on the radio. They kept up with the daily newspaper reports, eagerly awaiting the verdict. The jury found John Thomas Scopes guilty, and a judge charged him with a $100 fine. But the outcome of the case was a classic example of winning the battle but losing the war.

Clarence Darrow's questioning of William Jennings Bryan was a disaster for the creation camp as Bryan tried defending the Bible from a position of arrogance and ignorance. His poor responses to the criticism of scripture caused the second generation to lose even more confidence in traditional Christianity. Below are some of the excerpts from Clarence Darrow's questioning of William Jennings Bryan.

> **Darrow** --You have given considerable study to the Bible, haven't you, Mr. Bryan?
>
> **Bryan**--Yes, sir, I have tried to.
>
> **Darrow** --Then you have made a general study of it?
>
> **Bryan** --Yes, I have; I have studied the Bible for about fifty years, or some time more than that, but, of course, I have studied it more as I have become older than when I was but a boy.
>
> **Darrow** --You claim that everything in the Bible should be literally interpreted?
>
> **Bryan** --I believe everything in the Bible should be accepted as it is given there. Some of the Bible is given illustratively. For instance: "Ye are the salt of the earth." I would not insist that man was actually salt, or that he had flesh of salt, but it is used in the sense of salt as saving God's people.

Darrow --But when you read that Jonah swallowed the whale—or that the whale swallowed Jonah—excuse me please—how do you literally interpret that?

Bryan --When I read that a big fish swallowed Jonah—it does not say whale… That is my recollection of it. A big fish, and I believe it, and I believe in a God who can make a whale and can make a man and make both what he pleases.

Darrow --Now, you say, the big fish swallowed Jonah, and he there remained how long—three days—and then he spewed him upon the land. You believe that the big fish was made to swallow Jonah?

Bryan --I am not prepared to say that; the Bible merely says it was done.

Darrow --You don't know whether it was the ordinary run of fish, or made for that purpose?

Bryan --You may guess; you evolutionists guess…

Darrow --You are not prepared to say whether that fish was made especially to swallow a man or not?

Bryan --The Bible doesn't say, so I am not prepared to say.

Darrow --But do you believe He made them—that He made such a fish and that it was big enough to swallow Jonah?

Bryan --Yes, sir. Let me add: One miracle is just as easy to believe as another

Darrow --Just as hard?

Bryan --It is hard to believe for you, but easy for me. A miracle is a thing performed beyond what man can perform. When you get within the realm of miracles, it is just as easy to believe the miracle of Jonah as any other miracle in the Bible.

Darrow --Perfectly easy to believe that Jonah was swallowed by a whale?

Bryan --If the Bible said so. The Bible doesn't make as extreme statements as evolutionists do…

Darrow --The Bible says Joshua commanded the sun to stand still for the purpose of lengthening the day, doesn't it? And you believe it?

Bryan --I do.

Darrow --Do you believe at that time the entire sun went around the earth?

Bryan --No, I believe that the earth goes around the sun.

Darrow --Do you believe that the men who wrote it thought that the day could be lengthened or that the sun could be stopped?

Bryan --I don't know what they thought.

Darrow --You don't know?

Bryan --I think they wrote the fact without expressing their own thoughts.

••••••••••••••••••••

Darrow--Can you answer my question directly? If the day was lengthened by stopping either the earth or the sun, it must have been the earth?

Bryan --Well, I should say so.

Darrow --Now, Mr. Bryan, have you ever pondered what would have happened to the earth if it had stood still?

Bryan --No.

Darrow --You have not?

Bryan --No. The God I believe in could have taken care of that, Mr. Darrow.

Darrow --I see. Have you ever pondered what would naturally happen to the earth if it stood still suddenly?

Bryan --No.

Darrow --Don't you know it would have been converted into molten mass of matter?

Bryan --You can testify to that when you get on the stand, I will give you a chance.

Darrow --Don't you believe it?

Bryan --I would want to hear expert testimony on that.

••••••••••••••••••••

Darrow --You believe the story of the flood to be a literal interpretation?

Bryan --Yes, sir.

Darrow --When was that flood?

Bryan --I would not attempt to fix the date...

Darrow --About 4004 BC?

Bryan --That has been the estimate of a man that is accepted today. I would not say it is accurate.

Darrow --That estimate is printed in the Bible?

Bryan --Everybody knows, at least, I think most of the people know, that was the estimate given.

Darrow --But what do you think that the Bible, itself says? Don't you know how it was arrived at?

Bryan --I never made a calculation.

Darrow --A calculation from what?

Bryan --I could not say.

Darrow --From the generations of man?

Bryan --I would not want to say that.

Darrow --What do you think?

Bryan --I do not think about things I don't think about.

Darrow --Do you think about things you do think about?

Bryan --Well, sometimes.

(Laughter in the courtyard.)

Policeman--Let us have order...

Bryan --These gentlemen have not had much chance. They did not come here to try this case. They came here to try revealed religion. I am here to defend it and they can ask me any question they please.

The Court--All right.

(Applause from the courtyard.)

Darrow--Great applause from the bleachers.

Bryan --From those whom you call "yokels."

Darrow--I have never called them "yokels."

Bryan --That is the ignorance of Tennessee, the bigotry.

Darrow--You mean who are applauding you? (Applause)

Bryan --Those are the people whom you insult.

Darrow--You insult every man of science and learning in the world because he doesn't believe in your fool religion.

The Court--I will not stand for that.

Bryan --For what he is doing?

The Court--I am talking to both of you...

Darrow --Wait until you get to me. Do you know anything about how many people there were in Egypt 3,500 years ago, or how many people there were in China 5,000 years ago?

Bryan --No.

Darrow --Have you ever tried to find out?

Bryan --No, sir. You are the first man I ever heard of who has been in interested in it. (Laughter)

Darrow --Mr. Bryan, am I the first man you ever heard of who has been interested in the age of human societies and primitive man?

Bryan --You are the first man I ever heard speak of the number of people at those different periods.

Darrow --Where have you lived all your life?

Bryan --Not near you. (Laughter and applause)

Darrow --Nor near anybody of learning?

Bryan --Oh, don't assume you know it all.

•••••••••••••••••••

Darrow--I want to take an exception to this conduct of this witness. He may be very popular down here in the hills...

Bryan--Your honor...the only reason they have asked any question is for the purpose as the question about Jonah was asked—for a chance to give this agnostic an opportunity to criticize a believer in the word of God; and I answered the question in order to shut his mouth so that he cannot go out and tell his atheist friends that I would not answer his questions. That is the only reason, no more reason in the world.

• • • • • • • • • • • • • • • • • • •

Darrow --Mr. Bryan, do you believe that the first woman was Eve?

Bryan --Yes.

Darrow --Do you believe she was literally made out of Adams's rib?

Bryan --I do.

Darrow --Did you ever discover where Cain got his wife?

Bryan --No, sir; I leave the agnostics to hunt for her. (Laughter)

Darrow --You have never found out?

Bryan --I have never tried to find

Darrow --You have never tried to find?

Bryan --No.

Darrow --The Bible says he got one, doesn't it? Were there other people on the earth at that time?

Bryan --I cannot say.

Darrow --You cannot say. Did that ever enter your consideration?

Bryan --Never bothered me.

Darrow --There were no others recorded, but Cain got a wife.

Bryan --That is what the Bible says.

Darrow --Where she came from you do not know. All right. Do the statements, "The morning and the evening were the first day," and "The morning and the evening were the second day," mean anything to you?

Bryan -- I do not think it necessarily means a twenty-four hour day.

Darrow --You do not?

Bryan --No.

Darrow --What do you consider it to be?

Bryan --I have not attempted to explain it. If you will take the second chapter— let me have the book (examines the Bible). The fourth verse of the second chapter says: "These are the generations of the heavens and of the earth, when they were created in the day that the Lord God made the earth and the heavens." The word "day" there in the very next chapter is used to describe a period (of time). I do not see that there is any necessity for construing the words, "the evening and the morning," as meaning necessarily a twenty-four hour day, "in the day when the Lord made the heavens and the earth."

Darrow --Then, when the Bible said, for instance, "...and God called the firmament heaven. And the evening and the morning were the second day," that does not necessarily mean twenty-four hours?

Bryan --I do not think it necessarily does.

Darrow --Do you think it does or does not?

Bryan --I know a great many think so.

Darrow --What do you think?

Bryan --I do not think it does.

Darrow --You think those were not literal days?

Bryan --I do not think they were twenty-four hour days.

Darrow --What do you think about it?

Bryan --That is my opinion. I do not know that my opinion is better on that subject than those who think it does.

Darrow --You do not think that?

Bryan --No. But I think it would be just as easy for the kind of God we believe in to make the earth in six days as in six years or in 6,000,000 years or in 600,000,000 years. I do not think it important whether we believe one or the other.

Darrow --Do you think those were literal days?

Bryan --My impression is they were periods, but I would not attempt to argue as against anybody who wanted to believe in literal days.

•••••••••••••••••••

Bryan--Your Honor, I think I can shorten this testimony. The only purpose Mr. Darrow has is to slur at the Bible, but I will answer his question. I will answer it all at once, and I have no objection in the world, I want the world to know that this man who does not believe in a God is trying to use a court in Tennessee to...

Darrow--I object to that!

Bryan--(Continuing) ...to slur at it, and while it will require time, I am willing to take it.

Darrow--I object to your statement. I am exempting you on your fool ideas that no intelligent Christian on earth believes.

The Court--Court is adjourned until 9 o'clock tomorrow morning.

The good that came from the trial was overshadowed by the bad. Scopes may have been slapped with a $100 fine, but the eyes of the American public were opened. The concept of evolution began to make more sense, not less sense. Those who took the Bible literally, whether using it to explain creation or any other issue, were suddenly seen as foolish. This incident set the stage for the third generation to reverse the creation statute.

While the church succumbed to modern liberalism, the public embraced their new-found freedom from accountability to a creator. A belief system entirely new to America was organizing. That system was secular humanism.

Secular Humanism

In 1933, the original Humanist Manifesto was signed by thirty-four people and published in the May/June issue of the *The New Humanist*. It began like this:

"The time has come for widespread recognition of the radical changes in religious beliefs throughout the modern world. The time is past for mere revision of traditional attitudes. Science and economic change have disrupted the old beliefs. In every field of human activity, the vital movement is now in the direction of a candid and explicit humanism. In order that religious humanism may be better understood, we, the undersigned, desire to make certain affirmations which we believe the facts of our contemporary life demonstrate."

"There is great danger of a final, and we believe fatal, identification of the word religion with doctrines and methods which have lost their significance and which are powerless to solve the problem of human living in the Twentieth Century...Today man's larger understanding of the universe, his scientific achievements, and his deeper appreciation of brotherhood, have created a situation which requires a new statement of the means and purposes of religion...To establish such a religion is a major necessity of the present. It is a responsibility which rests upon this generation."

The Humanist Manifesto then went on to list fifteen articles (or affirmations). Here are a few of those articles:

#1)   "Religious humanists regard the universe as self-existing and not created."

#3)   "Holding an organic view of life, humanists find that the traditional dualism of mind and body must be rejected."

#8)   "Religious humanism considers the complete realization of human personality to be the end of man's life and seeks its development and fulfillment in the here and how. This is the explanation of the humanist's social passion."

#9)   "In place of the old attitudes involved in worship and prayer, the humanist finds his religious emotions expressed in a heightened sense of personal life and in a cooperative effort to promote social well-being."

#11) Man will learn to face the crises of life in terms of his knowledge of their naturalness and probability...We assume that humanism will take the path of social and mental hygiene and discourage sentimental and unreal hopes and wishful thinking."

Number eleven hints at a core belief for all secular humanists: man's problem is not a sin nature but simply a lack of knowledge. The application of number eleven has resulted in our society emphasizing the attainment of knowledge above all else. Everyone who's been influenced by secular humanist thinking believes that, to some degree, their "salvation" will be found in the area of education. By gaining more information, a person will be able to better solve life's problems, thereby creating his own destiny and controlling his universe.

Knowledge is obviously a good and necessary thing. In scripture, a lack of knowledge is presented as a sure path to destruction (Hosea 4:6). But there is a contrast between the knowledge humanists seek and the knowledge believers should seek. The Bible stresses the importance of knowledge alongside wisdom and understanding. The humanist tells us that knowledge can be gained through experimentation. They tell us *all* knowledge gained from experience or otherwise is always good. This is simply not true. For instance, gaining knowledge about something while violating God's laws is wrong (e.g. learning what it's like to lie, cheat, get high, engage in adultery, etc.).

The manifesto says we should discourage "sentimental and unreal hopes and wishful thinking." The unreal hopes and wishful thinking it is referring to are anything related to a traditional sense of religious values. The humanists' goal is to cleanse America of Christianity. After all, they believe man is pure and good. There is, therefore, no reason to teach our children that their natural inclinations should be controlled. Humanists do not believe that sin exists at all. They are the generation described in Proverbs 30:12 as "men who are pure in their own eyes."

Most second generation Christians embraced these liberal humanist ideas on some level. Many consciously accepted them, but most just allowed them to seep into their subconscious. Everyone alive and living in America now will have a tendency towards secular humanist thinking. It's nearly impossible for us to separate our thoughts from that philosophical system because we were raised in it.

The Humanist Manifesto ends like this:

> "So stand the theses of religious humanism. Though <u>we consider the religious forms and ideas of our fathers no longer adequate</u>, the quest for the good life is still the central task for mankind. Man is at last becoming aware that he alone is responsible for the realization of the world of his dreams, that he has within himself the power for its achievement. He must set intelligence and will to the task."

Thirty-four people signed underneath these closing comments. The ninth signature at the bottom of Humanist Manifesto is John Dewey, father of our public school system.

Dewey is described by biographers and commentators as "America's foremost philosopher and educator." It is said that he:

> "...refashioned the educational system in America, moving it from the so-called static concepts of the past into a wholly new era in education. In the process, he redefined almost everything from the nature of truth to the responsibilities of the teacher and the capacity of the human personality... That the 'new thinking' at the turn of the twentieth century became 'the

way the world thinks' can be laid at the feet of this man who more than all others made education in America what it is today."

John Dewey said:

> "The educational system must move one way or another, either backward to the intellectual and moral standards of a pre-scientific age or forward to ever greater utilization of scientific method in the development of the possibilities of growing, expanding experience."

Dewey suggested that society would return to a hopeless and barbaric past if they didn't embrace the modern wave of the second generation. This barbaric past included such silly things as: recognizing a creator, believing in an inerrant Bible, and trusting that the savior of the world is Jesus Christ. According to Dewey, such concepts must be abandoned in favor of more scientific thinking. Dewey managed to convince an entire generation that they can't truly enjoy the advances of modern man if they remain crippled by the weight of archaic Christianity.

1961-2000: The Haughty and Disdainful: The 'Me' Generation

> "There is a generation, O how lofty are their eyes and their eyelids are lifted up." Proverbs 30:13 KJV

The third generation engaged in behavior that our society had never before witnessed. As America continued to make scientific advances, introducing new technology and medicine, Christian truth and a sense of morality were traded en masse for a culture of self-expression.

Proverbs 30:13 calls the third generation "haughty and disdainful." They are egotistical and condescending. Their personal arrogance and disregard for others is manifested in much of what they do. It's all about them.

The third generation immediately overthrew any remaining legal hold Christianity had on society. In 1962, the *Engel v. Vitale* case resulted in prayer being removed from public schools. In 1963, the *Abington Township School District v. Schempp* case ended with the Supreme Court ruling that school-sponsored readings of the Lord's Prayer were unconstitutional. In 1980, the *Stone v. Graham* case resulted in a 5-4 decision that declared the posting of the Ten Commandments illegal. According to the court, the Ten Commandments "had no educational function" and were thus banned from public schools. In 1987, the case of *Edwards v. Aguillard* ended with all teaching of creationism banned from public schools on the grounds of "separation of church and state." (The Supreme Court voted 7-2 in this decision.) In 1989, in *Allegheny County v. Greater Pittsburgh ACLU*, the Supreme Court ruled that setting a Nativity scene in a public place was unconstitutional. In a later case, it accepted a Nativity scene in public *only if* the scene also included other *fictional*, secular Christmas items such as Frosty the Snowman, Santa, Rudolph, etc.

The third generation pursued the "heightened sense of a personal life" encouraged in the manifesto, but this personal life came at a great cost. Those who paid the highest price were discarded spouses and children. The landscape of our society became a landfill of broken marriages and broken homes. We still don't understand the total cumulative effect this will have on the fourth generation.

Although we don't know exactly what the kids who grew up rummaging through this social landfill will be like when they're older, we do have some early indication. A study of more than one million children who were tracked for more than a decade found that children raised in broken homes were twice as likely to suffer from serious psychiatric disorders. They were twice as likely to attempt or commit suicide and twice as likely to develop an addiction to alcohol. Girls from broken homes were three times more likely to become drug addicts, and boys from broken homes were four times more likely to become addicted to drugs. Studies with findings similar to this are countless.

Because of this new relational environment, two-parent, intact families could no longer be used as the measuring rod for a "good" home. So the third generation rushed to create a new measuring stick. First, they determined that a "good" parent would now be anyone who was overly involved in their children's lives. To make up for their inability to stay together, unhealthy moms and dads became emotionally-intertwined with their children. A "good" home then became any home where the children were loaded down with performance-based, extra-curricular activities (music, clubs, sports, etc.). These activities were essential to the overall evaluation because the primary indicator of a "good" home was now any home where children were given the best and most educational opportunities. Education was again deemed the highest virtue.

The fourth generation will have a deep hunger that will never be satisfied.

2001-2040: The Fourth and Final Generation

"There is a generation, whose teeth are as swords, and their jaw teeth as knives, to devour the poor from off the earth, and the needy from among men." Proverbs 30:14, KJV

The fourth generation is described as a generation who will "devour the poor and the needy from among mankind." In other words, anyone who is not productive has no value. Abortion is just the beginning of how this prophecy will play out. Euthanasia will soon become a reality as well.

Their "teeth are swords" and their "jaws are set with knives." Teeth and jaws are used to chew and devour food, thus satisfying hunger. The fourth generation will have a deep hunger that will never be satisfied. They will have insatiable desires created by the decline of society and the rampant display of sin and unrestrained greed. They will be a heartless and violent generation, not caring about the poor. Since those who are rich can more quickly attain fame and power, money will become everything. ⁻

The fourth generation is now entering adulthood. Most were raised in broken homes, taught in humanistic schools, and bombarded by the media at every turn. They were taught there is no creator, no such thing as sin, no judgment day, and no afterlife. They are maneuvering in a culture sick with hedonism and materialism.

The fourth generation doesn't even wonder about the God of the Bible. To them, the idea of living according to traditional Christian values is laughable. This generation doesn't believe in absolutes. They believe that each man should decide for himself what is good. They think having tolerance for all people and all behavior is the only acceptable way to live. The truth has been lost, and all the information that's been acquired in this age of technology can't bring it back.

Chapter 16: The United States and
Its Five Cycles of Judgment

Five Cycles of Judgment in the United States from 1880-2040

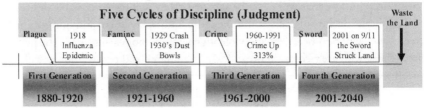

E ACH OF THE four generations has been met with a new cycle of judgment, as declared by God in Leviticus 26. What will God's response be after the fourth generation in America? Will it be the same response he had when "the sin of the Amorites was full?" Will it be like the end of the fourth generation in Israel in 70 AD? *Or* will our nation heed God's warnings before it's too late?

The Warnings

The first generation (1880-1920) received their warning via disease and plague as promised in Leviticus 26:14-16:

> "But if you will not listen to me and carry out all these commands, and if you reject my decrees and abhor my laws and fail to carry out all my commands and so violate my covenant, then I will do this to you: <u>I will bring upon you sudden terror, wasting diseases and fever that will destroy your sight and drain away your life."</u>

The 1918 Influenza Epidemic infected 28% of all Americans. The disease was so devastating that the average American lifespan decreased by ten years in a twenty-four month period. Ten times more Americans died from this plague than died in World War I (also fought during this time).

The second generation (1921-1960) was disciplined with the promises of Leviticus 2:18-20:

> "If after all this you will not listen to me, I will punish you for your sins seven times over. I will break down your stubborn pride and make the sky above you like iron and the ground beneath you like bronze. Your strength will be spent in vain, because <u>your soil will not yield its crops, nor will the trees of the land yield their fruit."</u>

The stock market crashed in 1929. In one day, $30,000,000,000 disappeared from the American economy. The Great Depression devastated families living in the 1930s. The country watched as crop prices fell 40-60%. Added to these problems were the dustbowls that ravaged America's plains and ruined 50,000,000 acres of land. The dustbowls are, believe it or not, known as "the most devastating weather event in American history." The drought peaked in 1936 when the summer heat set temperature records that still stand today. During this time, FDR said, "I see one-third of our nation is ill-housed, ill-clad, and ill-nourished."

The next generation (1961-2000) entered the third cycle of judgment described in Leviticus 26:21-22:

> "If you remain hostile toward me and refuse to listen to me, I will multiply your afflictions seven times over, as your sins deserve. <u>I will send wild animals against you, and they will rob you of your children</u>, destroy your cattle and make you so few in number that your roads will be deserted."

Crime rates rose dramatically in the third generation. The United States Crime Index Rate per 100,000 people went from 1,887.2 in 1960 to 5,897.8 in 1991. The crime rate in this generation was 313% higher than the last. There were an additional 55,775 deaths from the Vietnam War during these years—most of the deaths were young people ages 17-29.

According to Leviticus 26:23-25, the fourth cycle of discipline begins the day the Lord brings "the sword upon you" to strike the land.

> "If in spite of these things you do not accept my correction but continue to be hostile toward me, I myself will be hostile toward you and will afflict you for your sins seven times over. And <u>I will bring the sword upon you</u> to avenge the breaking of the covenant."

On September 11, 2001, the sword did indeed strike the United States. If this fourth generation (2001-2040) continues without repentance, we should prepare to meet more turmoil before our enemies finally overtake us (Leviticus 26:25-26).

> "When you withdraw into your cities, <u>I will send a plague among you, and you will be given into enemy hands.</u> When I cut of your supply of bread, ten women will be able to bake your bread in one oven, and they will dole out the bread by weight. You will eat, but you will not be satisfied."

The fifth cycle of judgment will be the overthrow of our nation as described in Leviticus 26:27-32:

> "If in spite of this you still do not listen to me but continue to be hostile toward me, then in my anger I will be hostile toward you, and I myself will punish you for your sins seven times over. You will eat the flesh of your sons and the flesh of your daughters. I will destroy your high places, cut

down your incense altars and pile your dead bodies on the lifeless forms of your idols, and I will abhor you. <u>I will turn your cities into ruins and lay waste your sanctuaries</u>, and I will take no delight in the pleasing aroma of your offerings. <u>I will lay waste the land, so that your enemies who live there will be appalled.</u>"

Summary

In the late 1800s, our nation threw out the old idea of God in favor of new ideas. In the early 1900s, those new ideas were developed into a philosophy. During the second half of the 1900s, that philosophy was applied to our homes, schools, churches, governments, and businesses. We are now reaping the harvest of the past one hundred and twenty years. The humanists' advice to abandon traditional Christianity has not made our society better. Our families and children are not stronger or happier. John Dewey's call to "pursue knowledge" hasn't solved our problems. We are not a greater nation because we finally shook off the shackles of a Creator and Savior.

As a nation we must begin the recovery process from secular humanism. We must realize we've been brainwashed through our schooling. We must recognize that our uber-tolerant, anything-goes society is moving us further away from what God wants. If we hope to see a fifth generation in America, we must change now.

Chapter 17: Israel's Revelation
Compared to Gentile Revelation

FROM THE TIME Israel became a nation until the day Jesus Christ died, God spoke to the world through Israel. God's plan was that Israel would preserve his truth and be a light on earth. After all other nations had turned to idol worship, God called a man named Abram out of the land of the Chaldeans (an area in ancient Babylon which is modern day Iraq). God told Abram:

"All peoples (nations) on earth will be blessed through you." Genesis 12:3

Without Israel, there would be no Old Testament, no prophets, no Messiah, and no foundation for the Christian church. The truths of God's kingdom have been preserved by Israel throughout history.

Prophets like Isaiah, Jeremiah, Ezekiel, Daniel, and Zechariah consistently harkened the Israelites back to the Law of Moses. When these same prophets spoke to Gentile nations, however, they didn't reference the Law of Moses, the Ten Commandments, or other special revelations God had given to Israel. They instead spoke of another standard—a standard of morality God had established through "general revelation."

General vs. Special Revelation

God reveals himself to mankind in two ways: "general" revelation and "special" revelation. General revelation is granted to all people, but special revelation only comes to people through Israel (in the Old Testament) and the church (in the New Testament). Special revelation is found in the written word of God and deals with things that cannot be seen or explained scientifically. Special revelation includes Jesus Christ paying for our sins at the cross. It includes the indwelling of the Holy Spirit in believers. Paul tells Timothy:

"I am writing you these instructions so that, if I am delayed, you will know how people ought to conduct themselves in God's household, which is the church of the living God, the pillar and foundation of the truth." I Timothy 3:15

General revelation, on the other hand, is revealed to all men, in all times, and all nations. It involves the truths of God that are evident in the created world. Scientists can study these things; philosophers can reason over them; and common men can live by the principles found in them. Nations should base their laws on general revelation because there is no one exempt from it. It's something that people from every culture and every time period should be able to agree upon because it's been written on their hearts. Romans 2:14 says:

"When Gentiles, who do not have the law, do by nature things required by the law, <u>they are a law for themselves</u>, even though they do not have the law, since they show that the requirements of the law are written on their hearts, their consciences also bearing witness."

There is something inside each man that lets him know what's right and what's wrong. Anytime we judge someone else's behavior, we instantly reveal that we have the law written on our hearts. We each have a conscience built by a creator. So when it comes to sin, we are without excuse.

"Since what may be known about God is plain to them, because God has made it plain to them. For <u>since the creation of the world God's invisible qualities – his eternal power and divine nature – have been clearly seen</u>, being understood from what has been made, so that men are without excuse." Romans 1:19, 20

As for people who've never heard the gospel, God's invisible qualities are clear to them through the created world. This general revelation should perpetuate righteous living whether or not a person has been exposed to Christianity.

Even the most hardened atheist will not be surprised on judgment day. He will have always known deep down that there is some kind of higher power. In fact, the leading atheist of the 20th century, Anthony Flew, became a confessing deist in 2004. This man, who used to passionately debate C.S. Lewis, renounced atheism altogether. Flew said:

"It now seems to me that the findings of more than fifty years of DNA research have provided materials for a new and enormously powerful argument to design."[13]

Flew always claimed he would go "wherever the evidence led." Now, at the age of 81, Flew has followed the evidence down a very surprising path. He finally discovered what Romans 1:19 confirms—God's invisible qualities are clearly seen. Flew said:

"...It seems to me that the case for an Aristotelian God who has the characteristics of power and also intelligence is now much stronger than it ever was before." [14]

During the 1900s, philosophy taught us there were no absolutes. Many people tried applying this idea to their lives, but it didn't produce the utopia it promised. Instead it left many people stranded on a dead-end road, ready to turn back and search for something that made more sense—something they saw in the brilliance of nature and felt deep in their hearts. Like a rubber band, our philosophy was stretched in the 1900s, but that stretching could not prevent the old form from returning. There are absolutes, and our society will continue to unravel until we embrace those absolutes once again.

Special revelation is found in God's written word and imparted by the Holy Spirit. It includes truths that cannot be discovered in the physical realm, like the existence of heaven, hell, angels, Satan, and the trinity. Only by reading scripture do we discover that salvation comes through faith. Special revelation also tells us God's attitude toward sin, his plan for resurrecting the dead, and holding a final judgment of all men. Anyone can read the Bible and obtain some knowledge, but not everyone can understand the spiritual depth of the scriptures. The Holy Spirit is needed for that. Paul refers to this in I Corinthians 2:12-14:

> "We have not received the spirit of the world but the Spirit who is from God, that we may understand what God has freely given us. This is what we speak, not in words taught us by human wisdom but in words taught by the Spirit, expressing spiritual truths in spiritual words. <u>The man without the Spirit does not accept the things that come from the Spirit of God, for they are foolishness to him</u>, and he cannot understand them, because they are spiritually discerned."

Hamas

As already discussed, the prophets did not have the same expectations for Gentile nations that they had for Israel. However, they did demand that Gentile nations conduct themselves with a certain level of integrity and morality. Any nation guilty of "violence," (the Hebrew word "hamas"), would be severely judged. In the Old Testament, the word "hamas" is used to refer to oppression, violence, injury, or harm. To commit "hamas" is considered a direct offense against God and will result in his judgment.

Violence ("hamas") can take on these forms:
    a) Physical violence – such as the shedding of innocent blood
    b) Psychological violence – such as oppression
    c) Judicial violence – such as a corrupt court system
    d) Social violence – such as injustice

Character traits associated with violence in the Bible:
    a) Pride
    b) Deception
    c) A false witness (lying in court)
    d) Domestic abuse
    e) Uncontrolled anger
    d) Treacherous behavior
    e) Dishonest business practices
    f) Destruction of animals
    g) Destruction of land

God's response to violence in a nation:
   a) He puts an end to the people; they are forever destroyed
   b) No wealth or anything of value is left
   c) He scatters the people
   d) Evil spirits are sent to the people
   e) The people are covered with shame

What can a violent nation do to avoid God's judgment?
   a) Humble themselves—they can stop being so arrogant
   b) Call urgently upon God
   c) Give up their evil ways
   d) Renounce their violence
   e) Guard their spirits—they can control what is allowed into their souls through the gates of their eyes and ears so they can resist any thoughts that might corrupt them
   f) Stop breaking covenants and promises—they can let their yes be yes and their no be no

God uses the "hamas" of one nation to punish another nation:

"The day is here! It has come! Doom has burst forth, the rod has budded, and arrogance has blossomed! <u>Violence (hamas) has grown into a rod to punish wickedness</u>; none of the people will be left, none of that crowd – no wealth, nothing of value." Ezekiel 7:10, 11

"Woe to the Assyrian, the rod of my anger, in whose hand is the club of my wrath! <u>I send him against a godless nation, I dispatch him against a people who anger me</u>...but this is not what he intends, this is not what he has in mind; his purpose is to destroy, to put an end to many nations...I will punish the king of Assyria for the willful pride of his heart and the haughty look in his eyes." Isaiah 10:5, 6, 7, 12

Note: "Destroy" in the above verse is the word "shamad" which means "to completely and utterly bring to nothing, to utterly overthrow, to completely cause to perish."

Additional scripture references concerning violence or "hamas":
   1) Genesis 6:11: "Now the earth was corrupt in God's sight and was <u>full of violence</u>."
   2) Genesis 6:13: "So God said to Noah, 'I am going to put an end to all people for the <u>earth is filled with violence</u> because of them.'"
   3) Psalms 73:6: "Therefore pride is their necklace; <u>they clothe themselves with violence</u>."
   4) Proverbs 3:31: "<u>Do not envy a violent man</u> or choose any of his ways."
   5) Isaiah 53:9: "He was assigned a grave with the wicked and with the rich in

his death, <u>though he had done no violence</u>, nor was any deceit in his mouth."

6) Jonah 3:7, 8: "Then he issued a proclamation in Nineveh, 'By the decree of the king and his nobles: Do not let any man or beast, herd of flock, taste anything; do not let them eat or drink. But let man and beast be covered with sackcloth. Let everyone call urgently on God. <u>Let them give up their evil ways and their violence</u>.'"

7) Proverbs 10:6: "<u>Violence overwhelms</u> the mouth of the wicked."

8) Malachi 2:16: "'I hate divorce,' says the Lord God of Israel, 'and <u>I hate a man's covering his wife with violence</u> as well as with his garment.' So guard yourself in your spirit and do not break faith."

9) Genesis 49:7: Simeon and Levi are brothers and <u>their swords are weapons of violence</u>... for they have killed men in their anger and hamstrung oxen as they pleased. Cursed be their anger so fierce and their fury so cruel! I will scatter them in Jacob and disperse them in Israel." (This was a reference to their slaughter at the city of Shechem.)

10) Judges 9:24: "God sent an evil spirit between Abimelech and the citizens of Shechem, who acted treacherously against Abimelech. God did this in order that <u>the crime ("hamas")</u> against Jerub-Baal's seventy sons, the shedding of their blood, might be avenged."

11) Obadiah 10: "Because of the <u>violence against your brother</u> Jacob, you will be covered with shame; you will be destroyed forever."

12) Micah 6:13-15: "Shall I acquit a man with dishonest scales, with a bag of false weights? <u>Her rich men are violent;</u> her people are liars and their tongues speak deceitfully. Therefore, I have begun to destroy you, to ruin you because of your sins."

13) Habakkuk 2:17: "<u>The violence you have done</u> to Lebanon will overwhelm you, and your destruction of animals will terrify you. For you have shed man's blood; you have destroyed lands and cities and everyone in them."

In Genesis, we learn the whole earth was full of "hamas" at the time of the flood—which is the reason God decided to wipe everyone out. God is always in control, and when things get out of control on earth, he intervenes. As you probably know, there is a terrorist group in the Middle East today called Hamas. God makes it clear that although he may use a nation full of "hamas" to punish another nation, he will eventually destroy them as well.

Amos Warns the Violent Nations

Elijah and Elisha were "professional prophets." They started a school for training other prophets, (e.g. Jonah). The prophet Amos, however, was not a professional prophet by any means. He was a successful sheep breeder and an arborist (Amos 1:1). Amos says:

"I was neither a prophet nor a prophet's son, but I was a shepherd, and I also took care of sycamore-fig trees. But the Lord took me from tending the flock and said to me, 'Go, prophecy to my people Israel.'" Amos 7:14

Amos came from Judah and lived in the town of Tekoa, about ten miles south of Jerusalem. He walked across the border into the northern kingdom of Israel to proclaim his message, telling the people to repent. They rejected him and sent him back home. He responded by writing down his message and sending it to them in letter form. We can read this message in Amos 1 and 2. The message is written to eight nations, including Judah and Israel and six Gentile nations. Amos first speaks to the Gentile nation of Aram.

1. Aram (Syria):

Amos 1:3-5, "This is what the Lord says:
'For three sins of Damascus,
even for four, I will not turn back my wrath.
Because she threshed Gilead
with sledges having iron teeth,
I will send fire upon the house of Hazael
that will consume the fortresses of Ben-Hadad.
I will break down the gate of Damascus;
I will destroy the king who is in the Valley of Aven
and the one who holds the scepter in Beth Eden.
The people of Aram will go into exile to Kir,'
says the Lord."

The people of Aram (modern day Syria) fought a war with the land of Gilead and won. But after they secured their victory, they used a threshing sled with iron teeth on their prisoners of war. A threshing sled was used to crush grain and separate the good seed from the shaft. An animal would pull the sled with a driver sitting on top of it for weight. The people of Aram were using these threshing sleds to drive over captives and tear flesh from their bodies.

The statement "for three sins, even for four" is a way of saying that Aram had reached God's limit of patience. The prophecy is clear: a judgment will come upon them for their behavior and the punishment will be fair.

2. Philistia:

Amos 1:6-8, "This is what the Lord says:
'For three sins of Gaza,
even for four, I will not turn back my wrath.
Because she took captive whole communities
and sold them to Edom,
I will send fire upon the walls of Gaza
that will consume her fortresses.

> I will destroy the king of Ashdod
> and the one who holds the scepter in Ashkelon.
> I will turn my hand against Ekron,
> till the last of the Philistines is dead,'
> says the Sovereign Lord."

The sin of the Philistines (now the Gaza Strip) is that they captured and sold entire tribes of people into slavery. Gaza is near the coast on the edge of a desert which made it a prime location for trading with sea merchants and land caravans. The people of Gaza, along with the other Philistine cities mentioned, felt it was okay to profit financially from the sale of people.

3. Phoenecia:

Amos 1:9, 10, "This is what the Lord says:

> 'For three sins of Tyre,
> even for four, I will not turn back my wrath .
> Because she sold whole communities of captives to Edom,
> disregarding a treaty of brotherhood,
> I will send fire upon the walls of Tyre
> that will consume her fortresses.'"

The Phoenicians (now the land of Lebanon) were also great merchants and legends of sea travel. They practiced the slave trade as well, but did something even worse than the Philistines. They captured and sold the very people they had previously signed a peace treaty with. They sold these people to the land of Edom, south of the Dead Sea.

4. Edom:

Amos 1: 11, 12, "This is what the Lord says:

> 'For three sins of Edom,
> even for four, I will not turn back my wrath.
> Because he pursued his brother with a sword,
> stifling all compassion,
> because his anger raged continually
> and his fury flamed unchecked,
> I will send fire upon Teman
> that will consume the fortresses of Bozrah.'"

The people of Edom are portrayed as having no natural affection for their brother. Instead they are consumed with raging anger and the flames of unchecked fury.

5. Ammon

Amos 1:13-15, "This is what the Lord says:

> 'For three sins of Ammon,
> even for four, I will not turn back my wrath.

Because he ripped open the pregnant women of Gilead
in order to extend his borders,
I will set fire to the walls of Rabbah
that will consume her fortresses
amid war cries on the day of battle,
amid violent winds on a stormy day.
Her king will go into exile,
he and his officials together,'
says the Lord."

Throughout the Old Testament, Ammon was always attempting to expand its borders to include more fertile ground. (Their nation was a desert land.) They actually slaughtered pregnant women on this quest, a level of violence that is obviously unacceptable.

6. Moab:
Amos 2: 1-3, "This is what the Lord says:
'For three sins of Moab,
even for four, I will not turn back my wrath.
Because he burned, as if to lime,
the bones of Edom's king,
I will send fire upon Moab
that will consume the fortresses of Kerioth.
Moab will go down in great tumult
amid war cries and the blast of the trumpet.
I will destroy her ruler
and kill all her officials with him,'
says the Lord."

Moab (modern day Jordan) had a heart for violence. This was expressed by the way they treated the corpse of the former King of Edom. In an act of desecration, they burned his body. They may have done this in the hope that they'd cause him additional suffering in his afterlife.

7. Judah:
Amos 2: 4, 5, "This is what the Lord says:
'For three sins of Judah,
even for four, I will not turn back my wrath.
Because they have rejected the law of the Lord
and have not kept his decrees,
because they have been led astray by false gods,
the gods their ancestors followed,
I will send fire upon Judah
that will consume the fortresses of Jerusalem.'"

When it comes to judging Judah, God uses a completely different standard. Judah is not judged for their crimes against humanity like the Gentile nations. Judah is instead accused of:

a) Rejecting the law of God (the Mosaic covenant) and not keeping his decrees

b) Following false gods

If we were to examine the Gentile nations, we'd find that they too were guilty of all these things. They worshipped false gods, and they didn't even know the Law of Moses let alone follow it. But the Gentile nations weren't held accountable for these things.

8. Israel:

Amos 2: 6-16, "This is what the Lord says:

'For three sins of Israel,
even for four, I will not turn back (my wrath).
They sell the righteous for silver,
and the needy for a pair of sandals.
They trample on the heads of the poor
as upon the dust of the ground
and deny justice to the oppressed.
Father and son use the same girl
and so profane my holy name.
They lie down beside every altar
on garments taken in pledge.
In the house of their god
they drink wine taken as fines.
I destroyed the Amorite before them,
though he was tall as the cedars
and strong as the oaks.
I destroyed his fruit above
and his roots below.
I brought you up out of Egypt,
and I led you forty years in the desert
to give you the land of the Amorites.
I also raised up prophets from among your sons
and Nazirites from among your young men.
Is this not true, people of Israel?'
declares the Lord.
'But you made the Nazirites drink wine
and commanded the prophets not to prophesy.
Now then, I will crush you

as a cart crushes when loaded with grain.
The swift will not escape,
    the strong will not muster their strength,
    and the warrior will not save his life.
The archer will not stand his ground,
    the fleet-footed soldier will not get away,
    and the horseman will not save his life.
Even the bravest warriors
    will flee naked on that day,
declares the Lord."

The northern kingdom of Israel hadn't necessarily committed crimes against other nations, but they had oppressed their own people.

Israel had:
a) trampled on the poor
b) denied justice to the oppressed
c) engaged in sexual abuse
d) corrupted the financial system
e) enacted government penalties and taxes that only benefited their leaders
f) forced people to compromise their convictions
g) refused to let prophets of God speak

For the rich and powerful in Israel, these were the best of times. People who occupied prestigious positions had many advantages. The financial, judicial, and governmental systems were all set up to benefit them (having first been corrupted by them). While the rich continued to profit, the poor were further oppressed.

God teaches that the rich have a social responsibility to society. God *does not* teach socialism or communism but calls for social responsibility. Men are to care for and assist those who are less fortunate. This is tempered with Paul's words to the Thessalonians: "When we were with you, we gave you this rule: 'If a man will not work, he shall not eat'" (II Thessalonians 3:10).

Here are a few things God says in Deuteronomy and James regarding the rich and their duty to the poor:

"Give generously...and do so without a grudging heart; then because of this the Lord your God will bless you in all your work and in everything you put your hand to. There will always be poor people in the land. Therefore I command you to be openhanded toward your brothers and toward the poor and needy in your land." Deuteronomy 15: 10, 11

"You have hoarded wealth in the last days. Look! The wages you failed to pay the workmen who mowed your fields are drying out against you. The cries of the harvesters have reached the ears of the Lord Almighty.

You have lived on earth in luxury and self-indulgence. You have fattened yourselves in the day of slaughter." James 5: 3-5

Many of Israel's problems involved the way they treated the poor. Amos prophesied about this to Israel in 760 BC, during the prosperous reign of Jeroboam II. But Israel did not change. Jeroboam II died six years later, (754 BC), he was succeeded by six kings, four of which were assassinated.

In 743, seventeen years after Amos sent his first letter to Israel, the Assyrian king Tiglath-Pileser invaded Israel and demanded thirty-seven tons of silver. In 722 BC, Samaria fell to Assyria's new king, Sargon II. Survivors from the northern ten tribes of Israel were dispersed into the Assyrian Empire (300-800 miles away from home). In 721, a mere forty years or one generation after Amos warned Israel, the people were swept away and scattered. Their nation was destroyed.

An Example of a Gentile Nation Repenting

As Amos was warning Israel, God called a prophet named Jonah to go to the Gentile land of Assyria and warn a city called Nineveh (500 miles away). The Assyrians were evil and violent. God had already sent several warnings to let them know their days were numbered.

Amos had prophesied:

> "'In that day,' declares the Sovereign Lord, 'I will make the sun go down at noon and darken the earth in broad daylight.'" Amos 8:9

Sure enough, an Assyrian historical record called the Eponym Canon contains documentation from a scribe in Nineveh that tells about a great eclipse that occurred on June 15, 763 BC. It was the warning sign foretold.

Ninevah also suffered two plagues. Records reveal that the first plague swept through Ninevah in 765. The second one took place in 759. Jonah would have arrived in Ninevah at the very end of the second plague.

Jonah had been trained under Elisha in the school of the prophets. His message to Ninevah is recorded in just five Hebrew words and translates: "Forty more days and Nineveh will be overturned." The king and his officials responded positively to Jonah's message. They understood what God expected of them without Jonah having to spell it out. They knew they didn't need to start following Jewish laws, observing the Sabbath, or worshipping at the temple. Jonah never mentioned the Levitical Law or the Ten Commandments. All that God required from the people of Ninevah was sincere repentance of the violence in their culture.

Because of Jonah's prophecy, King Ashur-dan III issued a decree calling for "national repentance" in Nineveh. It said:

> "By the decree of the king and his nobles: 'Do not let any man or beast, herd or flock, taste anything; do not let them eat or drink. But let man and

beast be covered with sackcloth. Let everyone call urgently on God. <u>Let them give up their evil ways and their violence ("hamas")</u>. God may yet relent and with compassion turn from his fierce anger so that we will not perish.'" Jonah 3:7, 8

YEAR	WARNING SIGNS OF AN ANGRY GOD
780-759 BC	Invaders force people into Nineveh
765	A plague sweeps through Nineveh
June 15, 763	Total eclipse of the sun
759	Second plague strikes Nineveh
759	Jonah announces their destruction will come in forty days

Jonah 3:10 says:

> "When God saw what they did and how they turned from their evil ways, <u>he had compassion</u> and did not bring upon them the destruction he had threatened."

America, like Ninevah, has been in decline for quite some time, and there have been many events in our recent history that signify warning signs of an angry God. The people of the United States can, like Nineveh, repent and flee immorality, oppression, deception, injustice, etc. God does not require that our nation collectively turn toward Christ and say a sinner's prayer; he asks only that we begin living according to standards he's made clear through general revelation. Proverbs 14:34 says:

> "Righteousness exalts a nation, but sin is a disgrace to any people."

The words of some great men who served America confirm this idea:

> "No people can be great who have ceased to be virtuous." -Samuel Johnson

> "Only a virtuous people are capable of freedom. As nations become more corrupt and vicious, they have more need of masters." -Benjamin Franklin

> "A state is nothing more than a reflection of its citizens; the more decent the citizens, the more decent the state." -Ronald Reagan

Chapter 18: What About the Terrorists?

Assyria Punishes Israel

The Assyrians were a cruel, militant people who struck fear in the hearts of the Israelites and eventually overthrew the ten northern tribes of Israel (701 BC). Isaiah 10:5 says that Assyria was the rod of God's anger used against the godless nation of Judah.

> "Woe to the Assyrian, the rod of my anger, in whose hand is the club of my wrath! I send him against a godless nation (Judah). I dispatch him against a people who anger me." Isaiah 10:5, 6

When we get to Isaiah 10:12, we see God talking about what he will do with the Assyrians after he is done using them for his purposes:

> "When the Lord has finished all his work against Mount Zion and Jerusalem he will say, 'I will punish the king of Assyria for the willful pride of his heart and the haughty look in his eyes…Therefore, the Lord Almighty will send a wasting disease upon his sturdy warriors…in a single day it will burn and consume his thorns and his briers…it will completely destroy." Isaiah 10:12-19

This situation is a good example of God using a violent nation to punish another godless nation. I think it's reasonable to suggest that we the United States are in the same position Israel was in long ago. The Assyrians could thus be likened to the terrorists of today at least concerning their purpose as a rod of anger in God's hands.

How we respond to God's judgment in the next few years will determine our future as a nation. In 760 BC, Amos spoke to the northern ten tribes of Israel, (Amos 2:6-9:10). He cited their sins against God and their fellow man. Amos urged the nation to seek holiness or risk God sweeping through their nation like fire to devour them (Amos 5:6). They chose not to respond and continued in sin, so God sent the Assyrians and King Tiglath-Pileser III into their land to plunder them.

Did this wake up the Israelites? No. Over the next twenty-years, four of Israel's kings were assassinated, but the people still refused to change. In 723 BC, the final siege on Israel's capital city of Samaria began. By 721 BC, just one forty-year generation after Amos' warnings, Samaria was destroyed and most survivors deported.

YEAR	EVENTS OF NORTHERN ISRAEL'S FINAL GENERATION
760	Amos prophesies to Israel.
753	After a six month reign, King Zechariah is assassinated by Shallum who then takes the throne.
752	After a one month reign, King Shallum is assassinated by Menahem who then becomes king.
752	Menahem reigns as king of Israel for ten years.
743	Tiglath-Pileser III, the King of Assyria, invades Israel and carts away thirty-seven tons of silver (II Kings 15:19).
740	Pekahiah is assassinated after two years by Pekah who then becomes the second to last king of Israel.
732	Tiglath-Pilesar takes possession of the northern part of Israel's land (II Kings 15:29).
732	Pekah is assassinated by Hoshea who becomes the final king of Israel.
723	Hoshea betrays Assyria's new king Shalmaneser and is taken to Assyria when Shalmaneser lays siege to Samaria.
721	**Israel's capital city of Samaria falls to Sargon, king of Assyria; the people are deported.**

Israel is destroyed by the Assyrians, the rod of God's judgment. All the political violence and social chaos they'd experienced had been warning signs of impending doom. God gave Israel numerous prophecies to help them make the connections, but they still didn't repent.

Babylon Punishes Judah

Judah would also face an enemy that God had raised up to help punish them. Habakkuk and Jeremiah were prophets living in Jerusalem around 620-580 BC. Habakkuk had already seen the first deportation of the people from Judah in 605 BC when Nebuchadnezzar, king of Babylon, took Daniel and other young men from the royal family back to Babylon with him (Daniel 1:3-7). Babylon invaded again in 597, after which Ezekiel and other craftsmen were deported back to Babylon.

As Habakkuk watched these things take place, he complained to God about the wicked Babylonians and how they dominated Jerusalem and God's chosen people.

"How long, O Lord, must I call for help, but you do not listen? Or cry out to you, 'Violence!' ('hamas') but you do not save? Why do you make me look at injustice? Why do you tolerate wrong? Destruction and violence ('hamas') are before me…" Habakkuk 1:2-4

The Lord responds to Habakkuk saying:

> "Look at the nations and watch—be utterly amazed. For I am going to do something in your days that you would not believe, even if you were told. I am raising up the Babylonians." Habakkuk 1:5, 6

The Lord then describes the Babylonians in the verses that follow. He says they are:

- Ruthless (bitter) – the Hebrew word means "angry, chafed, discontented"
- Impetuous (hasty) – the Hebrew word means "to be liquid or to flow easily," so the word suggests the idea of being carried headlong, suddenly, quickly
- Quick to take land that's not theirs
- Feared
- A law unto themselves
- Self-promoting
- Bent on violence ("hamas") – they believe they are superior to other nations, and this idea justifies their evil
- Guilty
- Enamored with their own strength; their strength is their god (Habakkuk 1:6-9)

The Lord also describes the Babylonians' abilities and the methods of war they use:

- They have horses swifter than leopards and more fierce than wolves
- They are a people others dread
- Their cavalry gallops headlong
- They swoop down to devour like a vulture
- They advance like a storm
- They gather prisoners like sand
- They deride kings and scoff at rulers
- They laugh at fortified cities
- They build ramps and capture those cities (Habakkuk 1:6-11)

Habakkuk couldn't believe what God was telling him. He didn't understand why God would continue to let the Babylonians prosper even though he himself called them "guilty men whose own strength is their god" (Habakkuk 1:11). Habakkuk then says:

> "O Lord, are you not from everlasting?
> My God, my Holy One, we will not die.
> O Lord, you have appointed them to execute judgment.

O Rock, you have ordained them to punish.
Your eyes are too pure to look on evil;
You cannot tolerate wrong.
Why then do you tolerate the treacherous?
Why are you silent while the wicked swallow up those more righteous
than themselves?"

The Babylonians have been "ordained" by God to "punish" another nation. In verse seven the Babylonians are said to be a "law unto themselves," and yet their sinful system of law will soon come to Jerusalem. Habakkuk is horrified by this thought.

Habakkuk asks God:

"Why then do you tolerate the treacherous? Why are you silent while the wicked swallow up those more righteous than themselves?" Habakkuk 1:13

Habakkuk fully intends to receive an answer from God, and he closes his questioning by saying:

"I will stand at my watch and station myself on the ramparts. I will look to see what he (God) will say to me, and what answer I am to give to this complaint." Habakkuk 2:1

Jeremiah heard God reveal the same plan concerning the coming judgment at the hands of the Babylonians:

"From the north disaster will be poured out on all who live in the land. I am about to summon all the peoples of the northern kingdoms…their kings will come and set up their thrones in the entrance of the gates of Jerusalem…I will pronounce my judgments on my people because of their wickedness in forsaking me." Jeremiah 1:14-16

Nebuchadnezzar was going to move with his Babylonian forces across the face of the Middle East to destroy all those who wouldn't cooperate with him. The Babylonian army would become the "hand of God," bringing judgment to the nations, just like the Assyrians did in 721 BC and the Romans would do in 70 AD.

Isaiah tells us what God said to Babylon:

"I was angry with my people and desecrated my inheritance; I gave them into your hand, and you showed them no mercy." Isaiah 47:6

God Controls History

The point here is that God will raise up nations or people groups to bring his judgment on other cultures that have rebelled against him. Many times the nations or groups he raises up are extremely evil. God's answer to Habakkuk may be the same answer for us today as we consider world events. The descriptions used to identify Babylon also apply to modern-day terrorists. They are angry, discontented, rash, ready to take land that is not theirs, feared, a law to themselves, self-promoting, violent.

The rise of terrorism may be God's hand of judgment on America and the West. If we ignore this possibility, we might miss God's warning signs. We must not be like the people of Jesus' generation who were wise concerning the physical world but could not perceive what was happening in the spiritual realm. Jesus said:

> "When you see a cloud rising in the west, immediately you say, 'It's going to rain,' and it does. And when the south wind blows you say, 'It's going to be hot,' and it is." Luke 12:54-55

In the next verse, Jesus says:

> "Hypocrites! You know how to interpret the appearance of the earth and the sky. How is it that you don't know how to interpret this present time?" Luke 12:56

We must not be like Jerusalem in 30 AD or northern Israel in 760 BC or Judah in 640 BC. We have to begin correctly analyzing the signs of the time in light of God's word. If we do this, we will we see that the righteousness of our country has faded, and God has raised a group of people to bring judgment on us. We must respond correctly to avoid disaster (like Ninevah did), because if we don't, we'll soon face more judgment.

What Will Happen to the Terrorists?

If you're still wondering why God would want to use terrorists to punish us, you're not alone. As we already discussed, Habakkuk wondered similar questions concerning the Babylonians in 600 BC. He asked God:

> "Why are you silent while the wicked swallow up those more righteous than themselves?" Habakkuk 1:13

God answered his question by saying:

> "Will not all of them taunt him (Babylon) with ridicule and scorn saying, 'Woe to him (Babylon) who piles up stolen goods and makes himself wealthy by extortion! Will not your debtors suddenly arise? Will they not wake up and make you (Babylon) tremble? Then you (Babylon) will become their victim. Because you (Babylon) have plundered many nations, the peoples who are left will plunder you (Babylon)." Habakkuk 2:6-8

In other words, Babylon was going to be used by God just before he wiped them out altogether. Similar warnings in Isaiah and Jeremiah reveal the same plan:

"Sit in silence, go into darkness, Daughter of the Babylonians; no more will you be called queen of kingdoms. I was angry with my people and desecrated my inheritance; I gave them into your hand, and you showed them no mercy. Even on the aged you laid a very heavy yoke. You said, 'I will continue forever – the eternal queen!' But you did not consider these things or reflect on what might happen…Disaster will come upon you, and you will not know how to conjure it away…" Isaiah 47:5-15

Because Judah eventually repents, God will bring his people out of Babylon. But Babylon itself will be overthrown.

"'In those days, at that time,' declares the Lord, 'the people of Israel and the people of Judah together will go in tears to seek the Lord their God. They will ask the way to Zion and turn their faces toward it…My people have been lost sheep; their shepherds have led them astray and caused them to roam on the mountains…Whoever found them devoured them; their enemies said, we are not guilty…flee out of Babylon; leave the land of the Babylonians…for I will stir up and bring against Babylon an alliance of great nations from the land of the north. They will take up their positions against her, and from the north she will be captured. Their arrows will be like skilled warriors who do not return empty-handed. So Babylonia will be plundered; all who plunder her will have their fill,' declares the Lord." Jeremiah 50:6-10

The violent kingdom of Babylon was ultimately destroyed by God. The same was true of the Assyrian empire. God can lift up leaders or nations as tools of his judgment to accomplish his will. After he is finished with them, he can eliminate them.

"No one from the east or the west or from the desert can exalt a man. But it is God who judges: He brings one down, he exalts another." Psalm 75:6, 7

It would then appear that God can use terrorists or terrorist states as a warning to other nations that they need a course correction. What does this course correction consist of? Amos said:

"And what does the Lord require of you? To act justly and to love mercy and to walk humbly with your God." Amos 6:8

Likewise, Isaiah describes God's expectations for man:

"Maintain justice and do what is right, for my salvation is close at hand and my righteousness will soon be revealed." Isaiah 56:1

God's Advice

God's advice to nations facing his judgment includes:
1) Be just in all your decisions and maintain justice in your land.

2) Do what is right continually.
3) Be merciful to men.
4) Be humble before God.

Consider Ourselves Warned

The Assyrians, Babylonians, and Romans were allowed to invade the land of Israel to punish the people for violating their covenant with God (II Kings 17:7). The same has been true for other once righteous nations that decided to reject God's standards. The terrorists may also be used as the rod of God's judgment against America. But we must remember that God does not let violent cultures continue for very long on earth, and he will eventually deal with the terrorists.

The question we must answer now is: Are we as a nation going to respond to God's discipline and change our ways, or will we march ahead, oblivious to the divine cycle of judgment we're experiencing? On September 11, 2001, we were given a warning, but it will not be our last. What we choose to do in the next few months and years will determine our future.

Will The United States Respond to God's Fourth Cycle of Discipline??

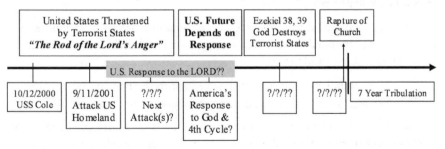

If God decides to use terrorist states against us as his rod of his anger, it won't be long before the events of Ezekiel 38 and 39 will rapidly unfold. These are the next events on the timeline of God's plan for mankind. We know this because in Ezekiel 36 and 37, Israel becomes a nation again. The process is compared to bodies of dead, dry bones coming together and having life breathed into them. Israel's return is specifically detailed in Ezekiel 37:1-11 as a time when:

1) Dry bones come together
2) Tendons and flesh appear
3) Skin covers them
4) Breath enters them
5) They come to life to form a vast army

The verses say that, through a series of steps, God will bring his people back together and turn them into a vibrant and powerful nation again. In Ezekiel 37:12-14, God says:

> "O my people, I am going to open your graves and bring you up from them; I will bring you back to the land of Israel. Then you, my people, will know that I am the Lord, when I open your graves and bring you up from them. I will put my Spirit in you and you will live, and I will settle you in your own land."

Over the last 60+ years, the world has watched as the dry bones of Israel have take on new life. The grave of the nation of Israel, buried in 70 AD by the Romans, recently opened, and the physical nation of Israel has emerged onto the stage of world history again. But this process is far from over. The Bible clearly tells us that after Israel's return as a nation, their enemies will come against them again, finally angering God to the extent that he will wipe them off the face of the earth. The end result will be total destruction of the terrorist and their allies that practice violence ("hamas") as a way of life.

Ezekiel Chapter 38

Ezekiel prophesied about Israel's return on January 8, 585 BC. On this same date, Ezekiel prophesied about other events yet to take place. He talks about the now infamous God and Magog.

> "Son of man, <u>set your face against Gog, of the land of Magog, the chief prince of Meshech and Tubal</u>; prophesy against him." Ezekiel 38:2

Gog is the name of a man who is a leader from the land of Magog. Meshech and Tubal are two locations within Magog. We must then identify where the land of Magog and the locations of Meshech and Tubal would be several thousand years later.

1) **Magog** was one of Noah's grandsons, and, after the tower of Babel was built, he settled in an area known as Caucasus. Linguists believe the name "Caucasus" means "Gog's Fort."

2) **Meshech** was the son of Japheth. In the writings of Josephus we find out that Meshech settled in Cappadocia. The country of Georgia (formerly part of the Soviet Union) has traditionally traced its ancestry back to Meshech. In addition to Georgia, ancient Cappadocia is also currently occupied by Armenia, Azerbaijan and Kazakhstan.

3) **Tubal** was another son of Japheth. Josephus records that Tubal also occupied modern day Georgia. The capitol of Georgia is T'bilisi which some say still preserves the name Tubal as "Tubal-isi" or "land of Tubal."

4) **Gog** then is the leader of a future people who will reside in the modern countries of Georgia, Azerbaijan, Armenia, Kazakhstan, and possibly further north.

God gives Ezekiel a message for this coming leader named Gog:

> This is what the Sovereign Lord says: 'I am against you, O Gog, chief prince of Meshech and Tubal.'" Ezekiel 38:3

Ezekiel tells Gog that the Lord is against him. Gog has rebelled and rejected the Lord's ways. Gog, like the Assyrians and Babylonians before, will be used by God to discipline other nations before facing his ultimate destruction. The Lord says of Gog:

> "I will turn you around, put hooks in your jaws and bring you out with your whole army—your horses, your horsemen fully armed, and a great horde with large and small shields, all of them brandishing their swords." Ezekiel 38:4

Just as ancient empires used to lead foreign kings off to captivity with a ring in their nose or their jaw (II Chronicles 33:11), the Lord is going to take control of Gog and his army. He is going to draw them out of their land and prepare them for war. Gog's army will have incredible military strength. They will be a massive offensive force with a variety of defense systems as well.

Gog's military ("from the North") will be joined by a coalition that includes the five nations referenced in Ezekiel 38:5:

> "Persia, Cush, and Put will be with them, all with shields and helmets, also Gomer with all its troops, and Beth Togarmah from the far north with all its troops—the many nations with you."

Regarding these nations we know:

1) **Persia** is the modern land of Iran.

2) **Cush** was one of Ham's sons (the grandson of Noah). He was also the father of Nimrod. Cush settled first in Shinar and then Southern Arabia. His people eventually moved from Southern Arabia across the Red Sea into Ethiopia and Sudan. Whenever the Bible mentions Cush, it it is refering to the land of southern Iraq, Kuwait, Yemen, Ethiopia, Eritrea, Sudan, and southern Saudi Arabia.

3) **Put** is Ham's third son. Josephus records, "Put also was the founder of Libia." In Isaiah 66:19, the land of Put is described as the land between Tarshish (Spain) and the "land of the Lydians" (the western part of Egypt). Therefore, Put would be the nation just west of Egypt—which is Libya.

4) **Gomer** is one of Japheth's seven sons. His brothers include Magog, Tubal, and Meshech. Josephus records that the people of Gomer migrated out of

southern Russia around 600 BC. Some went east into Media (Iran), while others went west to Cappadocia (western Turkey). Most settled in Galatia and became the New Testament Galatians. Today, Gomer would be the land of Turkey.

5) **Togarmah** was one of Gomer's sons. Modern day Armenians claim to be descendents of Togarmah. Thus, Togarmah would be the land of Armenia.

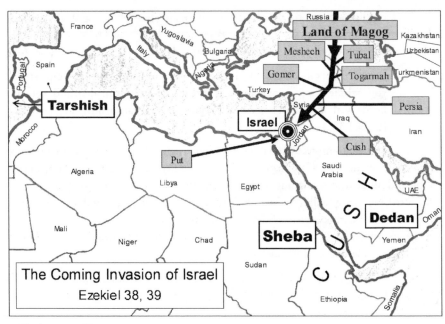

The Coming Invasion of Israel
Ezekiel 38, 39

God says to Gog:

> "'Get ready; be prepared, you and all the hordes gathered about you, and take command of them." Ezekiel 38:7

Gog will take command of this coalition in latter days. The coalition will include Georgia, Armenia, Azerbaijan, Kazakhstan, Uzbekistan, Afghanistan, Turkmenistan, Turkey, Iran, Iraq, Kuwait, and Libya. Together they will invade the land of Israel.

The Lord tells Gog he will be called to go to war against Israel. The Lord then describes what the social, economic, and political conditions of Israel will be at that time:

> "After many days you will be called to arms. In future years you will invade a land that has recovered from war, <u>whose people were gathered from many nations to the mountains of Israel, which had long been desolate.</u> They had been brought out from the nations, and now all of them live in safety." Ezekiel 38:8

This type of invasion has never occurred in recorded history. It didn't happen before Ezekiel's lifetime, and it has not occurred since Ezekiel prophesied about it in 585 BC. In fact, it was not until after WWII that the land of Israel was reclaimed, and the people were "gathered from many nations to a land that had long been desolate."

The Lord tells Gog and his allies what his mighty military force will look like on the day they are called to invade Israel:

> "You and all your troops and the many nations with you will go up, advancing like a storm; you will be like a cloud covering the land." Ezekiel 38:9

General Gog will lead one of history's largest invasions. His army will enter Israel with the hope of plundering it:

> "This is what the Sovereign Lord says: on that day thoughts will come into your mind and you will devise an evil scheme. You will say, 'I will invade a land of unwalled villages; I will attack a peaceful and unsuspecting people—all of them living without walls and without gates and bars. I will plunder and loot and turn my hand against the resettled ruins and the people gathered from the nations, rich in livestock and goods, living at the center of the land.'" (Ezekiel 38:10-12)

We see from these verses that before God calls upon Gog's army to invade Israel, there will be an unprecedented peace in the Middle East. According to Ezekiel, before this great invasion, we find:

1) a peaceful Israeli people
2) an unsuspecting Israeli people
3) villages without walls, gates, or bars
4) an extremely prosperous Israeli people
5) a national economy based on industry and agriculture

I believe it is safe to assume that one of the key reasons Gog and his allies will attack Israel is economic in nature. As Israel's economy flourishes in the near future, many countries will become jealous of their wealth.

Ezekiel also tells us that three nations or groups of nations speak out in defense of Israel and make it clear that they are against Gog's coalition:

> "Sheba and Dedan and the merchants of Tarshish and all her villages will say to you, 'Have you come to plunder? Have you gathered your hordes to loot, to carry off silver and gold, to take away livestock and goods and to seize much plunder?'" Ezekiel 38:13

The modern-day breakdown of these nations:

1) Sheba – is the area on both sides of the Red Sea which today is Ethiopia (on the west) and Yemen (on the east). This area is part of the land of Cush that refuses to participate in the invasion.

2) **Dedan** – is where the descendents of Cush ended up (Genesis 10:7), beginning with Abraham and his second wife Keturah (Genesis 25:3). Isaiah tells us this group of people went to Arabia with their caravans. This would be the middle section of the land of Cush which today is Saudia Arabia.

3) **Tarshish** – was a Phoenician port based in Spain. The word "Tarshish" was usually associated with large ships and merchandise being transported by sea and was a reference to "the distant lands of the western world." Tarshish would then be a reference to Spain, Western Europe, and the Americas. (Phoenician sailors and merchants of the ancient world are believed to have sailed past Spain to the Americas. Evidence of these trade routes has been found in America, including the discovery of ancient Phoenician, Egyptian, and Roman trade objects. Various places in the western hemisphere also have Phoenician, Egyptian, Greek, and Roman inscriptions engraved in stone.)

From this information, we can presuppose that Saudia Arabia, parts of Africa, Europe, and the Americas will stand in opposition to Gog. They will be outraged by the way the terrorist states are treating Israel.

When Gog decides to invade Israel, his decision will not be justified in the eyes of the world. This is because his coalition will have become so entrenched in "hamas" by this time that their façade of religion will no longer be valid. They will be exposed to the world for the fraud they are. They are countries uniting in the name of a higher purpose (religion) but are really only unified in their hatred for Israel and their envy of Israel's wealth.

The Lord goes on to say:

> "Therefore, son of man, prophesy and say to Gog, 'This is what the Sovereign Lord says: In that day, when my people Israel are living in safety, will you not take notice of it? You will come from your place in the far north, you and many nations with you, all of them riding on horses, a great horde, a mighty army. You will advance against my people Israel like a cloud that covers the land." Ezekiel 38:14[15]

The creator of the universe is finally going to demonstrate to all the nations of the world that he, the God of Israel, is the one true God.

> "In days to come, O Gog, I will bring you against my land, so that the nations may know me when I show myself holy through you before their eyes. This is what the Sovereign Lord says: 'Are you not the one I spoke of in former days by my servants the prophets of Israel? At that time they prophesied for years that I would bring you against them." Ezekiel 38:16-17

We finally learn what the outcome will be after Gog invades Israel:

> "This is what will happen in that day: When Gog attacks the land of Israel, my hot anger will be aroused, declares the Sovereign Lord." Ezekiel 38:18

The Lord will begin his counterattack with an earthquake. It will be an earthquake that originates in Israel but shakes the entire globe. The effects of this earthquake will extend through the sea to all continents and will have a lasting effect on the atmosphere. The earth's plates will shift and mountains will literally disappear.

> "In my zeal and fiery wrath I declare that at that time there shall be a great earthquake in the land of Israel. The fish of the sea, the birds of the air, the beasts of the field, every creature that moves along the ground, and all the people on the face of the earth will tremble at my presence. The mountains will be overturned, the cliffs will crumble and every wall will fall to the ground." Ezekiel 38:19-20

Terror from the earthquake will send Gog's army into panic and confusion. The coalition will begin firing on each others' armies believing they are firing on Israel.

> "I will summon a sword against Gog on all my mountains, declares the Sovereign Lord. Every man's sword will be against his brother." Ezekiel 38:21

The earthquake will result in volcanic activity, and the earth's cracked plates will spew molten lava into the air. The fallout from these emissions will include massive thunderstorms with driving rain and hail.

> "I will execute judgment upon him with plague and bloodshed; I will pour down torrents of rain, hailstones, and burning sulfur on him and on his troops and on the many nations with him." Ezekiel 38:22

The other nations that watched Gog begin the invasion will understand that something very great has just happened, something even greater than the parting of the Red Sea. The Lord is indeed in heaven, watching the goings-on of mankind. A new fear of God will sweep through the hearts of men worldwide.

> "And so I will show my greatness and my holiness, and I will make myself known in the sight of many nations. Then they will know that I am the Lord." Ezekiel 38:23

Ezekiel Chapter 39

God makes it clear that he is the one who brought the enemy down from the North and into the land of Israel, but he did this in order to *destroy* them there.

> "Son of man, prophesy against Gog and say: 'This is what the Sovereign

Lord says: I am against you, O Gog, chief prince of Meshech and Tubal. I will turn you around and drag you along. I will bring you from the far north and send you against the mountains of Israel." Ezekiel 39:1, 2

Gog and his men will not have time to retreat. After entering Israel, their weapons will be knocked out of their control. Whatever the modern counterpart of an ancient bow and arrow may be—it will be rendered useless against Israel on that day. Hordes of soldiers will die in the mountains of Israel and on the battlefield. Birds and wild animals will immediately begin to devour their carcasses.

"Then I will strike your bow from your left hand and make your arrows drop from your right hand. On the mountains of Israel you will fall, you and all your troops and the nations with you. I will give you as food to all kinds of carrion birds and to the wild animals. You will fall in the open field, for I have spoken, declares the Sovereign Lord." Ezekiel 39:3-5

As the army is dying in the mountains of Israel, a fire will break out back in the army's homeland of Magog. Magog isn't the only place struck by the fire of God. Other nations will watch as fire breaks out in their cities and along their coastlands.

"I will send fire on Magog and on those who live in safety in the coastlands, and they will know that I am the Lord." Ezekiel 39:6

Finally, the people of the world will recognize that God is who he's always said he is. Even the current secular attitude of the Jewish people will change. Their deliverance from Gog will remind modern Jews that they are still God's chosen people. They will recognize that their existence as a nation is possible only because the Lord willed it.

"I will make known my holy name among my people Israel. I will no longer let my holy name be profaned, and the nations will know that I the Lord am the Holy One in Israel. It is coming! It will surely take place, declares the Sovereign Lord. This is the day I have spoken of." Ezekiel 39:7-8

After Gog's destruction, the people of Israel will gather up Gog's weapons to burn them. We learn that Israel will not need to produce energy for seven years because the burning of these weapons will supply their energy needs. The weapons will be disassembled to remove some element of power that can be converted into a usable energy source.

"Then those who live in the towns of Israel will go out and use the weapons for fuel and burn them up—the small and large shields, the bows and arrows, the war clubs and spears. For seven years they will use them for fuel. They will not need to gather wood from the fields or cut it from the forests, because they will use the weapons for fuel." Ezekiel 39:9-10

Gog's army had intended to loot Israel and "carry off silver and gold and take away livestock and goods and seize much plunder." Yet ironically, the dead army of Gog's coalition will instead be looted by the people of Israel.

> "And they will plunder those who plundered them and loot those who looted them, declares the Sovereign Lord." Ezekiel 39:10

There will be an enormous number of dead soldiers to deal with. The location of the mass burial for these soldiers will be a huge ravine in the mountains on the eastern side of the Dead Sea. It will be a grave so massive that the road system in that area will have to be altered in order to logistically accommodate it. Ezekiel tells us this place will be called "Hamon Gog" which means "hordes of Gog."

> "On that day I will give Gog a burial place in Israel, in the valley of those who travel east toward the Sea. It will block the way of travelers, because Gog and all his hordes will be buried there. So it will be called the Valley of Hamon Gog." Ezekiel 39:11

The number of dead will be so great that it will require many Israelites to be employed full-time for seven months just to bury them. Life in Israel will stop until the remains of the hordes of Gog have all been carted away.

> "For seven months the house of Israel will be burying them in order to cleanse the land. All the people of the land will bury them, and the day I am glorified will be a memorable day for them, declares the Sovereign Lord. Men will be regularly employed to cleanse the land. Some will go throughout the land and, in addition to them, others will bury those that remain on the ground." Ezekiel 39:12-14

After seven months, workers will do a thorough search of the land, looking for human body parts leftover from the slaughter. This search team will place a marker by each bone they find so the transportation department can take the last remains to Hamon Gog to be buried. There will be so many people working at the Hamon Gog burial site that a temporary city will be constructed there. It will be called "Hamonah" which simply means "horde" or "multitude."

> "At the end of the seven months they will begin their search. As they go through the land and one of them sees a human bone, he will set up a marker beside it until the gravediggers have buried it in the Valley of Hamon Gog. Also a town called Hamonah will be there. And so they will cleanse the land." (Ezekiel 39:14-16)

The date that God overthrew the armies of Gog will become a national holiday in Israel alongside other Jewish holidays like Passover and Hanukkah. This great and final war may be God's way of dealing with terrorism once and for all. In the end, the terrorist states will fall just like the Assyrians and the Babylonians did.

The Church Age is Our Place in World History

Chapter 19: The Seven Kingdom Parables

ISRAEL HAS BEEN God's mouthpiece to the world since the day he met them on Mt. Sinai until the moment Jesus arrived in Israel. During that 1400 year period, every prophet came from Israel and every written word of revelation came from Israel. Even the Messiah himself came from Israel. Jesus told the Samaritan woman, "Salvation is from the Jews" (John 4:22). Jesus told the Phoenician woman, "I was only sent to the lost sheep of Israel" (Matthew 15:24).

John the Baptist and Jesus both told the Jewish people that the kingdom of heaven was near:

> "In those days, John the Baptist came, preaching in the Desert of Judea and saying, 'Repent, for the kingdom of heaven is near.'" Matthew 3:2

> "From that time on, Jesus began to preach, 'Repent, for the kingdom of heaven is near.'" Matthew 4:17

This message was first brought to Israel, and the plan was for them to take the message to the world. Abraham was called around 2000 BC for the purpose of becoming a nation that God would use to bless all nations (Genesis 12:2, 3). Israel was supposed to proclaim the coming of the kingdom of heaven and a king who would rule that kingdom.

Approximately 2000 years after God called Abraham, that king arrived. Matthew 12:22 says:

> "Then they brought him a demon-possessed man who was blind and mute, and Jesus healed him so that he could both talk and see. All the people were astonished and said,

> 'Could this be the Son of David?'"

The people who saw Jesus drive out the demons and restore the man wondered if he might be the king promised to Israel in the Old Testament. The crowd asked their religious leaders if there was any way that Jesus could be the promised Son of David.

> "But when the Pharisees heard this, they said, 'It is only by Beelzebub the prince of demons that this fellow drives out demons.'" Matthew 12:24

To explain the implications of the Pharisees' response to Jesus, consider this analogy for a moment. Let's say that the Kingdom of God is like a huge corporation—we'll say for the sake of the example that it's the Pepsi Corporation.

One day, the president of Pepsi arrives at his weekly meeting with the marketing department and asks the team what their latest ideas are. They tell him that the next campaign should include the tagline, "Pepsi—it tastes terrible and it's bad for you." The president of Pepsi would likely fire the entire marketing department and immediately start interviews to find a new marketing team.

That is exactly what is going on in Matthew 13. This interaction between Jesus and the religious leaders of Israel is similar to the business meeting above. The Jews, the ambassadors of the kingdom, have been approached by Jesus, the king of the kingdom. Instead of receiving the king for who he is, the ambassadors identify the king as Satan himself and begin a negative advertising campaign against him. Jesus will eventually fire his whole marketing department just like the president of Pepsi would. You simply can't have a marketing team that perpetuates terrible public relations and negative press. Jesus is going to announce a new marketing approach for the advancement of the Kingdom of God. This new approach will leave Israel unemployed, as Jesus hands their job assignment over to a new team of people.

Jesus will now reveal seven aspects of this new phase in his kingdom. He will use seven parables to describe seven truths about where the kingdom of God is headed now that Israel has been temporarily rejected as God's way to reach the world.

"That same day Jesus went out of the house and sat by the lake. Such large crowds gathered around him that he got into a boat and sat in it while all the people stood on the shore. Then he told them many things in parables." Matthew 13:1

	Parable	Basic Truth about the Next Phase of the Kingdom of Heaven on Earth – The Church Age	Scripture
1	The Sower and the Seed	Growth during this next phase of the Kingdom of God will be based on receiving and responding to the word (seed) which will cause production.	Mt.13:3-9; 18-23
2	The Sowing of the Weeds	False teaching (imitation seeds) will also be sown and allowed to grow and develop during this age.	Mt. 13:24-30; 37-43
3	The Mustard Seed	This new group of kingdom representatives will begin very small but will grow to be the biggest.	Mt. 13:31-32
4	The Yeast	Once this truth is mixed into the world, even in the smallest amount, it will spread throughout the world into every nation and every part of society.	Mt. 13:33

5	The Hidden Treasure	Israel is the treasured nation and although it is now set aside (hidden in the field), Israel (the treasure) will be dug up to be used again later.	Mt. 13:44
6	The Pearl	The Lord (the merchant) has been trying to gain the nations (the pearls). He will now purchase all the nations on the cross	Mt. 13:45-46
7	The Net	At the end of this age, the next event is the day of judgment or the separating of people (separating good and bad fish).	Mt. 13:47-50

The same day the religious leaders called Jesus Beelzebub, Jesus shares seven parables with the crowd. The first parable explains how the kingdom of heaven will advance on the earth. It will not advance through military force. It will not advance through legislation. It will not advance through family heritage or national descent. The kingdom of God will be spread in the same way a farmer scatters his seed.

> "A farmer went out to sow his seed. As he was scattering the seed, some fell along the path, and the birds came and ate it up. Some fell on rocky places where it did not have much soil. It sprang up quickly because the soil was shallow. But when the sun came up, the plants were scorched, and they withered because they had no root. Other seed fell among thorns which grew up and choked the plants. Still other seed fell on good soil, where it produced a crop—a hundred, sixty, or thirty times what was sown. He who has ears, let him hear." Matthew 13:3-9

Teaching in parables was a new technique Jesus was using in his ministry. Up until this time, he had spoken very plainly to the people of Israel, as seen in the Sermon on the Mount in Matthew 5-7.

> "When Jesus had finished saying these things, the crowds were amazed at his teaching, because <u>he taught as one who had authority</u>, and not as their teachers of the law." Matthew 7:28

On this day, as Jesus "told them many things in parables" (Matthew 13:3), his disciples immediately noticed the difference in his communication style. They were confused by so much abstractness. After the strange message about planting seeds in the middle of a road, the disciples decided to question Jesus about his new parable technique.

> "The disciples came to him and asked, 'Why do you speak to the people in parables? He replied, 'The knowledge of the secrets of the kingdom of heaven have been given to you, but not to them. <u>Whoever has will be given more</u>, and he will have an abundance. <u>Whoever does not have, even that which he has will be taken from him.</u> This is why I speak to them in

parables: 'Though seeing, they do not see; though hearing they do not hear or understand.'" Matthew 13:11-14

Jesus told them that because they had accepted him for who he actually was—the Messiah—the parables would make sense to them. But the people of Israel who rejected him would have no idea what he was talking about. For those who understood the basic truths he taught, their knowledge would increase and their understanding would expand. For those who rejected his teachings from the beginning, even the little bit they did understand would be lost and they would be confused by the parables. Nothing would make sense to them after this.

Without understanding that Jesus was the Messiah, the promised king, people could still hear his teachings, but wouldn't fully grasp what they meant. It would be like hearing one side of a phone conversation;

"Well, if he messes up the house again he can stay outside."

- - - - - - -

"I know…I know…he probably won't like it, but whatever. I just hope he doesn't bother the neighbors."

- - - - - - -

"Yeah, I'll just take some food out to him, and he can stay out there until he learns his lesson."

This phone conversation is about a pet. But if the person eavesdropping didn't know the person speaking was a pet owner, he or she might have wrongfully believed the conversation was about a young child.

This was the problem whenever Jesus spoke to crowds. The believing Jews could put his words in perspective because they knew he was speaking as the Messiah. But the unbelievers who heard him speak thought he was a mere man. They were always trying to figure out what was really being said. After listening to him speak, they'd walk away saying things like:

"Now we know that you are demon-possessed!" John 8:52

"He is demon-possessed and raving mad. Why listen to him?'" John 10:19-21

Those who believed in Christ continued to understand his words and parables. But, for those who did not believe, their anger intensified each time he spoke until finally they nailed him to a cross.

Jesus finally explained the parable of the sower:

"Listen then to what the parable of the sower means: When anyone hears the message about the kingdom and does not understand it, the evil one comes and snatches away what was sown in his heart. This is the seed sown along the path. The one who received the seed that fell on rocky places is the man who hears the word and at once receives it with joy. But since he has no root, he lasts only a short time. When trouble or persecution comes because of the word, he quickly falls away. The one who received the seed that fell among the thorns is the man who hears the word, but the worries of this life and the deceitfulness of wealth choke it, making it unfruitful. But the one who received the seed that fell on good soil is the man who hears the word and understands it. He produces a crop, yielding a hundred, sixty, or thirty times what was sown." Matthew 13:18-23

This parable explains how a person enters the kingdom of heaven and grows in faith. This explanation will remain true throughout the next dispensation—the one that will replace the age of Israel until the last days. The word of God will now be proclaimed to the world and many people will receive the seed of his word. How they respond to that seed will determine whether or not they enter the kingdom.

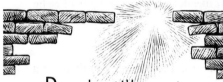

Some will reject it like the hard packed dirt of the road rejects a seed. Some will get excited about the advantages of the kingdom but will only seek the pleasant fruit from the harvest. Some will begin to grow, but the problems of life will consume them and they will fail to produce anything of lasting value. Just like different types of soil produce different yields in the same crop, some believers will produce thirty times what has been sown in their lives, others sixty times, and still others one hundred times more. How they care for the growth of the seed in their lives will determine how much they produce for the kingdom of God in the next age.

People still want Jesus to heal their bodies and multiply bread but have little interest in their own spiritual health.

We in the church age have a simple job description: teach the word of God to everyone (or sow the seed along the path.) The response we receive from people will range from rejection to shallow understanding to distracted indifference to acceptance followed by much fruit. The response part is not up to us. The sowing part is.

The **second kingdom parable** warns the people that their will be weeds or false teaching sown in the hearts of men at the same time the truth is being proclaimed. Whatever God does, Satan counterfeits. The important message of this parable is that, during this next dispensation, God will not do anything to hinder the advance of these false doctrines. He will allow the weeds to grow alongside the seeds.

> "Jesus told them another parable: <u>The kingdom of heaven is like a man who sowed good seed in his field. But while everyone was sleeping, his enemy came and sowed weeds among the wheat</u>, and went away. When the wheat sprouted and formed heads, then the weeds also appeared. The owner's servants came to him and said, 'Sir, didn't you sow good seed in your field? Where then did the weeds come from?' 'An enemy did this,' he replied. The servants asked him, 'Do you want us to go and pull them up?' 'No,' he answered, 'because while you are pulling the weeds, you may root up the wheat with them. Let both grow together until the harvest. At that time I will tell the harvesters: First collect the weeds and tie them in bundles to be burned; then gather the wheat and bring it into my barn.'" Matthew 13:24-30

In the parable of the weeds, (Matthew 13:37-43) even the angels ask if they can rip out the weeds, but the Lord says, "No...let them both grow together until the harvest" (Matthew 13:29, 30). During the church age, there will be a lot of false teaching that men will receive and develop. This false teaching will be one of the ways God separates the noble from the wicked. If you desire false teaching and deception, it will be there for you. Your choice will reveal what's in your heart.

> "They will perish because they refused to love the truth and so be saved. For this reason <u>God sends them a powerful delusion so that they will believe the lie</u> and so that all will be condemned who have not believed the truth but have delighted in wickedness." I Thessalonians 2:10-12

The **third kingdom parable** is a prophecy concerning the growth of the number of believers.

> "He told them another parable: <u>The kingdom of heaven is like a mustard seed, which a man took and planted in his field</u>. Though it is the smallest of all your seeds, yet when it grows, it is the largest of garden plants and becomes a tree, so that the birds of the air come and perch in its branches.'" Matthew 13:31-32

The day Jesus spoke, the believers were just a small minority in Israel (which, as a nation, was itself a minority in a land of Gentiles). Some of the most amazing prophecies in scripture deal with Jesus' predictions for the growth of the church. Here he promises that a mustard seed, the smallest of all seeds, will grow to be the biggest plant in the garden. In other words, this small group of disciples, the smallest of all the religious groups in the world at that time, will, in the end, become the largest religious group on earth. The "birds of the air perching in its branches" may be a reference to people of all nations finding a place in this ever-expanding religion. This parable and the prediction it contains is another indiration that though Islam is the fastest growing religion today it will not outgrow the church during the church age.

The **fourth kingdom parable** uses the illustration of a small amount of yeast being placed into dough.

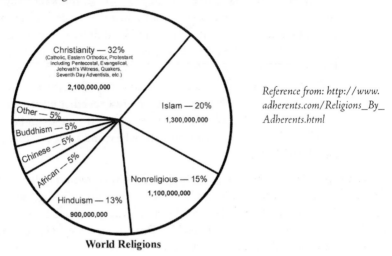

Reference from: http://www. adherents.com/Religions_By_ Adherents.html

World Religions

> "He told them still another parable: 'The kingdom of heaven is like yeast that a woman took and mixed into a large amount of flour until it worked all through the dough.'" Matthew 13:33

Just as the yeast grows and spread through the whole loaf, so it is with the truth. Once the truth is known on earth, it will spread throughout the world to every nation and every class of people within those nations. The young and old, rich and poor alike will embrace the truth.

The **fifth kingdom parable** talks about treasure buried in a field.

> "The kingdom of heaven is like treasure hidden in a field. When a man found it, he hid it again, and then in his joy went and sold all he had and bought that field." Matthew 13:44, 45

A man finds treasure buried in a field, so, in order to lawfully secure the treasure for himself, the man buries it again and then goes to the field's owner and buys the whole field. By purchasing the field, he also purchases the treasure that's buried there.

Israel is God's treasured nation, but, during the church age, it will be buried in the field of nations. God will purchase all the nations so that he can secure his treasure. After the earth has been secured, he will remove the treasure. In the final days, God will again use Israel. But this time they will successfully represent his kingdom to the world.

The **sixth kingdom parable** talks about a merchant who purchased fine pearls.

> "Again, the kingdom of heaven is like a merchant looking for fine pearls. When he found one of great value, he went away and sold everything he had and bought it." Matthew 13:45-46

In the Law of Moses, shellfish that produce pearls were viewed as unclean, just as foreign nations were viewed as unclean. Old Testament prophets associated the sea with distant Gentile lands. So the pearl mentioned here is a reference to the Lord purchasing the unclean Gentile nations. Jesus paid for the sins of all nations by giving up his life at Calvary. He "sold everything he had" for the opportunity to purchase what he'd always considered valuable, the Gentiles.

The **seventh kingdom parable** explains where the church age fits with regard to the history of mankind. It explains that the next thing that will happen will be the judgment or the separating of the good fish from the bad fish.

> "Once again, the kingdom of heaven is like a net that was let down into the lake and caught all kinds of fish. When it was full, the fishermen pulled it up on the shore. Then they sat down and collected the good fish in baskets, but threw the bad away. This is how it will be at the end of the age. The angels will come and separate the wicked from the righteous and throw them into the fiery furnace, where there will be weeping and gnashing of teeth." Matthew 13:47-50

The letting down of the net will include the restoration of Israel and the tribulation, which is referred to in Revelation as "the harvesting of the earth" (Revelation 14:14-20). Jesus uses various examples to show how people will be divided up at the end of time. In Matthew 25:31, it's sheep and goats that are separated.

When Jesus finished teaching the seven kingdom parables he asked his disciples:

> "Have you understood all these things?" Matthew 13:51

They said they did, and Jesus then told them that with this new information, they could explain both the previous revelation given to Israel and the new revelation given to the church. They could teach about how Israel has been set aside for a time while the new dispensation of the church age takes place. These seven kingdom parables can be used as a foundation for their teaching.

> "He said to them, 'Therefore every teacher of the law who has been instructed about the kingdom of heaven is like the owner of a house who brings out of his storeroom new treasures as well as old.'" Matthew 13:52

Jesus had revealed the plan for mankind to his disciples. He would finish his work as the suffering servant, and then the new dispensation would begin with this small group of men taking the seed of the word to all Gentile nations. The result would be an enormous amount of followers before Jesus returns to dig Israel out of the ground for the last days.

Chapter 20: "I Will Build My Church"

AFTER JESUS WAS rejected by the Jewish leadership in Matthew twelve, he moved back to his hometown (Matthew 13:53). There "they took offense to him" (Matthew 13:57), and Jesus made the comment, "only in his hometown and in his own house is a prophet without honor" (Matthew 13:57). This comment sets the stage for one of the disciples most important lessons. Jesus is not going to be accepted by his own nation.

When John the Baptist is beheaded (Matthew 14:1-12), Jesus withdraws from the crowd to spend time alone praying. What a temptation it must have been for Jesus to react aggressively to the decapitation of his cousin. We often see Jesus praying, sometimes all night long, when he's faced with a human desire or temptation that goes against God's plan for his life. For example:

1) Jesus fasted and prayed for forty days so he could overcome temptation. "Jesus, full of the Holy Spirit, returned from the Jordan and was led by the Spirit in the desert, where for forty days he was tempted by the devil" (Luke 4:1, 2).

2) In Capernaum, the people desperately wanted Jesus to stay with them, but, after a long night of prayer, Jesus told them, "I must preach the good news of the kingdom of God to the other towns also, because that is why I was sent" (Luke 4:43).

3) In the Garden of Gethsemane, Jesus prayed, "Father, if you are willing take this cup from me; yet not my will, but yours be done." After much anguish in prayer, Jesus "rose and went back" to face the mob that had come to arrest him and take him to his crucifixion (Luke 22:39-47).

In Matthew 14:13, Jesus "withdrew by boat privately to a solitary place." The crowds followed him however, and Jesus healed their sick and multiplied their bread. The multiplying of the bread was a sign to the crowd of Jews (John 6:14), revealing that Jesus was the bread of life (John 6:35). Sadly, the crowd did not want spiritual food, and by the time Jesus had finished explaining what it meant to the crowd, there was a lot of grumbling and arguing over his teaching (John 6:41).

> "From this time, many of his disciples turned back and no longer followed him." John 6:66

The masses that had followed Jesus into his solitary place for healing and food eventually rejected him when he started talking about their spiritual problems and sin. They wanted to make him king (John 6:15) because he could heal the sick and multiply their food (a sort of instant healthcare and welfare program). Meanwhile, they had no interest in confronting their own spiritual problems.

In Matthew 15:1, 2, some Pharisees challenged Jesus about his disciples' failure to wash their hands properly (according to the traditions of the elders of Israel). Jesus explains to the Jewish leaders that they have confused God's revealed truth with their own religious traditions. He then warns his disciples not to be misled by these blind guides (Matthew 15:14).

Matthew watches as the Jewish leaders reject Jesus even after he heals a blind and mute man. He hears the Jewish leaders attack Jesus for not following religious regulations. He watches a crowd of more than 5,000 people eat the bread that Jesus had multiplied; then he watched the very same crowd reject Jesus the next morning. He saw that the people from Jesus' hometown wanted nothing to do with him because, just as Jesus had warned, "Only in his hometown is a prophet without honor."

After Israel rejected Jesus, he took time to establish some foundational principles for his Jewish disciples. These principals would prepare them for the new spiritual age that would temporarily replace the age of Israel.

> "Leaving that place, Jesus withdrew to the region of Tyre and Sidon. A Canaanite woman from that vicinity came to him, crying out, 'Lord, Son of David, have mercy on me! My daughter is suffering terribly from demon-possession.'" Matthew 15:21-22

The N.I.V. leaves out a word in this verse that still remains in the Greek. It is the word "idou," and it's used to stress the amazing things Matthew saw and recorded. The word is often translated "behold!" J. B. Rotherham, a brilliant English Bible translator from the 1800s, translates the verse like this:

> "And going forth from thence Jesus retired into the parts of Tyre and Zidon. And lo! A Canaanite woman from those bounds coming forth..."

Matthew uses the modern names of Tyre and Sidon, but refers to the woman he meets by her ancient ancestry. She is, of all people, a Canaanite! Things had indeed come full circle. Israel, the chosen people of God, had driven out the Canaanites, but they had also rejected their Messiah. Now a Canaanite woman believed in the rejected Messiah. The Canaanite woman calls out, "Lord, Son of David, have mercy on me!" Her choice of words indicates that she understands Jesus is the promised one from the royal lineage of David.

The verse continues with Jesus' response to the woman:

> "Jesus did not answer a word. So his disciples came to him and urged him, 'Send her away, for she keeps crying out after us.' He answered, 'I was sent only to the lost sheep of Israel.' The woman came and knelt before him. 'Lord, help me!' she said. He replied, 'It is not right to take the children's bread and toss it to their dogs.' 'Yes, Lord,' she said, 'but even the dogs eat the crumbs that fall from their masters' table.' Then Jesus answered, 'Woman, you have great faith! Your request is granted.' And her daughter was healed from that very hour."

At first, Jesus ignored the woman while his disciples listened to her cry out for help. The woman's cries didn't solicit pity from the Jewish disciples, instead her cries annoyed them. When her hysteria finally became too much, the disciples urged Jesus to send her away. But instead of asking her to leave, Jesus says, "I was sent only to the lost sheep of Israel." He tells her this because it's true. Why was Jesus only sent to Israel? Because God's plan was for Israel to believe in Christ and then take his message to the entire world, thus fulfilling God's purpose in choosing Abraham to start a nation that "all peoples on earth will be blessed through" (Genesis 12:3).

When the woman again asks for help, Jesus continues to stress his point: salvation must first come to Israel so that Israel can lead other nations to God. He says, "It is not right to take the children's bread and toss it to their dogs." His comment shows the Jewish attitude toward the Gentile nations at the time. The Jews considered themselves superior to Gentile "dogs" who lived in sin and darkness. As Jesus said this, the disciples were probably nodding their heads, saying "amen," glad to see he put the Gentile woman in her place. In reality, Jesus was merely setting the stage to teach them something.

The "children" rejecting their "bread" refers to the Israelites rejecting Jesus, the bread of life. The woman explains she is more than willing to be "the dog" just as long as she and her daughter get some of the crumbs of bread that have fallen on the floor. She knows who Jesus is and she wants what he has to offer.

With the disciples still observing, Jesus says, "Woman, you have great faith! Your request is granted." By saying this, Jesus is showing the disciples that people in Gentile lands can also be part of this new group of believers. There are, in fact, many Gentiles eager to hear the good news.

Next Jesus goes from Tyre through Sidon down to the Sea of Galilee and into the region of the Decapolis (Mark 7:31). When passing through these Gentile areas, he draws more crowds of Gentile followers. For three days in Decapolis people brought their lame, blind, crippled, and mute for Jesus to heal. Jesus spoke to his disciples concerning the Gentile crowd:

> "I have compassion for these people; they have already been with me three days and have nothing to eat. I do not want to send them away hungry, or they may collapse on the way." Matthew 15:32

Jesus took seven loaves of bread and a few fish and performed a miracle by feeding the entire Gentile crowd. Again the disciples have an opportunity to watch Jesus ministering to Gentiles like he had to Jews. Prior to going into Phoenicia, Jesus had multiplied bread for a Jewish crowd of 5,000; now he does the same thing a few days later for a Gentile crowd of 4,000.

Jesus didn't have any conflict with Jewish leaders in these Gentile lands because Jews never mingled among "unclean dogs." But when Jesus sailed to Magadan

(Matthew 15:39) to return to the Israelites, he was immediately attacked by Pharisees and Sadducees who'd been awaiting his arrival (Matthew 16:1-12). And when Jesus returned to Galilee, the Pharisees demanded he give them a miraculous sign from heaven to prove he was the Messiah. This was Jesus' response to their request:

> "Jesus sighed deeply and said, 'Why does this generation ask for a miraculous sign? I tell you the truth, <u>no sign will be given to it.</u>' Then Jesus left them, got back into the boat and crossed to the other side."

Jesus took his disciples into Gentile territory one final time in the fall of 29 AD, just six months before his crucifixion.

Jesus had been rejected in Nazareth. About that time, he heard about John the Baptist's death, and he left for a solitary place on the shore of Galilee. After feeding 5,000 Jews, the disciples crossed the sea to Capernaum, during which time they saw Jesus walk on water. In the morning, the crowds who had eaten the multiplied bread found Jesus in Capernaum and rejected him as the bread of life. It was here also that the Pharisees and teachers criticized Jesus for not following their man-made religion. At this point, Jesus left Israelite territory and went into the Gentile land of the Phoenicians. There he met a woman who knew him as "Lord" and called him the "Son of David." Next, Jesus returned to Israel with a crowd of 4,000 Gentiles—the same crowd that would see him multiply the bread the second time. Jesus took the disciples away from Israel again for a lesson at "the Gates of Hades." All of this was done to prepare the disciples for the work of the church.

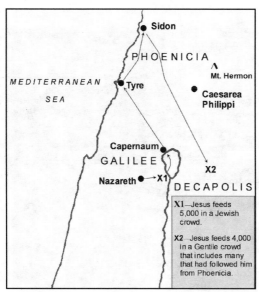

The Gates of Hades

Jesus left Israel and traveled twenty-five miles north of the Sea of Galilee into the area of Caesarea Philippi at the base of Mt. Hermon. A massive rock formation stood at the base of Mt. Hermon, and during that time (first century AD), a powerful spring of water gushed from the face of the rock, forming a stream that ran into the Sea of Galilee. This rock formation can be found in the Golan Heights today.

This large rock formation at Caesarea Philippi served as a temple to Pagan gods. Five niches, which can still be seen today in the rock formation, held the images of Pagan gods. Water flowed from the cave located to the left of these niches which is seen at the far left of this photo. This cave was thought to be a gate to Hades.

To the right of the cave called the Gates of Hades are five niches where idols sat. Three of the niches have Greek inscriptions mentioning Pan, Echo, Diopan, and Galerius. In this photo Galyn sits in one of the five niches with an inscription near it referring to Faleius, a priest of Pan. About three and a half feet above his head is one of the Greek inscriptions.

The original name for Caesarea Philippi was Panias because it was the birth place of the Greek god Pan. The modern name for the ancient city of Panias is Banias, which is just an Arabic corruption of the original name. Due to shifting plates, the flow of water from the rock formation has been greatly reduced over time. Today the water does little more than seep from the rocks.

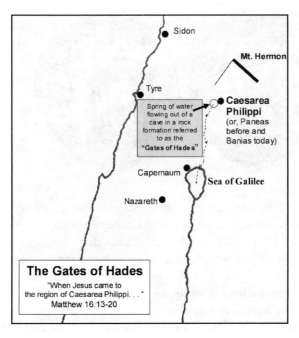

In Old Testament times, this rock formation was a place of Baal worship (Joshua 11:17; Judges 3:3). In 200 BC, it became a pagan shrine to honor Pan. Pan was portrayed as a half-man, half-god (a faun-like creature) who played a flute. In 20 BC, the territory was annexed to the kingdom of Herod the Great. This annexation was decided by Caesar Augustus. In turn, Herod built a temple on the sight and dedicated it to Caesar Augustus. So, in addition to the statues of Greek gods, the landscape was overflowing with white marble images that testified to the glory and deity of Caesar.

The pagan world believed the water gushing from this cave came directly from the abyss and was, therefore, the official doorway to the underworld. Thus, the cave in the rock formation became known as "the Gates of Hades." It was here that Gentiles met to worship the gods of the underworld and offer up sacrifices to Pan. Inscriptions were carved into the rock formation, and can still be seen today. They are Greek inscriptions recognizing the gods and the patrons who came there to worship and bring monetary offerings to them. There are five niches cut in the rock to the right of the cave. Statues and idols once sat in the niches of the cave.

Greek inscriptions in the rock by the niches mention Pan, Echo and a priest named Galerius. Below the niche closest to the cave an inscription says "to Pan and the Hymphs." Ancient coins from Caesarea also show which idols sat where. It appears a statue of Pan's consort, a nymph named Echo, sat in one niche, while Hermes, Pan's father, sat in another. Other gods were placed in various spots along the face

of the rock formation.

When Jesus and the disciples arrived in Caesarea Philippi, they were surrounded by idols and shrines to the cult of Caesar, along with reminders of the many immoral worship practices that had taken place there. It was a truly corrupt and wicked place, but it was to be the place where the disciples would go through a graduation ceremony of sorts. Jesus had one lesson left to teach them before they were left on their own in this new age of the church.

The disciples had learned by experience to take every word Jesus said as a word of power and prophecy. They knew by now that Jesus' words always produced results. Whether he spoke to the wind, the demons, the lame, or the blind, his word was the key. Now Jesus was facing the greatest pagan religious shrine in the world as he spoke to his disciples. The account of the conversation between Jesus and his disciples at the Gates of Hades (the great rock shrine) is recorded by Matthew, Mark, and Luke.

> "When Jesus came to the region of Caesarea Philippi, he asked his disciples, 'Who do people say the Son of Man is?' They replied, 'Some say John the Baptist; others say Elijah; and still others, Jeremiah or one of the prophets.' 'But what about you?' he asked. 'Who do you say I am?' Simon Peter answered, 'You are the Christ, the Son of the living God.' Matthew 16:13-16

By responding, "you are the Son of the living God" Peter was challenging all the gods standing in the niches of the rocks around them.

> "Jesus replied, 'Blessed are you, Simon son of Jonah, for this was not revealed to you by man, but by my Father in heaven. And I tell you that

you are Peter, and <u>on this rock I will build my church, and the Gates of</u>
<u>Hades will not overcome it</u>. I will give you the keys of the kingdom of
heaven; whatever you bind on earth will be bound in heaven, and whatever
you loose on earth will be loosed in heaven.'

Then he warned his disciples not to tell anyone that he was the Christ."
Matthew 16:17-20

In these verses, Jesus refers to Simon as Peter. The Greek word for Peter is
"petros" and is masculine in word form. The word is found 154 times in the Greek
New Testament, and, in all but one case, refers to Peter. In the Greek translation
of the Old Testament (Septuagint or LXX) the word is used twice and both times
it is referring to a stone. Greek dictionaries define "petros" as "a detached stone or
boulder," or "a stone that might be thrown or easily moved."

When Jesus says "on this rock I will build my church" he uses the word "petra"
meaning rock. This is the feminine form of the word "petros" but is used much
different in Greek writing. While other Greek writers used the masculine form
to denote a stone that is easily moved, this form of the word was used in secular
Greek to denote a large and solid rock, not easily moved.

In Exodus 17:6 in the Septuagint (LXX), the feminine word "petra" translates
as "cliff." In the New Testament, "petra" is used twice in the parable of the man who
built his house on a huge rock formation (Matthew 7:24, 25). Josephus uses the
word to describe the massive fitted stone blocks in the towers of Jerusalem. He
says they are "huge rocks suited for the foundation of buildings" as contrasted with
"ordinary rocks (petros) that men carry around."

Peter is called a "stone or a rock" and is told "on *this* rock formation or cliff" (the
one they're standing in front of), I will build my church. Jesus had traveled twenty-
five miles in order to show his disciples God's plan for the church. The church
would spread to Gentile lands and take over pagan temples, philosophies, and
cultures. It would eclipse pagan societies. And Jesus promised there was absolutely
nothing the Gates of Hades could do to stop it.

The church wasn't going to be a temple like the one in Jerusalem made of gold
and stone. The building materials for the church would instead consist of stones
like Peter—people who believed Jesus was the Christ. Peter writes:

"As you come to him, the living Stone – rejected by men but chosen by
God and precious to him – <u>you also, like living stones, are being built into</u>
<u>a spiritual house</u>." I Peter 2:4-9

Paul writes to the Gentiles in the Greek city of Ephesus:

"Consequently, you are no longer foreigners and aliens, but fellow
citizens with God's people and members of God's household, <u>built on</u>
<u>the foundation of the apostles and</u> <u>prophets, with Christ Jesus himself as</u>

the chief cornerstone. In him the whole building is joined together and rises to become a holy temple in the Lord. And in him you too are being built together to become a dwelling in which God lives by his Spirit." Ephesians 2:19

The church began in the pagan Roman world where Caesar was worshipped. But after the Roman Emperor himself converted, Caesar worship was abolished. Pagan temples turned into churches. Barbaric tribes consumed with darkness and superstitions found Christ. Some of those tribes turned into great civilizations over the next 2,000 years.

Jesus told the church that there was not a demon, philosophy, or society they could not overcome. If the truth about Jesus and his word were proclaimed, the church would overtake the Gates of Hades themselves. Just as ancient cities were destroyed by enemy forces and then resettled by the conquerors, so would pagan societies be conquered, not with the sword, but with the truth about Jesus Christ.

Two thousand years ago, my own ancestors (Germans, Scotch-Irish, French, Creek Indian) were, like yours, entrenched in pagan cultures with heathen philosophies. Although Christianity has wrongfully used force at certain times in history to overcome the pagan world, physical force was never what God intended for the church to use. God knew that the simple message of the gospel alone has the power to truly change men of every culture, tribe, and tongue.

But "Christianity" was never supposed to become a culture in itself. There is not a "Christian way of dressing" or a "Christian style of music." This idea may be frustrating to some Christians who've never fully understood their faith.

The gospel was never intended to become a culture of its own.

These days it seems new believers are immediately ushered into the bubble that is American Christian culture. Instead of learning about scripture and growing in righteousness, they learn about the latest pop Christian fad and are led away from denominational taboos. We must remember that God didn't want the gospel to become a culture—he wanted it to penetrate culture.

This confusion has been around since the beginning of the church, and it is the focal point of the first church council in Jerusalem (Acts 15) as well as the book of Galatians. Some Jewish Christians believed that pagans needed to both believe in Christ *and* convert to Judaism. The apostle Paul begged them to stop

this teaching. Paul understood that the gospel could be advanced in the pagan world without mixing it with Jewish culture. (Remember Paul was still overcoming his old lifestyle as a legalistic Pharisee.) Paul knew that a Greek could remain Greek and still be a Christian. An Ethiopian could remain Ethiopian and still be a Christian.

Jesus said, "Upon this rock of pagan worship I will build my church and the Gates of Hades will not stop it!" Sure enough, the dark philosophies of the heathen world and the idols once worshipped at pagan shrines began slowly disappearing. Societies were transformed as nations and tribes of all kinds began to follow God.

> "After this I looked and there <u>before me was a great multitude that no one could count, from every nation, tribe, people and language, standing before the throne and in front of the Lamb</u>. They were wearing white robes and were holding palm branches in their hands, and they cried out in a loud voice: 'Salvation belongs to our God, who sits on the throne, and to the Lamb.'" Revelation 7:9, 10

Chapter 21: A Multiplication Analogy

THERE'S A COP out many people take that bothers me. Whenever someone poses a question about the Bible or some theological issue, many people become uncomfortable and are quick to give the "right" answer." But the difference between knowing the right answer and understanding why that answer is right is huge.

The answers to math problems can be easily memorized (e.g. 7 x 7 = 49). In elementary school, my teacher told me to memorize my "times tables" so I could regurgitate the right answers on speed drills and math tests. However, if I had simply memorized the answers without truly understanding the concept of multiplication, I would have failed. Why? Because if I memorize 7 x 7 = 49 but the teacher asks me for the answer to 7 x 8, I won't be able to figure it out. I haven't really learned multiplication; I just know how to spit out a few right answers here and there. Only someone who understands how he got the answer to 7 x 7 will be able to figure out 7 x 8 on his own.

So it is with scripture. We should *never* simply accept an answer we're given without fully understanding it. But studying the Bible in order to understand is not a skill for the faint of heart. In fact, many Sunday school coffee drinkers don't think it's necessary at all. They ask, "Why can't you be satisfied with 7 x 7 = 49? Why do you question it? Why can't you just believe it? Can't you just take it on faith?" Yet we *must* continue to question because, even though we may already know the right answer, we will never have a deep understanding of the Christian faith if we stop questioning.

It takes time and discipline to go from knowing an answer to understanding it.

People who seek deeper understanding in church are often labeled "backsliders" by those who love to spout the "right" answers. Yet doubters and skeptics are usually the only people who have a true desire to achieve something most people of faith never achieve—a real understanding of what it's all about. It takes time and discipline to go from a basic knowledge of the Bible to a deep comprehension of it. Growing in faith is a much longer, more difficult, and often very frustrating process for those who take this longer route. But, in the end, it's the only route that leads to freedom.

Saying, "I don't understand" even in the midst of people who are perfectly

content to "know the right answer" can be scary. You have to stop worrying about what others think of you. You have to remember that seeking understanding with humility is the only way to honor the truth.

Chapter 22: Seven Letters to the Seven Churches

JESUS SPOKE TO his disciple John from the cross. He told John that he was now responsible for taking care of Jesus' mother Mary who would have been around 46-years-old at the time Christ died. In the book of John we learn that from that time on John took Mary into his home as Christ had asked (John 18:27). They lived together in Jerusalem during the early days of the church age. In 49 AD, Paul writes that, along with Peter and Jesus' brother James, John was "a pillar" in the church in Jerusalem (Galatians 2:9). John and Mary lived in Jerusalem up until the Roman armies destroyed the city just as Jesus had predicted. Jesus said:

> "When you see Jerusalem being surrounded by armies, you will know that its desolation is near. Then let those who are in Judea flee to the mountains, let those in the city get out, and let those in the country not enter the city. For this is the time of punishment infulfillment of all that has been written." Luke 21:20-22

When the Roman armies began to move into the land in 66 AD, John fled Jerusalem. A Jewish revolt broke out in Caesarea after the Gentiles desecrated a local synagogue, but John did not join this revolt. Instead he heeded the words of Jesus, "Let those in the city get out." John moved to Ephesus—a place he would call home for the next thirty years.

Ephesus would become the center of Christian activity for the next generation, (after Jerusalem, the birthplace of Christianity, fell). It was during this second generation of the church age that John's leadership and influence played an important role. His arrival in Ephesus filled a great gap since Peter had been martyred in 65 AD and Paul in the spring of 68 AD.

It was while he was in Ephesus that John wrote The Gospel of John (85 AD), as well as I, II, and III John (85-93 AD) and Revelation (95 AD). Many key leaders in the third generation of the church age would be trained by John. Those leaders included Ignatius, the pastor in Antioch who was thrown to wild beasts in the Roman coliseum in 117 AD, and Polycarp, the pastor in Smyrna who was burnt at the stake in 155 AD.

During John's later years in Ephesus, the Emperor Domitian took power (81-96 AD) and ushered in the second wave of severe Christian persecution. Domitian placed statues of himself in the temples and asked to be addressed "Our Lord and God." Anyone who refused to worship him was banished on grounds of treason. With Domitian practicing self-deification, we can only imagine how John, one of the "sons of thunder," got himself in trouble with the Emperor. John would not worship Domitian and was banished to the isle of Patmos "because of the word of God and the testimony of Jesus" (Revelation 1:9). The "word of God and testimony of Jesus" were the two very things that Jesus emphasized during his final months on earth. He said the Kingdom of Heaven would advance by sowing the seed of the word, and the church would only be established by men who believed Jesus was the Messiah.

On September 18, 96 AD, Domitian was assassinated by his political enemies in the senate. They stabbed him eight times as he sat at his desk signing decrees. Nerva, a member of the Italian nobility, had already been approached by the senate and asked if he would replace Domitian after the assassination. Historical records show that after Nerva came to power, he decided to release everyone who'd been banished or imprisoned for treason under the reign of Domitian. He even restored all previously confiscated property. So the apostle John was released from Patmos sometime after September 18, 96 AD, and he returned to Ephesus where he continued for two more years as the head of the Asian churches.

While John was on the isle of Patmos, Jesus appeared to him saying:

> "Write on a scroll what you see and send it to the seven churches:
> to <u>Ephesus, Smyrna, Pergamum, Thyatira, Sardis, Philadelphia and
> Laodicea</u>." Revelation 1:11

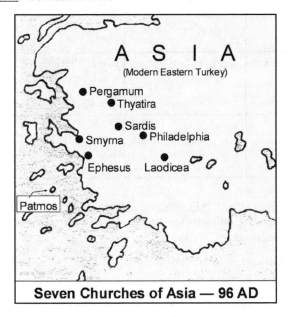

Seven Churches of Asia — 96 AD

The seven churches in Asia have interesting names with distinct Greek meanings:

	Name of City	Meaning of Name	Origin of Meaning	Rev.
1	**Ephesus** (30-98 AD)	"desirable"[1] "darling" "maiden of choice" "first"	**Greek** "Ephesos"	2:1

	Name of City	Meaning of Name	Origin of Meaning	Rev.
2	**Smyrna** *(98-313)*	"myrrh"[2] "bitter" "bitter affliction"	*Greek* "Smurna" "muron" – "myrrh" from Hebrew "mor" which means bitter from the taste of perfume produced by crushing the resin of a tree, used at burials[13]	2:8
3	**Pergamum** *(313-590)*	"thoroughly married"[4] "mixed marriage" "mountain"[3] "high tower"	*Greek* "Pergamos" "per" – a particle significant of abundance, thoroughness, emphasis, much "gamos" – marriage, wedding[14] "purgos" – a tower or castle[12]	2:12
4	**Thyatira** *(590-1517)*	"continual sacrifice"[4, 18]	"a perfume; sacrifice of labor"[16] " -teira" – goes on continually[18] *Greek* "thuateira" "thuo" – sacrifice[17] "odor of affliction"[19]	2:18
5	**Sardis** *(1517-1730)*	"those escaping"[4] "remnant"[18] "escaping one"[5] "come out"[5]	*Greek* "Sardeis"	3:1
6	**Philadelphia** *(1730-1900)*	"brotherly love"[5]	*Greek* "Philadelphia" "phileo" – tender affection[6] an unselfish love, ready to serve[7] adelphos – brother[8]	3:7
7	**Laodicea** *(1900-Rapture)*	"people ruling"[4]	*Greek* "Laodikia" "laos" – people[11] "dike" – judgment, decision; the execution of a sentence[9]	3:14

There were many churches in Asia that John could have written to—Colosse, Troas, Miletus, etc. But John was specifically told to address the seven churches outlined above. Jesus said:

"Write, therefore, what you have seen, what is now, and what will take place later." Revelation 1:19

The churches that Jesus chose and the order in which he chose to address them reveals much information both about the churches themselves and about the periods of church history each one represents.

When Jesus appeared to John he was standing among seven golden lampstands, holding seven stars in his right hand. The meaning of the lampstands and the stars was not clear to John at first. Scripture called it a "mystery." The Greek word for mystery is "musterion." This word is used several times in the New Testament to refer to information that is unknown and not to be revealed to mankind until the proper time. It was like secret information known only to those initiated into a fraternity. Jesus explained that he was now going to reveal to John the "mystery" of the seven churches. He said:

> "The mystery of the seven stars that you saw in my right hand and of the seven golden lampstands is this: The seven stars are the angels of the seven churches, and the seven lampstands are the seven churches." Revelation 1:20

The seven churches that Jesus is going to address are local churches that John oversaw and often ministered in. This is why Jesus tells John to "write...what is now." The "mystery" part regarding the churches is what Jesus refers to when he says "write...what will take place *later*" (Revelation 1:19).

The order of the churches explains the flow of church history. The churches are listed geographically in a clockwise circle beginning with Ephesus and ending with Laodicea. The messages to these Asian churches are extremely important to us today. Although each of the seven letters should be studied and taught in their historical settings with their exegetical meanings, they should also be deconstructed to show the flow of church history over the last 2000 years.

Ephesus (Revelation 2:1-7)

The Ephesian church correlates to the church age as the period of time from the founding of the church until the apostle John died. During that time, people heard tremendous Bible teaching and saw great miracles. Yet this group is told they have "left their first love." This is not a reference to God being their first love. It's a reference to how they've lost their love for the people they were supposed to be reaching. They were still faithful, busy, committed Christians, but they had lost sight of their purpose—to reach *all* nations with the knowledge of Jesus Christ.

This group is also warned about the Nicolaitans. The word "nicolaitans" comes from a compound Greek word that includes "niko," meaning "conqueror," and "laos," meaning "people." Nicolaitans means "conquer the people." Because the Ephesians had "forsaken their first love," they were going to soon be "conquered" in the form of a church hierarchy.

The Nicolaitans were an emerging group of men who called themselves "clergy." They were attempting to run the church and take the power away from the people they called "laity." These were the savage wolves that Paul had warned the Ephesians about in Acts 20:27-31:

> "For I have not hesitated to proclaim to you the whole will of God. Keep watch over yourselves and all the flock of which the Holy Spirit has made you overseers. Be shepherds of the church of God, which he bought with his own blood. I know that after I leave, savage wolves will come in among you and will not spare the flock. Even from your own number men will arise and distort the truth in order to draw away disciples after them. So

be on your guard!"

We know the wolves here refer to the Nicolaitans because John also warned about the same "wolves" Paul is describing. These wolves do not eat people; just as the Nicolaitans did not kill people. Instead they created followers and reduced people to cowering before them, thus conquering the flock.

Why would the Nicolatians or the "savage wolves" want to "draw away people as disciples after themselves?" Because they wanted the power that leadership imparts, as well as the money that accompanies it. After Paul warns the Ephesian leadership of the coming wolves, Paul reminds them what true leadership is:

> "<u>I have not coveted anyone's sliver or gold or clothing</u>. You yourselves know that these hands of mine have supplied my own needs and the needs of my companions. In everything I did, I showed you that by this kind of hard work we must help the weak, remembering the words the Lord Jesus himself said: 'It is more blessed to give than to receive.'" Acts 20:33-35

It may be a surprise to modern readers to see that the well-known verse "it is more blessed to give than to receive" is actually referring to church leadership and how they should serve people rather than take their money. Peter tells the church leaders to:

> "Be shepherds of God's flock that is under your care, serving as overseers – not because you must, but because you are willing, as God wants you to be; <u>not greedy for money</u>, but eager to serve." I Peter 5:2, 3

The power of the church should be found in the Spirit of God and the word. Great leaders in the church age are not supposed to come from seminaries. They are supposed to be average men and women who received the truth of God's word and were empowered by the Holy Spirit. Peter and Paul had very different training, yet the same spirit molded both a fisherman and a rabbi into useful tools for God's kingdom.

Smyrna (Revelation 2:8-11)

The word "Smyrna" is derived from the herb myrrh that was crushed to release a sweet aroma. Myrrh was used for embalming the dead at burials, and it was associated with bitterness. The age of Smyrna covered the period of time when Christianity was not recognized as a legal religion.

For much of first century, Christianity was viewed by the Romans as nothing more than a strange Jewish sect. But, after the fall of Jerusalem, Christianity could no longer hide under the cover of Judiasm. Jesus tells the age of Smyrna that they will suffer "afflictions" which in the Greek means "serious trouble" or "the burden that crushes." Believers are told they will face "poverty" which is the Greek word "ptocheia." This word means "desperate poverty and destitution." Another Greek word for poverty is "penichros" which means poor in the sense of not having many material things. The noun form of this second word is used to describe a laborer who works hard for his daily bread. The Christians of the Smyrna period of church history were not simply blue collar folks working hard for what they had. They faced the most serious form of poverty in the physical realm.

They are told the following things:

1) Know that suffering is coming
2) Do not fear the suffering
3) Know that the suffering will end
4) Realize that the suffering may cause death
5) Know that you will be rewarded

This period of time lasted from 100 to 313 AD and involved several major persecutions. Well-known martyrs from this time include Polycarp, Ignatius, Iraneus, Perpetura, and Leonides. Persecution was a regular part of the Christian experience during these years.

Pergamum (Revelation 2:12-17)

In 312, Constantine, a Roman general who had been declared emperor, crossed the Alps and conquered Northern Italy before moving into Rome. In 313, Constantine issued the Edict of Milan which ended all government-sanctioned persecution of Christians. It seemed like a glorious day for the church. Jesus had stood with his small group of disciples 282 years earlier at a pagan shrine outside Israel and said, "On this rock I will build my church." Now the Roman emperor not only recognizing Christianity but was a proclaimed Christ-follower himself. The age of Smyrna had ended and the age of Pergamum had begun.

The name Pergamum comes from two Greek words:

1) "per" – a particle indicating abundance, thoroughness, much, or very
2) "gamos" – marriage or wedding

Therefore, the name Pergamum means "thoroughly married" or "very married," and it refers to the complete mixing of two identities. This was the age when the church was completely mixed into the pagan system. Constantine may have confessed Christ and given the church many new freedoms, but he was still far from understanding the faith. Like everyone else in his culture, Constantine lived a life steeped in pagan tradition.

The church had moved into the Roman Empire, Satan's headquarters on earth. As a result, Christians began letting some pagan traditions slip into the church. Jesus tells this church:

> "I know where you live – where Satan has his throne...Nevertheless, I have a few things against you: <u>You have people there who hold to the</u>

teaching of Balaam who taught Balak to entice the Israelites to sin by eating food sacrificed to idols and by committing sexual immorality. Likewise you also have those who hold to the teachings of the Nicolaitans. Repent therefore!" Revelation 2:12-16

God likens this time to when the Israelites in the wilderness learned the ways of the Moabites from Balaam and Balak. Too many Christian practices and pagan traditions were being mixed together, and a lot of the customs we practice today come directly from this time period in church history. For example:

+ Constantine made Sunday a weekly holiday to honor the Sun. He then turned Sundays into a weekly church holiday to honor the Sabbath. The Latin Bible translator Jerome wrote in 420, "If it is called the day of the sun by the pagans, we willingly accept this name, for on this day the Light of the world arose, on this day the Sun of Justice shone forth.

+ Constantine gave many pagan shrines and public buildings (called basilicas) to Christians for their church services. Churches rarely owned buildings before he did this.

+ The Nicolaitans (the clergy or priesthood of the church) gained more strength and finally "conquered" the people by taking over church leadership. The new "clergy" were given costumes similar to those worn by pagan priests. They were also given seats in the front of the church buildings. They sat in lavish chairs next to marble altars. The non-clergy were required to bow and bring their offerings before the clergy.

+ The pagan festival dates for the winter solstice (December 21-25) were converted into a celebration of Christ's birthday.

+ Other Pagan festivals, such as the spring equinox honoring the Babylonian goddess Astarte or the Assyrian goddess Ishtar, were converted into the church calendar as Easter.

+ The ancient Roman fertility celebration commemorated on February 15 was "Christianized" by Pope Gelasius I around 496 and deemed St. Valentine's day. (It was to be celebrated one day earlier on February 14.)

+ All Saint's Day on November 1 was created by the church to counter the pagan's Halloween, celebrated one day before.

+ Roman gods took the names of Christian saints.

+ People started to discount former end-times teaching that said Christ would return to deliver Israel and establish his kingdom. Instead they started believing that the church had replaced Israel completely and would eventually produce the Kingdom of God on earth.

Jesus' prophecy that the church would be built on pagan societies (Matthew 16:18) indicated that the church would be "Christianizing" heathen practices. The negative outcome of this, however, was that many pagan practices were incorporated into the church.

The Pergamum church age began in 313 and continued until the arrival of the next age around 590 AD.

Thyatira (Revelation 2:18-29)

The name "Thyatira" comes from the Greek word "thuo" which means "sacrifice." Scholars suggest the full meaning of the name "Thyatira" is "continual sacrifice" and refers to a person who never grows weary of bringing sacrificial offerings.

Jesus first commends this church in Asia for their:

- Love   - Service
- Faith   - Perseverance

He also commends them, "For doing more than [they] did at first" (Revelation 2:19).

It was during this time period that the church put forth intense evangelism efforts. Christians traveled far from home to teach the barbaric Celts, the Teutons (a Germanic tribe), and the Slavic peoples (Russia and Poland). Believers learned the languages of these tribes and created written alphabets so they could translate Christian literature. They also taught more primitive tribes about agriculture and helped them set up a justice system.

Gregory became pope in 590, and, in 596, he commissioned more than thirty abbots and monks to convert the Anglo-Saxon people. Before long, much of England, Ireland, and Scotland had been converted to Christianity.

In 716, Boniface, a Saxon believer from England, left his home to start teaching the gospel in Germany. Many believers followed him there to help out. Boniface was later killed by a group of German pagans in 755, but the work he'd already done had laid an incredible foundation of faith for the Germans.

In 863, a man named Cyril went to Russia to translate scriptures and church liturgy for the people. Cyril invented a new alphabet for the Russians using Greek letters. (This system was the precursor for today's Russian alphabet.) Within one hundred years, Vladimir, the pagan prince of Russia, converted to Christianity, and the people of Russia destroyed their idols and began caring for the poor and building Christian schools.

After Jesus praises Thyratira for their evangelism efforts, he goes on to say:

> "Nevertheless, I have this against you: You tolerate that woman Jezebel who calls herself a prophetess. By her teaching she misleads my servants into sexual immorality and the eating of food sacrificed to idols...Now I say to the rest of you in Thyatira, to you who do not hold to her teaching

and have not learned Satan's so-called deep secrets, (I will not impose any other burden on you); only hold on to what you have until I come." Revelation 2:20-25

Thyatira is rebuked because:

- They tolerate a Jezebel-like woman who is really an imposter
- This woman brings false teaching that is misleading God's servants
- There is sexual immorality among them
- They are eating food sacrificed to idols
- There are idols around them
- There are newly-revealed "deep secrets" that the church seems eager to learn, (Jesus is crediting these secrets to Satan)

Jesus has said that any additional teaching or doctrine aside from what has already been revealed in the Bible is assuredly from Satan. The church has been told to simply hold onto the revelation they've been given until Christ returns.

During this same age, beginning during the time of Pope Gregory I in 590, the church tried to reinvent itself. Here are some things that occurred around this time:

- Gregory established "mass" for the dead so those suffering in the afterlife could have their pain eased.
- Gregory organized a "church army."
- Transubstantiation was introduced in 831 and fully established by 1215.
- Images and pictures were put up in churches to be honored.
- The pope became the Vice Regent of God in 1073 and began to dominate civil government.
- The clergy were forbidden to marry in 1050.
- Annual confessions to a priest were required beginning in 1215.
- "Dictatus Papae" (papal dictation) was released and claimed that the pope had universal power over all bishops and princes. They even had to physically kiss the pope's feet when they came into his presence.
- The church claimed it had never made errors with regards to decrees made by the pope.
- Newly created "holy days" were instituted in 1140, including Lent and Ash Wednesday, which required fasting from meat.
- The seven sacraments of the church were established: baptism at birth, confirmation, penance, communion, marriage, ordination, and last rites.
- False beliefs about the mission of the church caused the crusades to be launched in 1095.
- The "laity" were forbidden to read or even own a Bible.

- The doctrine of purgatory was introduced.
- The immaculate conception of Mary was declared, and Mary was proclaimed the Mother of the Church.
- The clergy began selling indulgences to the laity, offering forgiveness of any sins they'd committed after baptism.

It was during this time that the decrees of the pope and the teachings of the church began to be exalted above and beyond the word of God.

The name Thyatira means "perpetual sacrifice." In 1545, the Council of Trent declared that the bread and wine of communion underwent a physical change to become the literal blood and body of Christ (transubstantiation). This practice was canonized.

The Bible teaches that Jesus died as a sacrifice for the sins of mankind *once*. Scripture tells us this sacrifice should be remembered, not repeated. But the repeated or "perpetual" sacrifice was written into church law at the Council of Trent:

> Canon I – "If anyone saith that in the mass a true and proper sacrifice is not offered to God…let him be anathema."

> Canon III – "If any one saith, that the sacrifice of the mass is…not a propitiatory sacrifice…let him be anathema." [20]

Sardis (Revelation 3:1-6)

The age of Thyatira came to a sudden end on October 31, 1517, when, after years of turmoil, a German monk named Martin Luther nailed his "95 theses" to a church door in Wittenburg, Germany. Luther attacked the sale of indulgences, saying the only thing they guaranteed was an increase in financial profit among clergy. Luther also raised questions about the authority of the pope. Like many other reformers before him, Luther believed in the authority of scripture alone.

The recent invention of the printing press allowed for rapid mass distribution of Luther's "95 theses." And the end result was the Protestant Reformation (the "reforming of the church by protesters").

Jesus' words to Thyatira were:

> "I know your deeds; you have a reputation of being alive, but you are dead. Wake up!" Revelation 3:2

Jesus commanded them to "wake up" because their church was bordering on useless. He went on to tell the church entering the age of Sardis:

> "Strengthen what remains and is about to die, for I have not found your deeds complete in the sight of my God." Revelation 3:2

After 1500 years, nothing had changed in God's plan. Jesus calls the church of Sardis back to the word of God. It was time to return to what was written and repent of the distractions of the age of Thyatira. Jesus said:

> "Remember, therefore, what you have received and heard; obey it and repent." Revelation 3:3

Jesus then mentions his return. If Thyatira and Sardis do not "wake up" and "remember what they have received," Jesus tells them his second coming will surprise them like a thief in the night.

> "If you do not wake up, I will come like a thief, and you will not know at what time I will come to you." Revelation 3:3

The reformation restored the doctrine of justification by faith and the priesthood of every believer. The power of each individual's faith and their responsibility for individual ministry before God was also re-established. Sole dependence on scripture became a foundational doctrine, and it remains foundational in most Protestant churches today.

Many significant things happened during the age of Sardis, including:

1) The religious Revolution
2) The scientific Revolution
3) The democratic Revolution
4) The industrial Revolution

Philadelphia (Revelation 3:7-13)

By 1730, the reformation had established its doctrine but grown cold and ineffective in growth and outreach. The age of Philadelphia was the age of restoring "brotherly love." The two Greek words that make up "Philadelphia" are:

1) "phileo" – "tender affection" or "an unselfish love, ready to serve"
2) "adelphos" – "brother"

Jesus tells this generation:

> "See, I have placed before you an open door that no one can shut." Revelation 3:8

The First Great Awakening in the 1730s shook off old rituals and made Christianity more personal. Protestant denominations, including the Congregational, Presbyterian, Dutch Reformed, Baptist, and Methodist groups, were forever changed. Then, in the 1790s, the Second Great Awakening occurred. This awakening involved multitudes of people coming to Christ and was followed by a new wave of social activism and missionary work. Christian hospitals, schools, and publishing companies began popping up everywhere.

During the Philadelphia age, Jesus literally opened a door to the world that no one could shut. William Carey sailed to India (1793), and Hudson Taylor went to China (1854). Many of today's greatest Christian organizations were formed during these years, including the American Bible Society (1816), the American Education Society (1815), the American Sunday School Union (1824), the American Tract Society (1825), the American Home Missionary Society (1826), and the Salvation Army (1865).

This was the age when pre-millennial teaching was restored, along with the concept of dispensations. The clarification of the rapture of the church, the second coming of Christ, and the tribulation were explained scripturally by John Darby and others beginning around 1830. Regarding the rapture, Jesus said:

> "I will also keep you from the hour of trial that is going to come upon the whole world to test those who live on the earth. I am coming soon." Revelation 3:10

Ephesus	Smyrna	Pergamum	Thyatira	Sardis	Philadelphia	Laodicea
30-90 AD	98-313	313-590	590-1517	1517-1730	1730-1900	1900-rapture

Laodicea (Revelation 3:14-22)

The Laodicean age began around 1900. The name "Laodicea" comes from the Greek words:
1) "laos" – "people"
2) "dike" – "judgment, decision, the execution of a sentence"

This period would be known as a time when "the people ruled." The trends of this age began developing around 1900, and they include:

1) Higher biblical criticism that refuses to recognize the Bible as divine revelation. The Bible was reduced to a literary work that was more or less fabricated by ancient writers.

2) Cold formalism dominated most traditional churches. Rituals again took center stage.

The church had become powerless. So, in 1906, in an old building on Azusa Street in Los Angeles, the Pentecostal movement was born. An excitement about the power of the Holy Spirit, combined with zealous teaching that the rapture was near, fueled one of the most influential movements of the century. Pentecostals stressed missions, evangelism, and a worship style that would eventually permeate all of Christendom.

In an effort to counteract the rise of liberalism (1910-1915), Lyman Stewart, the wealthy president of Union Oil, organized a publishing project. He created twelve booklets that were compilations of articles written by pastors, scholars, and teachers. All these articles had one thing in common: they taught basic Christian doctrine and addressed modern issues like evolution, humanism, and money. Stewart and his brother paid for these booklets to be published, and within a few years, three million copies were distributed to every pastor, evangelist, missionary, theological student, and Sunday school superintendent that would take them. The booklets were simply called "The Fundamentals." Thus, in 1920, the term "fundamentalist" came to be used to describe anyone who held solely to the truth of God's word.

In Revelation 3:14-22, Jesus addressed the local church at Laodicea (96 AD). But he was also addressing those of us living during this church age of Laodicea. He said:

> "I know your deeds, that you are neither cold nor hot. I wish you were either one or the other! So, because you are lukewarm—neither hot nor cold—I am about to spit you out of my mouth." Revelation 3:15-16

The ancient city of Laodicea had tremendous wealth but a terrible water supply system. Six miles north of them, in the city of Hierapolis, were famous hot springs used for healing and medicinal purposes. The water from this city flowed towards Laodicea and spilled over a mile-long cliff that dropped the hot water 300 feet down into Laodicea. So by the time the water reached Laodicea, it was lukewarm and filled with minerals from the calcium carbonate that covered the cliff.

Cold drinking water, on the other hand, was found in Colosse, ten miles south of Laodicea. But, like the hot water from Hierapolis, the cold water had to travel a great distance and arrived at Laodicea lukewarm and filled with unnecessary minerals. This slimy, lukewarm salt water had a putrid taste and was useless as a refreshing drink.

Jesus tells the people in Laodicea that, like the hot and cold water flowing into their city, they'd become lukewarm. Jesus was not telling the Laodiceans they needed to "fire up" and "get hot" about God, or that they needed to "stop being cold and indifferent." He was telling them that they were useless, just like their lukewarm water.

The church has a purpose, just like hot and cold water. The hot water of Hieropolis was used for healing. The cold water of Colosse was used for drinking. The church of Laodicea could either be the hot water that healed broken lives or the cold water that refreshed the weary. Yet the Laodiceans were neither, and the church of today has the same problem. We are filled with the lukewarm, putrid water that Jesus says he will "spit" out of his mouth.

Jesus wants churches to be either hot or cold, but we must remember that "hot" has nothing to do with enthusiasm or commitment. Just because a church has enthusiasm and commitment doesn't necessarily mean they're useful and productive in the body of Christ. I have been a coach long enough to know that some of the most enthusiastic and committed kids are not necessarily the most productive athletes.

This is the age of the complacent church. Christians are no longer concerned with becoming mature in their faith. They are more interested in motivational speakers and pre-packaged programs that spell big business. This kind of ineffective church is distasteful to Christ. Notice that Jesus says, "I am *about* to spit you out of my mouth." This means there is still time for us to repent and change.

"Spit" is the Greek word "emesai" which means "to vomit, to reject with disgust." The same word is used in the Old Testament with Israel:

"Do not defile yourselves in any of these ways, because this is how the nations that I am going to drive out before you became defiled. Even the land was defiled; so I punished it for its sin, and the land *vomited* out its inhabitants…and if you defile the land, it will *vomit* you out as it vomited out the nations that were before you." Leviticus 18:24, 25, 28

"Keep all my decrees and laws and follow them, so that the land where I am bringing you to live may not *vomit* you out." Leviticus 20:22

The church in Laodicea tries to defend itself after the Lord offers his rebuke. Does their defense sound familiar?

"…I am rich; I have acquired wealth and do not need a thing." Revelation 3:17

The Laodicean church people already had everything they needed. Their material desires were met, so they saw no reason to invest heavily in their spiritual well-being. A yearning for physical wealth had replaced their longing for spiritual maturity.

False Teachings

The Pentecostal movement began in the early 1900s, and the charismatic movement followed in the 1960s. This was a direct response to the people's hunger for God's presence in their

A yearning for physical wealth has replaced our longing for spiritual maturity.

daily lives. Since that time, these moves of God have morphed into some corrupt theologies that have seriously infected the church. Groups like the "Word of Faith" movement and the "Third Wave" movement teach that financial prosperity is a fundamental right for all Christians.[21] Their message is that very claim, "I am rich; I have acquired wealth and do not need a thing."

Peter warns:

> "...There will be false teachers among you. They will secretly introduce destructive heresies...Many will follow their shameful ways and will bring the way of truth into disrepute. In their greed these teachers will exploit you with stories they have made up." II Peter 2:1-3

Jesus said to the "rich" Laodiceans:

> "But you do not realize that you are wretched, pitiful, poor, blind and naked." Revelation 3:17

The uselessness of the Laodiceans is only a symptom of the real problem. The real problem is that they are ignorant of their true condition. So it is with us. We are wretched, pitiful, poor, blind, and naked, but we don't know it.

1) **Wretched** means "distress, miserable." Wretched can be used to describe the physical life of a community when everything has been destroyed or plundered by war. A wretched person is in serious trouble because he has been overrun by his enemy. Satan has plundered him of anything worth taking. What does Satan plunder? Jesus said, "Satan comes and takes away the word that was sown in them" (Mark 4:15).

2) **Pitiful** means "one who is set forth as an object of extreme pity."[22] Of all the previous failings of the first six churches, this church is looked upon with the most pity. Laodicea is the biggest failure of all seven, yet they think they're on top of the world. The word "pitiful" indicates that people from other church ages in history are looking at us today, shaking their heads because we do not realize how poor we are spiritually.

3) **Poor** here means "poor as a beggar."[23] The people of Laodicea are rich in the natural sense, yet they are as "poor as a beggar" in the spiritual sense. Throughout John's letter, we see a repeated disconnection between physical wealth and spiritual wealth.

4) **Blind** eyes are completely insensitive to natural light. The Laodiceans were completely insensitive to the Holy Spirit's leading and plan.

5) **Naked** bodies were a symbol of judgment and total humiliation in the Roman world. The people of the Laodicean church will not be given distinguished clothing to wear at the reward seat of Christ. This group will be attending the event naked and full of shame.

A Knock at the Door of Laodicea

The good news is that change is still possible for those in the Laodicean age. Regarding the other ages, we learn:

1) Thyatira will continue to the end and will be asleep when Jesus comes (Revelation 3:3).

2) Sardis, the church that "began to wake up," will continue to the end not having fully completed the work (Revelation 3:2).

3) Philadelphia, the church of the Great Awakening, will continue to wait for the rapture of the church before the tribulation. (Philadelphia is the only church not rebuked by Jesus in these seven letters in Revelation.)

4) Laodicea, the final church, will end the dispensation of the church age in failure. This corresponds with all previous dispensations that also ended in failure: the fall of man, the flood, the tower of Babel, the rebellion of the nations, the setting aside of Israel, and Satan's final revolt at the end of the millennium (Revelation 20:7-10).

There is a word of rebuke and correction spoken to Laodicea that must not go unheeded by our generation. Jesus said:

> "I counsel you to buy from me gold refined in the fire, so you can become rich; and white clothes to wear, so you can cover your shameful nakedness; and salve to put on your eyes, so you can see. Those whom I love I rebuke and discipline. So be earnest, and repent. Here I am! I stand at the door and knock. If anyone hears my voice and opens the door, I will come in and eat with him, and he with me." Revelation 3:18-20

Jesus' advice is threefold and deals with wealth, clothing, and medicine. He tells us that we can be rich, but that wealth will only come through gold refined by fire. He also says we can still earn clothes to cover our nakedness on judgment day. Finally, he says he will provide salve for our blind spiritual eyes.

Wealth

The gold Jesus speaks of is faith that will be tested in the fire of life's afflictions. Peter says:

> "For a little while you may have had to suffer grief in all kinds of trials. These have come so that your faith – of greater worth than gold, which perishes even though refined by fire – may be proved genuine and may result in praise, glory and honor when Jesus Christ is revealed." I Peter 1:6, 7

Clothes

The clothes that will cover our nakedness are the good deeds we can do now to remove our shameful unproductiveness from the pages of history. Revelation 19:8 says, "Fine linen stands for the righteous acts of the saints." There is still time to do these righteous acts.

Medicine

We still have time to ask the Holy Spirit to become spiritual salve for our eyes. Paul writes to the church in Ephesus:

> "I keep asking that the God of our Lord Jesus Christ, the glorious Father, may give you the Spirit of wisdom and revelation, so that you may know him better. I pray also that the eyes of your heart may be enlightened in order that you may know the hope to which he has called you, the riches of his glorious inheritance in the saints and his incomparably great power for us who believe." Ephesians 1:17, 18

Jesus goes on to tell us why he even bothered to rebuke the seven churches. It is because he loves them and wants them to succeed. He says:

> "Those whom I love I rebuke and discipline. So be earnest, and repent. Here I am! I stand at the door and knock." Revelation 3:19, 20

There is still time. There is still grace. And there is still power to achieve the things God has called us to achieve in this Laocidean church age.

The mystery of the seven letters to the seven churches ends with Jesus saying:

> "He who has an ear, let him hear what the Spirit says to the churches." Revelation 3:22

What Do We Do?

Chapter 23: Can Our Nation Be Saved?

THERE WAS A time in United States history that sounds suspiciously similar to today. During that time, most Christians believed the golden age of our founding fathers' faith was fading away. United States had no sooner won its independence in 1783 and formulated its government in 1789 than the young nation was swept away by the philosophy that had fueled the French Revolution. Rationalism, with its stress on reason and scientific method, had created a society of skeptics. Pamphlets began appearing, attacking the church as an enemy of progress. Around 1800, it was said of the United States that "only the shell of orthodoxy was left."[1]

- Drunkenness was an epidemic. Our nation drank more alcoholic beverages per capita than ever before or ever since that time in history.[2] Lawyers drank before court and clergymen took drinks between services.[3]
- Out of a population of five million, 300,000 were alcoholics and fifteen thousand of them died each year.[4]
- Public profanity was shocking, filthy, and used often. [5]
- Women could not go into the streets at night because assaults were so frequent. [6]
- In 1795, the young Reverend Samuel Shepard arrived in Lenox, Massachusetts to pastor a Congregational church there (1795-1846). He said he found "the spiritual and moral aspects of the place gloomy."[7] A new member had not joined the church in sixteen years.[8] This means that during the years of the *Declaration of Independence*, the Revolutionary War, and Washington's two terms as president—Shepherd's church experienced zero growth.[9]
- The Lutherans and the Episcopalians were thinking about joining together since both denominations were failing. Methodist churches were losing members faster than they were gaining them.[10]
- Samuel Provost, an Episcopal Bishop in New York, offered his resignation in 1801 because it had been so many years since anyone in New York had been confirmed as an Episcopalian. [11]
- Voltaire taught that "Christianity will be forgotten in thirty years."
- Lyman Beecher,[12] a revival preacher who cried for morality among the citizens of this new country, said in 1811, "Our vices are digging the grave of our liberties and preparing to entomb our glory."[13]
- Lyman Beecher described a typical campus in 1795 while he was a student: "College was in a most ungodly state. The college church was almost extinct.

Most of the students were skeptical and rowdies were plenty. Wine and liquors were kept in many rooms; intemperance, profanity, gambling and licentiousness were common…most of the class before me were infidels and called each other Voltaire, Rousseau."[14]

* The influence of Voltaire, deism, and the French Revolution had created this anti-Christian climate in universities across the United States. Many of the culture's influential "free-thinkers" were given faculty positions at universities.
* Students disrupted worship services with profanity and burned down buildings, forcing the resignation of college presidents.[15]
* Christians had to meet in secret on campuses in 1790 and had to write any notes from meetings in code so they would not be discovered.[16]
* There wasn't one believer found among Harvard students. During the last decade of the eighteenth century, most Harvard were atheists.[17]
* There were just two Christians in the entire Princeton student body.
* Every student at Princeton (with the exception of five) had joined what was called "the filthy speech movement."[18] [19]
* Students held a mock communion at Williams College, and they put on anti-Christian plays at Dartmouth. [20]
* Students took a Bible from a local Presbyterian church in New Jersey and burned it in a public bonfire.[21]
* United States Chief Justice John Marshall wrote Bishop of Virginia James Madison to say that the church "was too far gone ever to be redeemed."[22]
* Charles Carroll, a *signer of the Declaration of Independence* wrote to James McHenry on November 4, 1800: "Without morals, a republic cannot subsist any length of time; they therefore who are decrying the Christian religion, whose morality is so sublime and pure…are undermining the solid foundation of morals, the best security for the duration of free governments."
* In 1780, a mere 10% of Americans claimed to be members of a church.[23] Most historians consider 1780 the lowest point for church affiliation.[24] .

The Second Great Awakening

It was with the country in this condition that the Second Great Awakening began. It started in many different places and involved a variety of personalities and denominations. It "grew out of the evangelical opposition to the deism associated with the French Revolution."[25] This spiritual awakening led to a series of meetings that reinvigorated church members to live more holy lives. It also brought many non-believers to faith in Christ. The final result was an improved culture and more productive society.

The Second Great Awakening began in 1787 among college students in Virginia. Many men went into Presbyterian ministry as a result and later led great revival meetings in Tennessee and Kentucky. These outdoor meetings that took place from 1796-1800 were attended by at least 10,000 people (some say there were as many as 25,000). This was at a time when the largest town in Kentucky had a population of 1,795. People came from up to one hundred miles away. In 1801, the president of Washington College in Virginia visited Kentucky. In his writings, he said he noticed a great lack of profanity there and recognized the morality and religious awe found among the citizens of Kentucky.[26]

In the 1790s, the Congregationalists held revival meetings in New England. Here men like Reverend Samuel Shepard saw their churches come alive, grow in membership, and bring about social change. Shepard, who had called his church "gloomy" in 1793, would refer to the entire city as "pleasant, healthful, and with little temptation to vice and immorality" by the 1830s.

In 1802, Yale President Timothy Dwight (grandson of Jonathan Edwards) addressed the student body with a series of Bible teaching lectures concerning the basics of Christian doctrine and godly living. His lectures undermined the roots of skepticism and doubt and resulted in a third[27] of the student body converting to Christianity. Half of these new believers went into full-time Christian work and, as a result, over 20,000 students went on to serve Christ in overseas missions throughout the 1800s.

From 1800 to 1835, church membership increased from 40% to 75%.[28] The number of congregations in most denominations also grew dramatically between 1776 and 1820:[29]

Denomination	Number of Congregations in 1776:	Number of Congregations in 1820:	Percentage Increase:
Anglican/Episcopalian	495	600	21%
Baptist	497	2700	443%
Congregational	668	1100	65%
Lutheran	150	800	433%
Methodist	65	2700	4050%
Presbyterian	588	1700	189%
Roman Catholic	56	124	121%

Baptists had 35,000 members in 1784 but grew to 170,000 members by 1810. During the same time period, the Methodists grew from 15,000 members to 200,000.[30]

Measured results of the spiritual awakening of the early 1800s:
  a) improvement of morals
  b) drunkenness was greatly reduced
  c) profanity became socially unacceptable
  d) churches began the tradition of a midweek prayer service that continues today
  e) Sunday school was introduced and accepted as a means to educate young people
  f) New universities were founded (1780-1830) to provide Christian higher education
  g) Missionary work grew until it reached a peak in the 1900s
  h) Many volunteer ministry and social outreach groups were formed, including:
    a. The American Bible Society (founded in 1816)
    b. The American Tract society (founded in 1825)
    c. The American Home Missionary Society (founded in 1826)
    d. The Salvation Army (founded in 1865)
    i) Financial giving "totaled hundreds of millions of dollars annually" by 1900.[31]
    j) Total church contributions since 1955 make up 1% of the GNP.

Because of the awakening:

  1) Local ministry groups were formed to reach their community and beyond.
  2) Publications and teaching material were produced and widely distributed.
  3) Bible teaching was promoted at all levels of society.
  4) Massive lifestyle changes occurred in the area of personal morality.
  5) Social justice and reform took place.

Signs That America is Ready for Another Great Awakening

We are now in the early years of the fourth generation. Here are some signs that a spiritual awakening is stirring in the United States:
  1) A surge of positive values in:
    a. Business
    b. Politics
    c. Schools

  2) Hollywood is corrupt and will always follow the money of consumers, but recently, Hollywood has been producing more movies with Christian themes and family values. Why? Because there are so many people willing to spend money to watch them.

3) A discussion about God and moral absolutes has returned to public debate because people recognize how bad things have gotten. In 2002, 67% of the people in the United States believed that morals were getting worse. In 2006, that number grew to 81%. People in the United States are ready for a shift toward morality.

4) Intelligent design is rocking the scientific world. Science is demanding that we recognize a creator.
   a. After decades of public educators teaching evolution, 64% of people still believe God created them.
   b. Only two out of every ten people believe they evolved.
   c. Why has evolution failed to capture people's hearts? Because God has made it clear through his creation that he does indeed exist, and forty-five minutes in a classroom won't change the truth.
   d. The percentage of people in the United States who believe evolution is true declined 6% from 1995 to 2005.

5) Atheism is losing the ground gained in the 1900s. Noted atheist Anthony Flew rejected atheism and became a deist because "science and DNA research demand that there is a creator."

6) Secular humanism is unraveling because it teaches that everything derived from chaos, by chance. There is no reason, logic, or order to it. The trouble is that they came to this conclusion using reason, logic, and order.

Church attendance has been steady for sixty years:

	Church for 60 years
1940	41%
1950	39%
1960	47%
1970	40%
1980	40%
1990	40%
2000	43%

Gallup statistics from Emerging Trends, Princeton Religion Research Center, IANNACCONE, ECONOMICS OF RELIGION MS: 8/31/2006, from http://www.religionomics.com/cesr_web/papers/iannaccone9620-9620ERel_book/Chap01Stats.pdf

Evangelicals have increased:

	Evangelicals
1976	34%
1981	38%
1992	36%
1995	41%
1999	46%

Gallup statistics from Emerging Trends, Princeton Religion Research Center, IANNACCONE, ECONOMICS OF RELIGION MS: 8/31/2006, from http://www.religionomics.com/cesr_web/papers/iannaccone9620-9620ERel_book/Chap01Stats.pdf

A majority of Americans believe in the existence of God, an afterlife, heaven and hell, and that Jesus was the Son of God.

U.S. Polls of Religious Beliefs, 1940-1995
Percentage of people in the U.S. who answered "yes" to these questions:

Year Poll Was Taken	"Do you believe in the existence of God or a universal spirit?"	"Do you believe in a life after death?"	"Do you think Jesus was God or just another leader like Mohammed or Buddha?"	"Do you think there is a heaven where people who have led good lives are eternally rewarded?"	"Do you think there is a hell to which people who have led bad lives and die without being sorry are eternally damned?"
1945	95	76			
1950	99	73	77	72	58
1955	97	74			
1960	97	74			
1965	97	75	75	68	54
1970	98	73			
1975	94	69			
1980	95	71	78	71	53
1985	94	74	76		
1990		71	84	75	60
1995	96	71			

NOTE: *Where data is lacking for a given year, but available for any of the four surrounding years, the average of these values has been entered.* SOURCE: *Gallup opinion polls reported in annual editions of Religion in America (Princeton Religion Research Center 1990, 1992/93, 1996.*

We are living in times that have seen these things occur:

1. A new mega-church (more than 2,000 people) is formed in the United States every two days.
2. Rick Warren's, *The Purpose-Driven Life,* has sold more than twenty-five million copies.
3. Lakewood Church in Houston, Texas welcomed 57,000 people for its opening day worship service.
4. *The Passion of the Christ* earned $370 million in domestic sales.
5. Tim LaHaye's *Left Behind* book series has sold over 65 million copies.
6. The media and both political parties recognized the influence of the evangelical vote in the 2004 presidential election as well as the 2006 election.
7. Willow Creek Church (20,000 members) and Harvest Bible Chapel (8,000 member) have an enormous impact on the Chicago region.[32]

We Can Make a Difference Today

God wants to reach our generation. Believers and non-believers alike are looking for answers to life's questions. But many people, especially fundamental evangelicals, have hid their heads in their *Left Behind* novels claiming they are simply waiting for Jesus to return.

Jesus said:

Our responsibility is to wait faithfully for Jesus while we serve him productively.

> "Who then is the faithful and wise servant, whom the master has put in charge of the servants in his household to give them their food at the proper time? It will be good for that servant whose master finds him doing so when he returns. I tell you the truth, he will put him in charge of all his possessions." Matthew 24:45-46

Our responsibility is to wait faithfully for Jesus while we continue to serve him by fulfilling the commission he gave us. This way Jesus will be able to say to us:

> "Well done, good and faithful servant! You have been faithful with a few things; I will put you in charge of many things. Come and share your master's happiness." Matthew 25:23

Chapter 24: God and Government

WE ARE MEMBERS of two kingdoms—an earthly kingdom and a spiritual kingdom. As for our earthly kingdom, we are very fortunate to live in the United States of America with all the freedoms and resources we could ever want. But each person also belongs to one of two spiritual kingdoms which are called (among other names): The kingdom of darkness and the kingdom of light (Colossians 1:12, 13; Acts 26:18).

Just as there are legal requirements to be a citizen of the United States, there are also requirements to be a citizen of the spiritual kingdom of God. Jesus said, "I tell you the truth, no one can see the kingdom unless he is born again."

It is not unreasonable to believe that members of the Kingdom of Light can simultaneously cooperate with the rules of their earthly kingdom without compromising. In other words, it is scriptural to be both a good Christian and a good American.

We may work with fellow believers to accomplish goals in the spiritual kingdom; but we must also work with non-believers to accomplish goals in the earthly kingdom. Throughout history, people of all faiths have worked side-by-side to protect, defend, and achieve various objectives. Daniel worked with Nebuchadnezzar, Cyrus, and Darius (three great leaders of the ancient world). Paul cooperated with Festus and Herod Agrippa, the leaders of his earthly kingdom. Nehemiah worked with Artaxerxes. Esther married Xerxes. Even John the Baptist operated his ministry under the reign of Herod Antipas, and Jesus respected Pilate and his position.

Men of faith should do all they can to "maintain peace" in their land so they can continue living "quiet lives." In our postmodern world, however, the virtue of maintaining peace has been taken to an extreme and has somehow become the only right answer to every problem. When other nations threaten us, we rush to appease their demands and avoid conflict. This was also the trend in Israel around 1200 BC.

The Israelites had lived in the Promised Land for about two hundred years. By this time they had forgotten about the ultimate purpose of God and had adopted the philosophies and idols of surrounding nations. This left them weak and confused.

A Nation of Cowards

In Judges 5, we read about life in Israel at this time. The men of Israel had embraced a new philosophy which included a system of ethics that called for the disarmament of the military. They believed that using treaties and negotiation, they'd be able to broker peace with anyone. Judges 5:8 says:

> "When they chose new gods, war came to the city gates, and not a shield or spear was seen among forty thousand in Israel."

The Israelites were not virtuous for laying down their weapons; they were soft and self-absorbed. They had no concept of national identity. They were cowards. Men were too busy meeting their own desires and worrying about themselves to stand up and protect their people.

Judges goes on to explain that crime in Israel became so bad during this time that the streets were virtually deserted. The common citizen knew that something had gone terribly wrong with their culture. Those who had to deal with corruption in their daily lives realized that the nation had been led astray. The government was no longer doing what it was designed to do—protect the nation so its people can live "peaceful and quite lives" (I Timothy 2:2).

Deborah and the Singers

One Israeli citizen became extremely fed up with all this. Judges 5:7 says:

> "Village life in Israel ceased until I, Deborah, arose; I arose a mother in Israel."

Deborah is not identified as a great leader or some kind of warrior queen; she is a mother. She's a mother in a country that's failed her. She knows things aren't right, and she decides to do something about it. She was a very unique person at this time in history because she held to the ways of God even though her culture had become so corrupt. She wanted to stand up and fight for righteousness even though it wasn't popular to fight for anything.

Reading on, we find there were a few other people left in this corrupt society who still remember God. These people were called "the singers" because they sang and recited stories about God's goodness and the righteous ways of men from long ago. We read about these singers in Judges:

> "You who ride on white donkeys, sitting on your saddle blankets
> *(this is the rich and wealthy people of the land)*
> and you who walk along the road
> *(this is the poor or middle class)*
> consider the voice of the singers at the watering places
> *(everyone in society had to get water everyday; they would all
> continually visit the watering places)*
> They recite the righteous acts of the Lord, the righteous acts of his
> warriors in Israel
> *(The singers were reminding the people of the great things their former
> God had done and what great men of God had accomplished)*
> Then the people of the Lord went down to the city gates.
> *(The people who repented and wanted to return to God went to the
> place where the officials of the city and the government leaders sat
> which was literally in seats in the city gates)*

Wake up, wake up, Deborah! Wake up, wake up, break out in song! Arise, O Barak! Take captive your captives, O son of Abinoam."

(The people whose hearts had been changed by the message they heard at the watering places had decided it was time for a change in their society)

We are a nation full of soft, self-absorbed men.

The songs were about long-lost values and the noble character of men. These simple stories would become a catalyst to change the soul of the nation. These "singers" took their message to the one place where they would make contact with every family in town. Those that collected water not only returned to their homes with full buckets, but also with minds full of lyrics about standards that had been lost.

As the Israelites who came to the watering places heard the singers and remembered the days of old, their hearts were stirred. A group of them marched to the city gates, (the place where the nation's leadership met). The group told their leaders that the nation needed to change. In the chaos of their time, they demanded the government begin leading them according to God's law.

It isn't too hard to see that the United States has become like Israel. We are a nation full of soft, self-absorbed men. The "old days" of great warriors and righteous leaders is gone. It's now our turn to become the "voices of the singers" at the watering places of our generation. If we want to see a change, we must take our message directly to the people. Then hopefully the people will take the message to their politicians, and they can make decisions that will put us back in good standing with God.

The Establishment of Government

There was a time in the history of man that "government" as we know it had yet to be established. There was no government in the Garden of Eden or any time before the flood. There were good leaders and some loose form of culture, but it wasn't until Genesis 9:5 that God established the first human law. He explained that for the ultimate crime, the lawbreakers would have to pay the ultimate price. Murder would result in capital punishment. By initiating this law, God gave men the responsibility to rule.

Before the flood, the earth was filled with anarchy. Culture had become so corrupt that God said:

> "My Spirit will not contend with man forever…I will wipe mankind, whom I have created, from the face of the earth.' Genesis 6:3, 7

Regarding this time in history, we know:

> "Every inclination of the thoughts of men's hearts was only evil all the time." Genesis 6:5

Because this time was so evil, God made an extreme decision:

> "I am going to put an end to all people, for the earth is filled with violence ("hamas") because of them." Genesis 6:13

When Noah emerged from the ark, God gave the commission for men to rule their own societies:

> "From each man, too, I will demand an accounting for the life of his fellow man. Whoever sheds the blood of man, by man shall his blood be shed; for in the image of God has God made man." Genesis 9:5, 6

Unfortunately, there are no perfect forms of government today because there are no perfect people living on earth. A monarchy, democracy, and dictatorship all have strengths and weaknesses—obviously some have more strengths than others. A democracy is an excellent form of government only *if* that society is full of moral, upright people. If the people are moral, a democracy will flourish. If the people are immoral, the democracy will destroy itself. American democracy has survived because of its God-fearing, God-seeking people. But as the morality in our country declines, we will see our democracy gow more and more unstable.

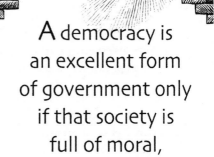

Our founding fathers believed that democracy and morality were deeply interwoven. Here are a few things they said:

A democracy is an excellent form of government only if that society is full of moral, upright people.

> "Our Constitution was made only for a moral and religious people. It is wholly inadequate to the government of any other." –John Adams 1798

> "I go on this great republican principle, that the people will

have virtue and intelligence to select men of virtue and wisdom. Is there no virtue among us? If there be not, we are in a wretched situation…If there be sufficient virtue and intelligence in the community, it will be exercised in the selection of these men. So that we do not depend on their virtue, or put confidence in our rulers, but in the people who are to choose them." – James Madison 1788

"Neither the wisest constitution nor the wisest laws will secure the liberty and happiness of a people whose manners are universally corrupt. He therefore is the truest friend of the liberty of his country who tries most to promote its virtue, and who, so far as his power and influence extend, will not suffer a man to be chosen onto any office of power and trust who is not a wise and virtuous man." –Samuel Adams

"If the public safety be provided, liberty and propriety secured, justice administered, virtue encouraged, vice suppressed, and the true interest of the nation advanced, the ends of government are accomplished…" –Algernon Sidney

"If we and our posterity reject religious instruction and authority, violate the rules of eternal justice, trifle with the injunctions of morality, and recklessly destroy the political constitution which holds us together, no man can tell how sudden a catastrophe may overwhelm us, that shall bury all our glory in profound obscurity." –Daniel Webster:

"Public virtue cannot exist in a nation without private [virtue], and public virtue is the only foundation of republics." –John Adams

"…Virtue, morality, and religion. This is the armor, my friend, and this alone that renders us invincible. These are the tactics we should study. If we lose these, we are conquered, fallen indeed…so long as our manners and principles remain sound, there is no danger." –Patrick Henry

"Religion, morality, and knowledge, being necessary to good government and the happiness of mankind, schools and the means of education shall forever be encouraged." –Article III of the "United States Annotated Code" passed by congress under President George Washington

"We have staked the future of all of our political institutions upon the capacity of mankind for self-government; upon the capacity of each and all of us to govern ourselves, to control ourselves, to sustain ourselves according to the Ten Commandments of God." –James Madison

The Separation of Church and State

When our nation was founded, the Ten Commandments were a reference of morality widely accepted by the general public. One of the great debates in our society today is whether or not to allow the Ten Commandments to be posted in any government-related building.

We must realize that absolute standards were set in place for all nations before the Ten Commandments were given to Moses. Those same standards still exist, having been woven into the very fabric of the universe. It doesn't really matter, then, whether or not the Ten Commandments are visibly displayed. It shouldn't be a big deal if they're taken out of courtrooms and schools. An external symbol of belief doesn't mean anything if no one really believes it. What matters is whether or not Americans are living moral lives and adhering to the Ten Commandments.

It is not the government's duty to impose the Christian faith. The purpose of government is to maintain order. This is the same message we get from Paul when he tells Timothy why the church should pray for the government:

> "I urge, then, first of all, that requests, prayers, intercession and thanksgiving be made for everyone—for kings and all those in authority, that we may live peaceful and quiet lives in all godliness and holiness. This is good, and pleases God our savior." I Timothy 2:1, 2

We need peace in our nation so that each man can pursue his own dreams. This is why the government has been given godly authority to punish wrong-doers and restore order. We can see this in Romans 13:2-4:

> "Consequently, he who rebels against the authority is rebelling against what God has instituted and those who do so will bring judgment on themselves. For rulers hold no terror for those who do right, but for those who do wrong. Do you want to be free from fear of the one in authority? Then do what is right and he will commend you. For he is God's servant to do you good. But if you do wrong, be afraid, for he does not bear the sword for nothing. He is God's servant, an agent of wrath to bring punishment on the wrongdoer."

There is no divine command for the government to convert all people to Christianity. Nor is there a command for the government to teach the word of God to people. In fact, throughout the Bible, many of the best leaders who provided peace and security for people were not believers themselves. There was Cyrus, the Persian emperor who sent the Jews back to Jerusalem. There was Artaxerxes who issued a degree that began the countdown of Daniel's "seventy sevens." There was Xerxes, the king who took Esther to be his queen. In the gospels we find Herod and Pilate maintaining peace for Rome in the land of Israel before the Messiah arrived.

The purpose of the government is to maintain order not impose the Christian faith.

Historically, nations do not need to be Christian nations in order to establish a good government and a peaceful land. Rome was not a Christian empire in the first century, but, nevertheless, there was order there. This was a very good thing because it enabled the early church to flourish. Both Peter and Paul explicitly tell believers to be submissive to their government (I Peter 2:13; Romans 13:1). At the time they said this, Nero was the emperor in charge of Rome, and Peter and Paul were both executed under Nero's command.

God established government in Genesis 9. He established the church in Acts 2. The government and the church are two clearly distinct entities, both created by God for specific purposes. The apostles never tried to convince their government to join them in spreading the gospel. The separation of church and state is a biblical principle designed long before the constitution or Thomas Jefferson came along. The government should not fulfill the role God assigned to the church. Public schools do not need to preach the gospel, nor do they need to hold prayer meetings.

The prophets in the Old Testament consistently talked about how governments should be just, but they never asked them to follow the Ten Commandments or adhere to Israel's sacrificial system. It is the church's responsibility alone to preach the gospel to all nations..

Character Counts

History shows that church-run governments often became oppressive. If our country suddenly became a religious state, it would be a mistake. We've seen this blunder at various times in the past. The Crusades are often used as the classic example, but there have been many other instances when nations were forced to embrace Christianity. People can coerce other people to follow God's rules, but it will never result in true faith. It will result in legalism and bitterness.

For the church to accomplish its mission in the United States, we must uphold freedom—the freedom to accept Jesus Christ and the freedom to reject him. To encourage people to live by certain common sense principles is not the same as proselytizing. While God's specific revelation cannot be taught in public schools, his general revelation is available to everyone and shouldn't be ignored.

Government-run schools have a responsibility to teach good morals to future generations.

This is the reason a new public school program called Character Counts makes so much sense. It's a great example of "general revelation" in action. This program promotes some of the traits we find in the righteous character of God without making anyone concede that those traits are exclusively Christian. The pillars of character taught through this program are: trustworthiness, respect, responsibility, fairness, caring, and citizenship.

The six traits taught in Character Counts are something both believers and nonbelievers can agree with and benefit from. If more children learn to demonstrate these traits in their lives, everyone around them will be better off. Character Counts is a way to begin turning our culture around without "Christianizing" it.

The six pillars of Character Counts are found below in bold type with some of the word-for-word phrases the Character Counts program uses to describe the pillars. My thoughts are in italics.

1) **"Trustworthiness – Be honest, don't deceive, cheat, or steal."**
   a) *Did you notice that this one pillar picks up two of the Ten Commandments now forbidden from being displayed in public schools:*
      i) *'Thou shalt not steal.'*
      ii) *'Thou shalt not bear false witness.'*

2) **"Respect – Follow the golden rule."**
   a) *If you remember from Sunday school, this is Christian code for Jesus' teaching, "Do unto others as you'd have them do unto you."*

3) **"Responsibility – Do what you're supposed to do. Use self-control. Be accountable for your choices."**
   a) *This is a basic theme throughout the Old Testament.*
   b) *Most churches today would look very different if the pastors were preaching this message, and their congregants were actually living it—doing what is right, using self-control, and being accountable.*

4) **"Fairness – Don't take advantage of others. Listen and be open to differing viewpoints. Be impartial."**
   a) *The entire presentation of the gospel is based on fairness:*

     i) *God is not partial concerning salvation and does not showing favoritism, I Timothy 5:2;*

     ii) *All we can ask is that people listen and be open-minded when we present the gospel;*

     iii) *As we deal with all kinds of people, we should treat them with fairness, Proverbs 3:27-30.*

5) "Caring – Be kind. Be compassionate. Express gratitude. Forgive. Help people in need."

   a) *Did someone use the Bible to come up with these definitions? Here is a simple scriptural list regarding these definitions:*

     i) *Character Counts says "Be kind" – The Bible says, 'The fruit of the Spirit is . . .kindness,' Galatians 5:22;*

     ii) *Character Counts says, "Be compassionate" – The Bible says, 'Be kind and <u>compassionate</u> to one another,' Ephesians 4:32; 'Love as brothers, <u>be compassionate</u> and humble,' I Peter 3:8;*

     iii) *Character Counts says, "Express gratitude" – 'Sing psalms, hymns and spiritual songs with <u>gratitude</u> in your hearts to God,' Colossians 3:16;*

     iv) *Character Counts says, "Forgive" – The Bible says, '<u>Forgive</u> whatever grievance you may have against one another. <u>Forgive</u> as the Lord forgave you,' Colossians 3:3;*

     v) *Character Counts says, "Help people in need" – The Bible says, 'Share with God's people who are in need," Romans 12:13.)*

6) "Citizenship – Make your school and community better. Get involved. Obey laws and rules. Respect authority."

   a) *Again, here are some scriptures that correspond with these definitions of citizenship from Character Counts::*

     i) *Character Counts says:"Get involved" – The Bible says: 'Live such good lives among the pagans that they may see your good deeds,' I Peter 2:12;*

     ii) *Character Counts says:"Obey laws" – The Bible says: 'Remind the people to be subject to rulers and authorities, to be obedient,' Titus 3:1;*

     iii) *Character Counts says:"Respect authority" – The Bible says: 'Everyone must submit himself to the governing authorities,' Romans 13:1, I Peter2:13.*

Though public schools should not be teaching religion, they should be teaching common sense values like these. To establish right from wrong in the hearts of young citizens is part of the process needed to maintain peace in our nation. The church is responsible to communicate the written revelation of God.

The government is responsible to reinforce the general revelation of God that is available to all people.

This view is not embraced by all Christians. I recently listened to a radio talk show host rail against the Character Counts program. He said now that Christianity has been removed from public schools, our culture wants to establish morality without Christ, which is wrong. But it's not wrong. He's wrong. He's like many other Christians who would rather foolishly crusade against something (Halloween, rock music, etc.) than have their souls penetrated with the word of God. The average Christian must realize that God is in the business of communicating to *all* people. There is a general standard of right and wrong that is found in all societies, even places without scripture. How is this possible? It's possible because the creator of the universe has made his standards very clear (Acts 17:27; Romans 1:19, 20; 2:15).

Something like the Character Counts program is a wonderful thing for our culture because it runs parallel with the scripture. We must not be like Christians from the Middle Ages who rejected Galileo and placed him under house arrest because he said the earth was round. God's word and his creation will always agree.

I am not giving the secular humanistic system of the public schools a free pass for what they've done over the last eighty 80 years. But I am giving them credit for recognizing after 80 years that absolutes are embedded in the hearts of people. A quote from the program Character Counts confirms that the way our schools have been running (entrenched in secular humanism) throughout the last century is a big part of our society's current lack of values:

> "Historically, education has had two great goals: to help people become smart and to help them become good. In establishing the first public schools, the American founders recognized that for democracy to work the country needed 'citizens of virtue.' In the 1800s, the Bible was the source book of both moral and religious instruction. By the beginning of the 20th century, as the nation became a melting pot of cultures, various ethnicities and religions began to challenge the propriety of promoting Judeo-Christian ethics, and the secularist became more adamant about keeping the Bible and religion out of schools. During the mid-20th century, three philosophical theories began to pervade and influence education."

> 1) "Logical positivism" – there is no basis for character education because there are no provable moral truths
> 2) "Moral relativism" – there are no universal ethical standards
> 3) "Personalism" – each person should choose his or her own values

Character Counts finally focuses on some values that exist whether or not we choose to follow them. In the last few years, it's become politically incorrect to claim there are absolutes. People who think there is a right way of behaving are deemed insane. Calling someone's behavior "immoral" can now land you in therapy.

Our country has adopted a "whatever feels right" approach to life. This has been disastrous to individuals, families, and our society as a whole. Yet much of our country still insists there are no absolutes. What they may not understand is that absolutes aren't created, they're discovered—in the same way a mathematician discovers the answer to 2+2. The mathematician himself did not create the answer; he merely recognized a truth that had always existed. The answer to the math problem 2+2 will be the same every single time. Even if the mathematician never discovers the right answer, it will still be 4.

So if absolutes are meant to be discovered, they can also remain undiscovered. But when people refuse to recognize certain absolutes, it doesn't mean they cease to exist. A person might claim that 2+2=5. And that person would be free to do so. But even if every student in a college-level math class agreed that 2+2=5, it still wouldn't make 5 the right answer.

Character Counts is a program that is presenting the fourth generation with the morality they desperately need. Although Character Counts does not tell people how to enter the kingdom of heaven, it does tell people how to live well in their earthly kingdom. A program such as Character Counts is for us what the singers at the watering places were for Deborah.

It is the job of the church alone to share the written revelation expressed in God's word:

> "[God] wants all men to be saved and to come to a knowledge of the truth. For there is one God and one mediator between God and men, the man Christ Jesus, who gave himself as a ransom for all men." I Timothy 2:3-6

Chapter 25: Church Work Today

W E ARE LIVING in a time of great polarization. The dark is getting darker, and the light is getting lighter. That is what this time is all about—forcing us to make a decision. Many will continue in confusion because they refused the light. For those who accept the truth of the scriptures, the light is going to continue to shine brighter and brighter.

This is a time were people's hearts are open and searching. The fourth generation is always a great time to be called to minister to the culture because there are a lot of things going on that corroborate the message

Prophets to the Fourth Generation

Jonah was sent to the Assyrians just forty days before their demise. His message was a simple one, but when it was combined with all the events of that day, it was powerful enough to grab the Assyrians attention. Jonah had no music ministry or sound crew. He didn't have a promotion team passing out flyers and selling his books at a back table. All he had was a message and a culture with people whose hearts had been prepared by God (they saw an eclipse, a foreign invasion, and plagues in their land). Jonah didn't do a lot of publicity in Ninevah in 759 BC. All he had to do was proclaim the message of truth. His sermon is recorded in Jonah 3:4, maybe in its entirety, "Forty more days and Nineveh will be overturned."

Because we are living in the days of Laodicea, we know that God is ready to reach our generation. Jonah's message was so uncomplicated that it could have been proclaimed by anyone who understood the times. Likewise, we, the members of the church, have a duty to proclaim the truth to this generation.

In the New Testament, Jesus spoke to the Samaritan woman at the well. After her conversation with Jesus, the woman ran back to the city of Sychar to tell people about her experience. She didn't offer a Bible lesson or use a great illustration, but her testimony struck a nerve with people in her city nonetheless. The Bible records her as saying:

> "Come, see a man who told me everything I ever did. Could this be the Christ?" John 4:29

The result of this situation was similar to what happened in Nineveh. Many people in her city believed and Jesus spent the next two days teaching in Sychar. This also occurred at the beginning of the fourth generation.

Another interesting thing about the woman at the well is that, after she hears what Jesus has to say, she leaves her water pitcher there so she can head back to the city right away. Jesus had actually just sent his Jewish disciples into the same city, asking them to get food. His intention was not that they get lunch, but that they look for spiritual opportunities in the city, that they "open their eyes and look at the fields ripe for harvest" (John 4:35). The disciples returned to Jesus with sandwiches, so Jesus has to explain exactly what he meant by "food." He says, "My food is to do the will of him who sent me to finish his work" (John 4:33).

While the disciples ate their sandwiches, Jesus told them that they failed because they were too preoccupied with earthly things (like lunch). In stark contrast, the woman at the well instinctively left her water pitcher where it lay right after she met Jesus. She ran back to the city to testify about a man she'd just met. A few minutes later, while Jesus was still teaching the disciples, the woman from the well returned with some people from Sychar who wanted to meet him.

We are at the right place in the right time. God is moving, and people are searching. But our problem is that we're preoccupied with "lunch." If we're going to see the fields ripe for harvest, it will require us to become less absorbed in the humanistic world, including our Laodicean churches. If we will lift up our heads, we will see that the greatest opportunity of the church age is before us. Jesus is knocking. Whoever opens the door will see the fields ripe for harvest *today*.

The Real Ministry

Change begins when someone like the Samaritan woman has an encounter with the living word of God and wants to tell everyone she knows. This should be what church is all about. Believers should come to meet the living word of God. Ephesians 4:11, 12 talks about how the body of Christ should be built up in the church age:

> "It was he (Jesus) who gave some to be apostles, some to be prophets, some to be evangelists, and some to be pastors and teachers, to prepare God's people for works of service <u>so that the body of Christ may be built up</u>."

God has given people in the church foundational gifts. He has made them apostles, prophets, evangelists, pastors, and teachers. These are not the best gifts or the peaks of ministry achievement. These gifts are actually the bottom of the ladder, the first steps of church ministry.

After just one conversation with Jesus, the Samaritan woman brought her whole city out to meet him. Jesus didn't go into the city, the woman went. When we start realizing that pastors aren't the only ones "in the ministry," but we each have a ministry to our family, community, and nation, the church will grow.

Pastors are not supposed to build the church; they are supposed to prepare God's people for works of service that will build the church. These works of service will not all happen on Sunday mornings between 10:00 and 11:30. Pastors often encourage people to get involved in "the ministry" by becoming an usher, greeter, parking lot attendant, nursery worker, choir member, offering taker, etc. These are not the "works of service" Paul is talking about in Ephesians 4. These are extensions of church administration. The works of service done by the people of God should happen outside the walls of the church building.

How Should the Church Operate?

A good pastor should focus on making God real to people. Their congregants must be equipped to go out and use the truth of God in their daily lives. They should heal the broken and refresh the weary (Revelation 3:15), and "strengthen, encourage, and comfort" people (I Corinthians 14:3). Pastors and teachers should not do this work for the congregants.

A common misconception is that the local church itself is "the ministry." It is not. Until the pastor realizes where he stands in the hierarchy of God's plan he is unable to fulfill his role.

Evangelists, pastors, and teachers are the beginning of ministry. They are not the pinnacle of ministry.

A church SHOULD NOT look like this:

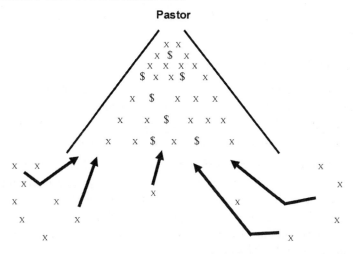

Here the pastor (or teacher) believes the church is the ministry. The people are there to support the greater vision of the church. This is usually done through giving money and helping the church become effective in the community. Here the ministry or "works of service" are taken from the people and replaced with the vision of men. It may be a great vision. It may include God's plan for the pastor himself. But, it is still not the type of service that believers should be prepared for. In this model, the pastor is at the top and the church takes joy in gathering more and more people.

A church SHOULD look like this:

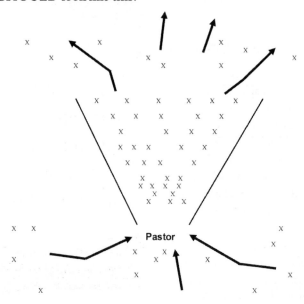

Here the pastor "prepares God's people" (not the pastor's people) for the gifts and ministries God has called them to. The pastor is a servant to those who go out and do works of service. People come to the local church to be refreshed. A healthy church will have people ministering at work and home, empowered by the Spirit. Teaching is not the pinnacle of ministry. It's foundational. A church that does not produce is underdeveloped and not grasping biblical teaching.

Gideon and the Angel of the Lord

In Exodus, the Lord came to Egypt to get Israel. After ten plagues and the parting of the Red Sea, he brought his people to Mt. Sinai where he made a covenant with them. Forty years later, he led them into the land of Canaan after he gave them (and their leader Joshua) a command and a promise:

> "Get ready to cross the Jordan River into the land I am about to give to them – the Israelites. I will give you every place where you set your foot, as I promised Moses. Your territory will extend from the desert to Lebanon, and from the great river, the Euphrates – all the Hittite country – to the Great Sea on the west. No one will be able to stand up against you all the days of your life." Joshua 1:3-5

In the days of Gideon, about four generations later, the Israelites had forgotten the promises of God. The mighty people of Israel who had swept through the land of Canaan in five years during the time of Joshua were now hiding in mountain clefts and caves while the Midianites, Amalekites, and other eastern peoples invaded their country (Judges 6:2, 3).

One day as Gideon was threshing wheat in a winepress to avoid being discovered by the Midianites, the Angel of the Lord appeared before him. The Angel of the Lord, (who throughout the Old Testament was a manifestation of the second member of the trinity or the Son of God), sat under a tree and watched as Gideon tried to separate the grain from the wheat in a valley instead of working on a hill where he'd have the help of the open breeze. Not only was Gideon trying to thresh in a valley with no wind, but he was also hiding in a winepress which was similar to a large bathtub-like vat. After watching this comic scene for a while, the Angel of the Lord speaks to Gideon and says, "The Lord is with you mighty warrior" (Judges 6:12).

The Lord addressed this oppressed young man as a mighty warrior and told him the Lord was with him. This was a reminder to Gideon of where he was at in time. The promises given to Israel in the days of Moses and Joshua had not been taken back, nor were they finished. The promises given two hundred years before had been forgotten by the people of Israel. Gideon did not know why they were being overrun by their enemies, but he did remember the stories from long ago when God would move on Israel's behalf. Gideon replied to the Lord:

"But sir, if the Lord is with us, why has all this happened to us? Where are all his wonders that our fathers told us about when they said, 'Did not the Lord bring us up out of Egypt?' But now the Lord has abandoned us and put us into the hand of Midian." Judges 6:13

The theology of the days of Gideon taught "the Lord has abandoned us." Their understanding was that the promises of God had been revoked. His plan had changed and they had been abandoned as a nation. The Lord replies to this mistaken theology by telling Gideon:

"Go in the strength you have and save Israel out of Midian's hand. Am I not sending you?" Judges 6:14

The promises of God had not been revoked; they had simply been forgotten. God's plan had not changed, but the older generations had failed to pass it down. God had not abandoned his people; they had abandoned God. Hosea 4:6 says, "My people are destroyed from lack of knowledge."

> The Lord said to Gideon, 'Go in the strength you have.' There was no new promise or anointing or move of God, simply a reminder."

The Angel of the Lord didn't give Gideon a new promise. He didn't anoint Gideon with oil or lay his hands on Gideon's head for a new special commission. There was no "move" of the Spirit. There was simply a reminder to "Go in the strength you have," nothing more. The Angel of the Lord was sitting under a tree because his work had been done for generations. Anything that happened in Israel now was just a matter of them recalling old commands and promises then acting on what God had long ago asked them to do. Everything else would fall into place.

The same is true in the church age. We were given promises and commands from God at the very beginning of our age. God's plan for the church has not changed nor will it change. There is nothing new to know. The original promise is still in effect because the original purpose has yet to be fulfilled. Gideon, although still in the age of Israel, found himself wondering, "Where are all God's wonders that our fathers told us about?" So it is with our generation in the church age. But God's response to us is the same as his response to Gideon, "Go in the strength you have."

I taught a high school construction class for several years. Every year we would build a house together as a class project. The students would arrive at the job site everyday for class. Aside from instructing them and leading them through the building process, my job was to make sure they each had a set of plans to follow. They also needed all the building materials readily available for each phase of the process. Likewise, when God calls *anyone* to do *anything* he provides:

1) The plans
2) The materials

In the Bible we find the plans and materials God has made available to those of us building the church in the church age.

The Plan for the Church

In Matthew 16, Jesus says his plan is to build the church right over the top of pagan philosophies as the powers of Hades stand helplessly and watch. We know from Matthew 16 and I Peter 2:4 that believers "like living stones are being built into a spiritual house where God can dwell." In Matthew 28:19 Jesus says, "Go and make disciples of all nations." Paul tells Timothy that "God's household, which is the church of the living God" is "the pillar and foundation of the truth" in the world during this present age (I Timothy 3:15). God's plan for the last 2000 years and beyond is to build his church across the globe. The church is to be "the salt of the earth" that will preserve societies from corruption, add flavor and meaning to life, and prevent false philosophies from growing in the hearts of men (Matthew 5:13). The church is "the light of the world" so that others can find their way to the father in heaven (Matthew 5:16).

The details of God's plan for the church age are found in the kingdom parables of Matthew 13. In these seven parables, Jesus teaches that the building of the Kingdom of God during the church age will involve these features.

Parable	Kingdom Feature of the Church Age
1. The Sower	Growth will come from spreading the Word.
2. The Weeds	There will be a lot of false teaching during this time.
3. Mustard Seed	The church will become the largest religious group.
4. The Yeast	The church will affect every culture in the world
5. Hidden Treasure	Israel, the treasured nation, will be set aside for a time.
6. The Pearl	Jesus will purchase the Gentile nations.
7. The Net	At the end of the church age, there will be judgment.

The Building Materials

The building materials are people. These people receive the truth, accept Jesus' payment for sins, and welcome the Holy Spirit into their lives.

> "Now you are the body of Christ, and each one of you is a part of it."
> I Corinthians 12:27

Jesus said at the Last Supper:

> "I will ask the Father, and he will give you another Counselor to be with you forever – the Spirit of truth. The world cannot accept him because it neither sees him nor knows him. But you know him, for he lives with you and will be in you." John 14:16, 17

Anyone who believes in Jesus receives the Holy Spirit. This is something the average person may not understand. Jesus goes on to say that the Holy Spirit will do these things for believers:

- Teach them (John 14:26)
- Remind them of what Jesus said (John 14:26)
- Testify about Jesus (John 15:26)
- Guide them and empower them to understand the word of God (John 16:13)

Paul tells the Corinthians:

> "Now to each one the manifestation of the Spirit is given for the common good." I Corinthians 12:7

Believers indwelt by the Holy Spirit are living stones (I Peter 2:5) that serve as building blocks for God's church. Each person in the church body will have the

Spirit of God manifest in him and will be endowed with a unique gift (or gifts) from the Spirit. These gifts are not the same as natural talents like intelligence, industrial skills, musical ability, or anything passed down through genes at birth. Spiritual gifts are supernatural gifts given to people at their second birth (when they accept Jesus Christ). Just like natural talents come from natural parents, spiritual gifts come from our spiritual father.

The Gifts of the Spirit

I Corinthians 12:4 says:

> "There are different kinds of gifts, but the same Spirit. There are different kinds of service, but the same Lord. There are different kinds of working, but the same God works all of them in all men. <u>Now to each one the manifestation of the Spirit is given for the common good.</u>"

From these verses and others we learn that God gives many types of gifts to people and the results they produce will be very unique. This is because when spiritual gifts are combined with people's natural talents and personalities—anything can happen. A listing of all the manifestations of all the spiritual gifts (were it possible) would look like an enormous rainbow of color as one shade gradually moves into another shade. As the gifts manifest through each person, the gift becomes as unique as that person's finger print. So although we can learn from other people with similar spiritual gifts, but we should never lower ourselves to imitating them. We should plan on being unique and getting used to it.

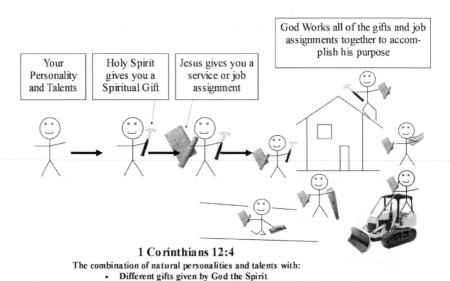

1 Corinthians 12:4
The combination of natural personalities and talents with:
- Different gifts given by God the Spirit
- Different services assigned by God the Son
- Different kinds of Workings worked by God the Father

The gifts of the spirit are:

1) for the good of the church (I Corinthians 14:3, 12; Ephesians 4:12)
2) not earned or deserved
3) given to every believer at the point of new birth
4) to be developed by each believer
    a. "Do not neglect your gift..." I Timothy 4:14, 15
    b. "I remind you to fan into flame the gift of God..." II Timothy 1:6
5) distributed by the Holy Spirit
    a. "All these are the work of one and the same Spirit, and he gives them to each one, just as he determines." I Corinthians 12:11
    b. "For by the grace given me I say to every one of you...we all have different gift, according to the grace given us..." Romans 12:3, 6
    c. "Each one should use whatever gift he has received to serve others faithfully administering God's grace in its various forms." I Peter 4:10
    d. "God is able to make all grace abound to you, so that in all things at all times, having all that you need, you will abound in every good work." II Corinthians 9:8

Everyone receives a gift the moment they accept Christ, but that gift must be discovered and developed. I accepted Jesus as my savior when I was 16, but it wasn't until I was teaching a fifth grade boys Sunday school class ten years later that I discovered my gift of teaching. Since that time, I have been practicing and developing that gift. Still today, I become more familiar with my gift each time I preach. Our spiritual gift comes from God but we must be diligent to develop it. An undeveloped gift is useless and will not produce anything.

I Corinthians 14:32 says, "The spirits of prophets are subject to the control of prophets."

At no time is a spiritual gift "in charge" of the person who has it. The gift can be turned on or turned off. If my spiritual gift is teaching, do I wait for God to cause me to start teaching? Or do I send out a flyer that says, "I'll be hosting a Bible study on Monday nights at 7:30 at my house"? Do I put a little disclaimer at the bottom that says, "Warning: Spiritual gift of teaching may not be available on Mondays... we will wait on God"? No, I don't.

How about when I'm preaching on a Sunday morning? Maybe I've been preaching for sixty minutes and still have a lot of information rolling around in my head. I don't want to quit, but I have to keep to the schedule of the church service. I make the excuse that "I am under the influence of my spiritual gift and I just can't quit"? Or, can I turn it off Sunday morning at 11:30 a.m. just like I turned it on at

Learn from others but do not lower yourself to imitation. Plan on being very unique and getting used to it.

7:30 p.m. Monday night? If "the spirits of the prophets are subject to the control of the prophets" then "the spirits of the teachers are subject to the control of the teachers."

List of the Gifts

A list of gifts is below, as recorded by the apostles. There is no indication that this list is exhaustive. There is also no reason to think that all of these gifts must be in operation throughout the entire church age. For example, there is no reason to think that each generation must have apostles who establish apostolic revelation like Peter and Paul.

Try not to immediately dismiss certain gifts on the list because they sound too "supernatural." This list is not like programs offered at college. You don't get to pick your own major. Also, just because someone is a member of "the clergy" and is licensed and ordained by men doesn't mean that person has a pastor/teacher/evangelist gift. Pastors should identify their specific gifts and let their congregants take care of the rest. The main reason I have listed the gifts is to help you identify what God the Spirit may have gifted to you so you can develop it.

Romans 12:3-8
+ Prophesying
+ Serving
+ Teaching
+ Encouraging
+ Contributing
+ Leadership
+ Mercy

I Corinthians 12:8-10
+ Message of wisdom
+ Message of knowledge
+ Faith
+ Healing
+ Miraculous

powers
+ Prophecy
+ Distinguishing between spirits
+ Tongues
+ Interpretation of tongues

I Corinthians 12:28-31
+ Apostles
+ Prophets
+ Teachers
+ Miracles
+ Healings
+ Administration
+ Tongues

Ephesians 4:11
+ Apostle
+ Prophet
+ Evangelist
+ Pastor
+ Teacher

I Peter 4:8-11
+ Hospitality
+ Speaking
+ Serving

244

Chapter 26: What Should We Do?

WITH ALL THE information we have about our responsibility at this time in history, what would be some reasonable goals or next steps?

1) We should continue to proclaim the truth, but we must remember that no matter how compelling we make our message, some people simply won't want to hear it. It's their choice. God gave them free will and wants them to use it. He allows everyone to choose, and so should we.

2) We need to become more biblically literate concerning our past and future so we can understand where we are today and what we should be doing. This is one of the most important roles of the local church and its pastors and teachers. If we don't communicate past revelation and future prophecy, we will stay busy doing a variety of worthless and unproductive things.

3) Staying alert was a theme in Jesus' teachings. Scripture warns us how easy it is to become distracted from the spiritual dimension of life.

4) We will be rewarded for our service. Faithfully serving God for unseen future rewards is an act of faith. Teaching about rewards will provide a source of encouragement among believers.

5) False teachings and philosophies will continue to mislead people. We can't stop this from happening, but we can identify false teachings and speak out against them. We can always turn on a light in a dark room.

6) Do not forget that we are in the midst of a spiritual awakening. The darkness in our country became so dark that many people decided they liked the light better. Americans have had enough crime, immorality, and corruption. They are finally seeking some kind of standard that will produce better things in their lives.

7) Our nation is faced with problems that we can't solve by ourselves. God designed it that way. This is why the fourth generation must turn to him and let him lead us out of the disaster we face. Then we will see:
   a. good leadership in churches, government, business, and education
   b. favorable weather patterns
   c. production of natural resources
   d. good international relationships
   e. reversal of self-destructive cultural behaviors including alcoholism, drug abuse, pornography, etc
   f. compassion for people in our society

8) Church leadership needs to love people again. They can best do this by empowering them with the truth of God's word. Our culture will only change when individual people change.

9) We are in the fourth generation and are experiencing the beginning of the fourth cycle of judgment. These judgments are designed by God to bring people to a point of decision. Do you love God and his ways, or do you hate God and reject his standards? This is a decision we must all make.

10) The standards God has set for our nation here on earth are not the same standards he has set for the kingdom of God. Jesus told Nicodemus, "No one can see the kingdom of God unless he is born again" (John 3:3). Being born again is a requirement for enterance into God's kingdom not our earthly kingdom. Salvation is not a prerequisite to the success of a nation today. For a nation to prosper on earth requires only these few things identified in Amos 6:8 and Isaiah 56:1:

> "He has showed you, O man, what is good. And what does the Lord require of you? To <u>act justly</u> and to <u>love mercy</u> and to <u>walk humbly</u> with your God."

> "<u>Maintain justice</u> and <u>do what is right</u>, for my salvation is close at hand and my righteousness will soon be revealed."

11) We must remember the lesson of the "sin of Jeroboam." By the second, third, and fourth generations, people find it hard to identify the sin of the first generation. The sin of our great-grandfathers was secular humanism. They ushered in an idolatrous philosophy based on the assumption that there is no God and that man is the ultimate end of everything. This sin has not only infested our culture in the areas of government and education, but it has polluted the thinking of our churches as well. We must correct our own "sin of Jeroboam" which begins with identifying the fallacy of secular humanism.

12) Families must be restored. The hearts of the fathers must turn to their children and children to their fathers. This is the foundation of not just the Christian culture, but all culture. A society can't endure without fathers and families. Malachi 4:6 says, "He (Elijah) will turn the hearts of the fathers to their children, and the hearts of the children to their fathers; or else I (the Lord) will come and strike the land with a curse." The institutions that God set in place must be strengthened and maintained. Those institutions are: individual volition, marriage, family, government, and nationalism. Together they provide structure for the natural world. On the other hand, the two institutions God has used and is using to provide for man's spiritual well-being are: the nation of Israel (the past) and the church (the present).

13) The fourth generation always receives warnings through prophets and natural signs. If a society doesn't respond to these warnings, God pours out his wrath and judgment. There is no escaping his discipline.

14) The church's mission is to represent the spiritual kingdom of God to mankind at this point in history. This mission advances only when the seed of scripture is sown. The word of God in the heart of man combined with the Spirit of God in a believer is the most powerful force on earth today.

15) The true church is not a "holier than thou" separatist organization. From the very beginning, Jesus told his disciples that the church is made of common people who've come from pagan societies to build a spiritual body where the gates of Hades had previously stood. In the Old Covenant, if the holy was touched by the unholy, the holy thing became unclean. In this age of the New Covenant, the holy has been sent into the world of the unholy.

16) The church was derailed 1600 years ago when "clergy" were deemed "specially anointed people," holier than the average person. For centuries, believers have brought money to churches, providing a payroll for clergy and missionaries. Our churches will only see revival when lay people realize they have the same anointing as clergy and missionaries.

17) The end of the 1700s and the beginning of the 1800s was a time in American history that closely resembles today—drunkenness, crime, profanity, extreme skepticism, and universities that openly mock Christianity. The Chief Justice said the church "was too far gone ever to be redeemed." Voltaire said, "Christianity will be forgotten in thirty years." But the thirty years following his statement saw the greatest spiritual awakening America has ever experienced. The results of that awakening are still part of our culture today. Revival can happen again.

Believers have the hope of the coming Kingdom but also the responsibility to serve our nation today.

18) Revival must take place at two levels.
   a. The natural level: our culture must become just, humble, and moral. Institutions must be restored.

b. The spiritual level: the church must learn the word of God and let the Holy Spirit empower them.

Believers should encourage the natural virtues God requires of both Christians and non-Christians alike. The United States is fighting for its survival in this fourth generation. We have the hope of a coming kingdom as we pray, "Come Lord Jesus!" But we also have the responsibility to serve our earthly kingdom now so that we might hear the Lord say to us: "Well done, thou good and faithful servant."

May God find reason to bless the United States of America!

Epilogue

IN 2002, MY wife Toni and I decided to start a Bible teaching ministry aimed at reaching our generation with the truth of the Bible. On the first Monday of that April, we held a Bible study in our home in West Des Moines, Iowa. During the initial four weeks of the study, I taught the four generation cycle and how important it is that Christians understand scripture at this time in history. By the fourth week of the study, there were forty-five people crowded into our living room, (and sitting at our kitchen table, peering around the dining room wall, sitting on the stairs up to the bedrooms, and in the hallway on the second floor). Because there seemed to be so much interest, I started teaching up to four nights per week.

Over the next five years, I taught verse-by-verse through Galatians, Zechariah, Revelation, Romans, and Ezekiel. Most books of the Bible took at least one year for me to teach because I wanted to be thorough in explaining their historical/ cultural context, their translation from the original Hebrew/Greek, and what Biblical scholars say about each individual verse. I also taught several times through a 52-week set of curriculum I call simply "Bible School." This curriculum surveys both the Old and New Testaments and covers systematic theology, apologetics, hermeneutics, church history, the life of Christ, eschatology, and the history of the English Bible.

In 2003, I created the website www.generationword.com. We began recording my teaching on CDs and making them available at no cost to anyone interested in them around the world. Our first online order came from India. Before long, we were receiving up to fifty requests per day for teaching CDs. Toni and I did all the production, packing, and shipping of the materials, (although we did get a little assistance from our six boys—our very own child labor force). Our house quickly started to look more like a CD factory than a home.

We had never taken any offerings at Bible studies or asked for any money whatsoever. Yet people who attended our studies and had benefited from the teaching had actually asked us if there was any way they could give financially to our ministry. We used their generous support to pay for the growing cost of postage for CDs. Sending packages around the globe wasn't cheap.

By September of 2006, we had produced and shipped over 50,000 Bible teaching CDs to more than twenty-five countries. Our CDs were heard by people on every continent, and Bible schools were using them to train pastors and Christian workers in Nigeria, South Africa, India, Ghana, Kenya, and the Philippines. A group of high school boys in England emailed to say they'd started a Bible study using the CDs. We also learned that pastors in other countries were directing their congregants to our website for teaching materials.

Since many people, especially in Asian and African countries, couldn't afford their own Bible, we decided to include free Bibles with some of the teaching CDs.

Bishops, pastors, and evangelists sent us emails telling us how they'd distributed our CDs and Bibles in counties like Algeria, Libya, Egypt, Sudan, Ethiopia, and Liberia. In some instances, the materials were being given to Muslims, as missionaries from neighboring countries like Ghana, Nigeria, Kenya, and South Africa were attempting to evangelize them.

Requests for our "Bible School" set (which included fifty-two teaching CDs) became more frequent. Then, during the winter of 2006, we received 3,500 requests for the Bible School teaching set in a little over a month's time. We were still sending out everything free of charge and wanted to keep it that way, but the price to produce and ship all the new CD requests amounted to $250,000. It was far more than we could handle.

We spoke by phone and email with many people who'd requested our CDs so we could explain our predicament. The offerings that came from our Bible studies couldn't possibly support the current demands on the ministry. And my family definitely didn't have time to produce and package *all* those CDs in our home. (After all, I was still a full-time middle school teacher and coach.) I promised we'd continue investigating creative ways of solving our problem, but for now, we'd go ahead and make all the sermons downloadable from our website. We made both full-length audio and video messages available. We also started a daily podcast. It wasn't long before Generation Word appeared on the first page of Google and Yahoo searches for "Bible teaching" and "Bible teaching podcasts."

It was around this time that Toni and some friends asked me to put some teaching down in book form, specifically the information about the four generation cycle. They reminded me that the original purpose of Generation Word was to tell *this generation* of Americans that they're living at a very crucial time. Our goal was to teach them the word of God so they wouldn't become just another casualty of our culture, (hence the name Generation Word).

Do what is right in every area of your life – taking responsibility for all your choices.

It seemed so many Christians were confused about where they stand in relationship to world history, church history, and American history. I wanted nothing more than to help our society overcome its scriptural illiteracy. People didn't need more three-point sermons on marriage or evangelism. They didn't need more thematic Sunday morning messages on things they'd heard a hundred times. They longed to hear the word of God explained as plainly as possible. Believing this, I went to work on this book.

Now that you've finished reading this book, there's so much more to learn. I encourage you to get involved in a church were they actually *teach the Bible*. There is a difference between attending a church that believes the Bible (most do), and a church that actually teaches directly from the word on a weekly basis. I also suggest you check out www.generationword.com. In addition to our audio/video messages and podcasts, we have countless Bible study notes available for you to print out and use alone or in groups. We also have links to other sites that contain useful study tools and resources.

Generation Word will continue in its mission. We know we have a responsibility to our culture at this final period of church history. We hope you can help shoulder some of the responsibility with us. You can start by simply handing this book to a friend. If nothing else, the concepts discussed here might spark some debate and open up dialogue (as scripture revealed tends to do). The other, and perhaps most important, thing you can do is *change yourself*. Begin to do what is right in every area of your life—taking personal responsibility for all your choices. If you change the one institution you have control over, the rest of the institutions will fall in line. Marriages will change, families will change, and eventually society as a whole will look much better than it does now. Perhaps together we can prevent this generation from becoming our nation's last.

Chapter 4: Staying Alert
 1 *The New Linguistic and Exegetical Key to the Greek New Testament, Cleon L. Rogers Jr. &*
    Cleon L. Rogers III, Zondervan Publishing House, Grand Rapids, Michigan, 1998, p. 642..

Chapter 7: Ten Times Revealed by God
 1 *In Genesis 29:27-28 "shabu'im" speaks of the seven day bridal week. In Leviticus 25:3-5*
    "shabu'im" refers to a period of seven years.
 2 *Bernard Grun, The Timetables of History (Based upon Werner Stein's Kulturfahrplan) (Simon*
    and Schuster, Inc, NY, NY, 1979) 24.

Chapter 8: Punishing the Sins of the Fathers
 1 *Dr. John R. Abercrombie, Department of Religious Studies, University of Pennsylvania,* http://
    www.bu.edu/anep/LB.html, *January 27, 2007*
 2 *Henry H. Halley, Halley's Bible Handbook (Zondervan Publishing House, grand Rapids*
    Michigan, 1965) 166.
 3 *Ugarit was an ancient port city on the Mediterranean coast of Syria. The city's location was*
    discover in 1928 when a farmer accidentally opened a tomb from the ancient city while plowing.
    Libraries of the city were unearthed to reveal Ugaritic literature on tablets that included
    mythological texts, letters, legal documents, international treaties, and administrative material.
    The Ugaritic literature gave firsthand accounts of the Canaanite religious beliefs right before the
    Israelite invasion.

Chapter 13: Jesus, a Prophet to His Generation
 1 *Strong, James, The New Strong's Expanded Dictionary of Bible Words (Nashville, TN: Nelson*
    Publishers, 2000) p. 413

Chapter 14: Secular Humanism
 1 *"Creation News from Around the World" National Center for Science Education at http://www.*
    *ncseweb.org/resources/news/2006/XX/961_creationism_news_from_*
    around_t_11_2_2006.asp (July 9, 2007)
 2 *"Newsweek Poll: March 31, 2007: Conducted by Princeton Survey Research Associates*
    International" Newsweek Politics, http://www.msnbc.msn.com/id/17875540/site/
    newsweek/ *(April 22, 2007.*
 3 *"Substantial Numbers of Americans Continue to Doubt Evolution as Explanation for Origin of*
    Humans" Gallup News Service, http://www.unl.edu/rhames/courses/current/creation/evol-poll.
    htm (December 14, 2006)
 4 *The Pew Research Center for the People and the Press: Reading the polls on evolution and*
    creationism, Pew Center Pollwatch. September 28, 2005. Available at: http://people-press.org/
    commentary/display.php3?AnalysisID=118. on December 19, 2006.
 5 *according to a Gallup Poll written and analyzed by Baylor University and reported in September*
    12, 2006 USA TODAY
 6 *as reported by Newsweek Dec. 5, 2004.*
 7 *Dec. 5, 2004, Newsweek, (updated Dec. 10, 2006) A Newsweek Poll http://www.msnbc.msn.*
    com/id/6650997/site/newsweek/
 8 *"U.S. Divorce Rates for Various Faith Groups, Age Groups, and Geographic Areas, Religious*
    Tolerance, http://www.religioustolerance.org/chr_dira.htm on April, 22 2007

Chapter 16: The United States and Its Five Cycles of Judgment
 9 *http://www.edwardtbabinski.us/lectures/mistakes_moses.html*
10 *http://www.edwardtbabinski.us/lectures/mistakes_moses.html*

11 http://www.agnosticuniverse.org/ingersoll-why_i_am_an_agnostic.html
12 (http://www.agnosticuniverse.org/ingersoll-why_i_am_an_agnostic.html

Chapter 17: Israel's Revelation Compared to Gentile Revelation
13 Philosophy Now magazine, August–September 2004. Reported in "Famous Atheist Now Believes in God" at http://www.simpletoremember.com/vitals/atheist_believes_in_god.htm
14 My Pilgrimage from Atheism to Theism: An Exclusive Interview with Former British Atheist Professor Antony Flew; Dr. Antony Flew, Professor of Philosophy, Former atheist, author, and debater, Dr. Gary R. Habermas.

Chapter 18: What About the Terrorists?
15 Even in the twenty-first century, the use of horses and cavalry remains the most effective means of transporting a large attack force through mountain terrain as described in Ezekiel 38 and 39. The cavalry has said for years that a horse can go wherever a man can. Modern tanks, trucks, and jeeps have to be abandoned in rugged terrain and troops are forced to march. General George S. Patton is quoted as saying, "It is the considered opinion, not only of myself but of many other general officers who took their origin from the infantry and artillery, that had we possessed an American cavalry division with pack artillery in Tunisia and in Sicily, not a German would have escaped, because horse cavalry possesses the additional gear ratio which permits it to attain sufficient speed through mountainous country to get behind and hold the enemy until the more powerful infantry and tanks can come up and destroy him." Other generals have made similar statements indicating that vehicles where useless in terrain similar to what Ezekiel is describing as the mountains of Israel. Horses and men on foot are the only thing that can move through this kind of terrain.

Chapter 22: Seven Letters to the Seven Churches
1 The International Standard Bible Encyclopaedia, General Editor James Orr, Hendrickson Publishers, Peabody, Massachusetts, 1956, Vol. II, p. 960.
2 The New Linguistic and Exegetical Key to the Greek New Testament, Cleon L. Rogers Jr. & Cle. Rogers III, Zondervan Publishing House, Grand Rapids, Michigan, 1998, p. 616.
3 The New Linguistic and Exegetical Key to the Greek New Testament, Cleon L. Rogers Jr. & Cleon L. Rogers III, Zondervan Publishing House, Grand Rapids, Michigan, 1998, p. 617.
4 Things to Come, J. Dwight Pentecost, Zondervan Publishing House, Grand Rapids, Michigan, 1964, p.153.
5 Dispensational Truth, Clarence Larkin, Rev. Clarence Larkin Est., Glenside, Pa., 1918, p. 131.
6 Expository Dictionary of New Testament Words, W. E. Vine, Zondervan Publishing House, Grand Rapids Michigan, 1952, Vol. III, p. 21.
7 The New Strong's Expanded Dictionary of Bible Words, James Strong, Thomas Nelson Publishers, Nashville, Tennessee, 2001, p.1439-1440
8 The New Strong's Expanded Dictionary of Bible Words, James Strong, Thomas Nelson Publishers, Nashville, Tennessee, 2001, p.913.
9 The New Strong's Expanded Dictionary of Bible Words, James Strong, Thomas Nelson Publishers, Nashville, Tennessee, 2001, p.1046.
11 Expository Dictionary of New Testament Words, W. E. Vine, Zondervan Publishing House, Grand Rapids Michigan, 1952, Vol. III, p. 172.
12 Expository Dictionary of New Testament Words, W. E. Vine, Zondervan Publishing House, Grand apids Michigan, 1952, Vol. IV, p. 146.
13 The New Strong's Expanded Dictionary of Bible Words, James Strong, Thomas Nelson Publishers, Nashville, Tennessee, 2001, p.631, 1246.

14 *Theological Dictionary of the New Testament, Gerhard Kittel, editor, Wm. B. Eerdmans Publishing Company, Grand Rapids, Michigan, 2006, vol. I, p. 648.*

15 *The New Strong's Expanded Dictionary of Bible Words, James Strong, Thomas Nelson Publishers, Nashville, Tennessee, 2001, p. 1305.*

16 *Hitchcock's Dictionary of the Bible Names, at http://www.christnotes.org/dictionary. php?dict=hbn*

17 *The New International Dictionary of New Testament Theology, Colin Brown, Editor, Zondervan Publishing House, Grand Rapids, Michigan, 1986, Vol. 3, p. 417.*

18 *Commentary on Revelation, H. A. Ironside, at http://www.ccel.org/i/ironside/revelation/ revelation.RTF*

19 *The New Testament Greek Lexicon, at http://www.studylight.org/lex/grk/view. cgi?number=2363*

20 *From the Council of Trent, The Twenty-Second Session, Edited and translated by J. Waterworth (London: Dolman, 1848), 158-159.*

21 *The Kingdom of the Cults, Walter Martin, Bethany House Publishers, Minneapolis, Minnesota, 1997, p. 495-516.*

22 *(The New Linguistic and Exegetical Key to the Greek New Testament, Cleon L. Rogers Jr. & Cleon L. Rogers III, Zondervan Publishing House, Grand Rapids, Michigan, 1998, p. 622.)*

23 *(The New Linguistic and Exegetical Key to the Greek New Testament, Cleon L. Rogers Jr. & Cleon L. Rogers III, Zondervan Publishing House, Grand Rapids, Michigan, 1998, p. 622.)*

Chapter 23: Can Our Nation Be Saved?

1 *Henry Adams, History of the United States of America During the Administration of Thomas Jefferson and James Madison, vol. 1, (New York: A. and C. Boni, 1930) 90.*

2 *W. J. Rorabaugh, "The Alcoholic Republic," Reviews in American History, vol. 8, no. 2 (Jun., 1980), 206-214.*

3 *Robert J. Allison, American Eras Development of a Nation 1783-1815 (A Manly, Inc. Book, Gale Research, 1997) 309.*

4 *Dr. J. Edwin Orr, Prayer and Revival, <http://www.pastornet.net.au/renewal/journal1/orr. html> (28 Dec 2006)*

5 *Orr, Prayer and Revival.*

6 *Ibid.*

7 *John Townes, "Town of Lenox, Massachusetts Homepage," 25 February, 2003, <http://www. townoflenox.com/Public_Documents/LenoxMA_WebDocs/about> (13 January 2007)*

8 *Orr, Prayer and Revival.*

9 *Shepard would pastor this Congregational church for 50 years. By the 1830s Shepard could write that "Lenox is pleasant and healthful, and probably presents fewer temptations to vice and immorality than almost any other place containing an equal population."*

10 *Orr, Prayer and Revival.*

11 *Ibid.*

12 *Lyman Beecher (1775 –1863) a Presbyterian clergyman and father of Harriet Beecher Stowe and a leader of the Second Great Awakening. He attended Yale in the 1790's and was a disciple of Timothy Dwight. Became a minister in Boston's Hanover Church and stood for Calvinism and a Christian democracy. He opposed liquor traffic, rationalism and slavery.*

13 *Sydney E. Ahlstrom, A Religious History of the American People, (New Haven and London: Yale University Press, London, 1972) 426)*

14 *Dr. Barry St. Clair & Keith Naylor, Bending Your Knees on Campus "Reach Out Youth Solutions Homepage," 13 January 2007 <http://www.reach-out.org/artic_principle1-1.asp> (13 January 2007)*

15 St. Clair & Naylor, *Bending Your Knees on Campus*

16 *Ibid.*

17 *Ibid.*

18 *Ibid.*

19 This was similar to the 1964–65 Free Speech and Filthy Speech Movement that occurred on the campus of the University of California, Berkeley when students. In an attempt to demonstrate and experience freedom from the restraints of Christianity and decent societal behavior students and faculty engaged in public us of profanity and vulgarity.

20 *Ibid.*

21 *Ibid.*

22 *Ibid.*

23 "It has been estimated that in 1800 only 6.9 per cent of the population had a church membership. (Kenneth Scott Latourette, *A History of Christianity: Reformation to the Present,* vol. 2, (Prince Press, Hendrickson Publishers, Peabody, MA, 2003) 1229.

24 Allison, *American Eras Development of a Nation 1783-1815*, p. 332.

25 Eric Foner and John A. Garraty, *The Reader's Companion to American History*, (Houghton Mifflin Company, Boston, 1991) 975.

26 Winthrop Hudson, *Religion in America* (Charles Scribner's Sons, New York, 1981) 138.

27 There often seems to be the 1/3 rule anytime there is a public move of God or a major public issue:1/3 supports the new move; 1/3 watches but accepts the benefits of the new move; 1/3 opposes the new move.

28 Hudson, *Religion in America*, 130.

29 Allison, *American Eras Development of a Nation 1783-1815*, p. 332.

30 *Ibid.*

31 *Ibid.* p. 1270.

32 John H. Armstrong, *Could Revival on College Campuses Be Near?* December 15, 2006, http://johnharmstrong.typepad.com/john_h_armstrong_/renewal/index.html (December 29, 2006)

257